David Jones

CHARTISM

AND

THE CHARTISTS

St. Martin's Press

NEW YORK

FOR GWENDA

CONTENTS

APPENDICES: CHARTIST ORGANIZATION

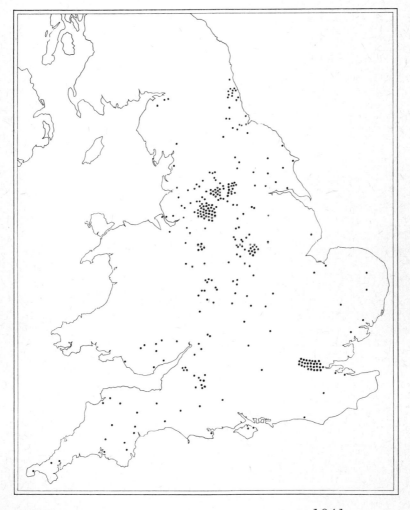

THE NATIONAL CHARTER ASSOCIATION IN 1841
Compiled from an official list in the *Northern Star*, 24 December 1841

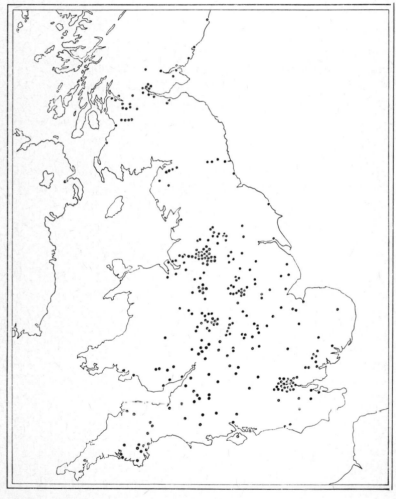

BRANCHES OF THE LAND COMPANY
IN THE SUMMER OF 1847
Source: *Northern Star*, 31 July 1847

PREFACE

The Chartists of the mid nineteenth century saw their movement as one stage of the long fight for human rights and happiness. They looked forward to a time when History and the
Future would merge in the glorious Present of a just society,
when kings, aristocracies and money-grabbing capitalists would
be of interest only to antiquarians. In the meantime the
Chartists called upon historians to 'curl up the tail of progress'.
Radicals like William Lovett, Julian Harney, Bronterre O'Brien
and Ernest Jones, who realized that the unenfranchised working class had to learn much of its politics from history, were
anxious to recover some of the lost battleground of the past,
and to provide future generations with a correct record of their
own particular struggle. The romantic literary productions of
a Benjamin Disraeli or the angry reminiscences of an R. G.
Gammage highlighted the urgency of the second task.

A century later the Chartist movement has been embraced by
a formidable army of Labour historians. Historical journals in
recent years have been full of debates over matters such as
Chartism and class, the extent of working-class militancy, the
relationship between middle- and working-class reformers, the
nature of Chartist interest in foreign revolutionary activities,
and the merits and strength of certain Chartist groups. Much
of this discussion is both stimulating and understandable. What
surprises the student is the lack of information about certain
vital aspects of the movement. We still know very little about
the organization of Chartism, the religious interests of its
leaders, the character of men like George White, James Leach
and Samuel Kydd, the reasons why certain communities rejected
the Chartist faith, the Chartist interest in history and poetry,

and the determination of working men to dominate the world of popular politics. It was this last point that made the greatest impression on contemporaries. 'The agitation for the Charter has afforded one of the greatest examples in modern history of the real might of the labourers,' wrote Dr Peter McDouall in 1841. 'In the conflict millions have appeared upon the stage and the mind of the masses has burst from its shell and begun to flourish and expand.'

I have tried, in the space at my disposal, to capture something of the atmosphere, integrity and complexity of this great movement. This small book is not in any real sense a comparative study, but in places it was necessary to define Chartism in relation to other movements. The individuals who appear in the story are not drawn, and the reader will be expected to know something of the narrative of events. Fortunately Dr J. T. Ward's comprehensive study, *Chartism* (Batsford) has just appeared in print, and those students seeking a detailed picture are referred to this.

I began writing this book in the spring of 1973. It was intended to be one volume in a Seminar Series for schools and colleges, but it was later decided to publish it as a separate essay. The documents which first appeared in the appendices have been incorporated into the text. But the original character and purpose of the book remain the same: to give students a pen portrait of Chartism, and to lead them on to the more substantial works of Mrs Dorothy Thompson, Professor Asa Briggs and other scholars.

Because of the problems of space, footnotes have been reduced to a minimum, and the important Scottish and Irish aspects of the movement were omitted. These can be studied in A. Wilson, *The Chartist Movement in Scotland*, 1970; R. O'Higgins, 'The Irish Influence in the Chartist Movement', *Past and Present*, 20, 1961; and J. H. Treble, 'O'Connor, O'Connell and the Attitudes of Irish Immigrants towards Chartism in the North of England 1838–48', in J. Butt and I. F. Clarke, eds, *The Victorians and Social Protest*, 1973.

I owe a particular debt of gratitude to my students; to those scholars who made their theses available to me; to Dr Brian Harrison, who allowed me to see material on Teetotal Chartism which has since been published; to Mrs Dorothy Thompson and Professor Glanmor Williams who read the manuscript; and above all, to my wife Gwenda. Mr Reg Groves, Mr Michael Shaw, Mr Peter Carson and the University College of Swansea have given me help and encouragement at various times, and Miss Ann Jones typed much of the manuscript. I thank them all. The mistakes, interpretation and Celtic enthusiasm are my own.

David Jones
December, 1973

TABLE OF EVENTS

1834	March	Tolpuddle Martyrs sentenced.
	July	Passing of Poor Law Amendment Act.
	August	Dissolution of the Grand National Consolidated Trades Union.
1835		Working Men's Associations and Radical Associations formed in Scotland and the North.
	September	Municipal Corporations Act passed. O'Connor on tour.
1836	March	Newspaper duty reduced.
	June	London Working Men's Association formed.
1837	January	East London Democratic Association formed.
	February	London Working Men's Association held its first public meeting. Petition to House of Commons adopted.
	April	Strike of the Glasgow Cotton-Spinners. The Birmingham Political Union revived.
	July	General Election. Defeat of many Radical M.P.s.
	November	*Northern Star* published. South Lancashire Anti-Poor Law Association established.
1838	April	The Great Northern Union formed at Leeds.

May	The People's Charter published in London.
	The National Petition published in Birmingham.
	Mass Glasgow meeting, attended by representatives from Birmingham Political Union and London Working Men's Association.
June	Northern Political Union formed at Newcastle.
August	Great Birmingham rally.
September	Kersall Moor Meeting, Manchester.
December	Calton Hill 'moral force' resolutions carried in Edinburgh.

1839	February	The General Convention of the Industrious Classes met in London.
	March	The Anti-Corn-Law League established.
	May	The Convention moved to Birmingham. Large demonstrations.
	Whitsun	
	July	The Bull Ring Riots in Birmingham, and arrest of Lovett and others.
		The Convention returned to London.
		The House of Commons rejected the first National Petition by 235 votes to 46.
		Troubles in the north-east.
	August	Rural Police Bill passed.
		'Sacred Month' demonstrations.
	September	The Convention dissolved.
	November	The Newport rising.
	Winter and spring	Chartist Arrests.

1840	January	Abortive Sheffield and Bradford risings.
	February – March	Chartist trials.
	March	Scottish Christian Chartist movement became popular.
	April	Northern Political Union reorganized in Newcastle.
	March – April	Delegates meet in Manchester and Nottingham.

	July	Chartist Conference in Manchester. The National Charter Association established.
	Autumn	Attempts to create Chartist–Radical alliance in Leeds.
	Winter	Attacks on 'Foreign Policy' Chartists.
1841	Winter and spring	Teetotal Chartist societies established.
	February	National Delegate Meeting at Manchester.
	April	National Association of the United Kingdom for Promoting the Political and Social Improvement of the People established. O'Connor's attack on Knowledge, Christian and Temperance Chartism.
	May	The Petition Convention. Petition defeated in Parliament.
	August	General Election, won by Sir Robert Peel and the Tories, with some help from the Chartists.
1842	April	Complete Suffrage Union Conference at Birmingham. Chartist Convention in London.
	May	The House of Commons rejected the second National Petition by 287 votes to 49.
	August – September	The Plug Riots and arrests of Chartist leaders.
	December	Conference of Chartist and Complete Suffrage representatives in Birmingham.
1843	March	Trial of O'Connor and other Chartists.
	September	Chartist Convention in Birmingham, where Land Reform was accepted. Chartist Executive moved to London.
1844	April	Chartist Convention in Manchester.
	May	Defeat of Master and Servants' Bill.
	August	Debate between O'Connor and Cobden at Northampton.

1845	April	Chartist Convention in London. Chartist Land Co-operative Society formed.
	Autumn	National Association of United Trades formed.
	September	Society of Fraternal Democrats established.
	December	Manchester Conference on the Land Plan.
1846	June	Repeal of the Corn Laws.
	December	Birmingham Conference on the Land Plan.
1847	May	Ten Hours Factory Bill passed. O'Connorville opened.
	July	General Election, won by Lord John Russell and the Whigs. O'Connor elected at Nottingham.
	August	Lowbands Conference on the Land Plan.
1848	February	Revolution in France.
	April	Chartist Convention in London. People's Charter Union formed. Kennington Common demonstration. National Petition ridiculed in Parliament. Joseph Hume's 'Little Charter' movement began.
	May	National Assembly met.
	Summer	Chartist disturbances and arrests.
	August	Chartist 'insurrection'. Publication of Reports of the Select Committee of the House of Commons on the Land Company.
1849	March	National Parliamentary and Financial Reform Association formed.
	June	Reform motion defeated in House of Commons by 286 votes to 82.
	December	Chartist delegate conference in London.

1850	January	O'Brien's National Reform League established.
		Harney and London Democrats capture the Chartist Executive.
	March	The National Charter League established in Manchester.
	June	Harney's *Red Republican* appeared.
	July	Ernest Jones released.
1851	January	Chartist Convention in Manchester.
	February	Bill to dissolve the National Land Company.
	March	Chartist Conference in London.
	May	Ernest Jones's *Notes to the People* published.
	Winter	Public discussions between Ernest Jones and Lloyd Jones over co-operation.
1852	January	Lock-out of engineers began.
	April	Harney bought the *Northern Star*.
	May	Ernest Jones launched the *People's Paper*.
		Chartist Convention in Manchester.
	June	O'Connor pronounced insane.
	July	General Election.
1853	Spring and summer	Revival of the Chartist movement.
	Winter	Mass Movement began.
1854	March	Labour Parliament met at Manchester.
		Britain entered the Crimean War.
1855	Spring	Chartist localities showed new vigour; Administrative Reform Association formed.
	August	Death of O'Connor.
1856	Autumn	'Welcome-to-Frost' meetings.
	Winter	Ernest Jones's 'Evenings with the People'.

1857 Spring   Ernest Jones and James Finlen clashed over Chartist propaganda.

       July   South Lancashire Chartists uncertain about value of a conference, but wanted an Executive of three people.

1858 February   Last national Chartist Convention, and birth of the Political Reform League.

       Spring   Northern Political Union formed.

National Political Union for Obtainment of the People's Charter established.

BACKGROUND

'The world has become nothing better than a great lunatic society' (Robert Owen, 21 August 1848). In 1848 the language of Robert Owen took on an alarming reality. A rash of bankruptcies and strikes, the return of hunger and unemployment, and the rumblings of revolution were enough to make a Gradgrind wonder. The confidence of free-traders gradually evaporated in the face of this discontent. The warnings of Thomas Carlyle and Richard Oastler now hung in the air: 'The People have now learnt their strength, the avalanche is descending . . .' Reformers of all persuasions had of course long predicted such a turn of events, and by a prophetic oversight the *Cheltenham Journal* had kept intact the type for its headline 'FRENCH REVOLUTION' since 1830.

The events of February–April 1848 released pent-up emotions and fears. Owen's apocalyptic despair found an echo in some of the novelists (76–83)*. Dickens, Charles Kingsley and others wrote about a deeply divided society in which personality was being consumed by progress. The curse was materialism, and its symbol the machine. Love, merriment and the fairy folk had been driven beyond the seas 'by the wickedness and want o' faith of men and women, and the building of mills and suchlike' (78). Another group of Victorians saw the state as the real enemy, but the victim remained the same – the individual and his 'spiritual freedom'. 'That lost,' said the journalist W.E. Adams, 'the nation becomes little better than a machine – a mere affair of cogs and wheels' (31). Caught in the crossfire of these criticisms were the Whig 'Steam Aristocrats', 'a pottering, dabbling, patching, pinching, meddling, poking, crew; a hypo-

* Numbers refer to entries in Bibliography.

critical canting set, doctrinaires, liberals, a freetrading, centralizing, concentrating, amalgamating, emigrating, accumulating, damnable crew' (S. G. Francis, Ipswich, Chartist, 1848).

The language, borrowed from William Cobbett, vibrates with the tension of an angry generation. Some working men acted out the novelists' dreams, and fled to the New World or turned to crime and drink. Most remained within the country and the law, finding solace and hope in Jesus Christ, Robert Owen and Tom Paine, three dominant figures of the early Victorian era. It was a difficult achievement; the social problems and economic oscillations of the period were unprecedented. Life for Stephen Blackpool was 'aw' a muddle'. Some tried too hard to change the world and themselves, and experienced breakdowns and madness. Among the casualties were prominent Chartists like the poet Thomas Cooper, the Scottish minister John Duncan, councillors Briggs and Ironside of Sheffield and the redoubtable Feargus O'Connor.

Who were the Chartists? Those who asked the question in the mid nineteenth century were provided with a popular pamphlet entitled 'The Question "What is a Chartist?" Answered'.
In this Mr Doubtful confronts a Radical:

MR DOUBTFUL Good morning to you, friend; I understand you profess Chartist principles, and as I confess, in common with many others, my ignorance of what Chartism means, I should be obliged by your informing me what is the meaning of the term 'Chartist'.

RADICAL It is one who is an advocate for the People's Charter.

MR DOUBTFUL The People's Charter, pray what is that?

RADICAL It is the outline of an act of parliament, drawn up by a committee of the London Working Men's Association, and six members of parliament; and embraces the six cardinal points of Radical Reform.

MR DOUBTFUL What are these points?

RADICAL They are as follows: 1. Universal suffrage – 2. Annual Parliaments – 3. Vote by Ballot – 4. Equal Representation – 5. Payment of Members – 6. No Property Qualification. . . .

In the remainder of this short tract the Radical proceeds to examine and justify these six points. A few purists wanted to confine the term 'Chartist' to the original supporters of Lovett's document or to paid-up members of the National Charter Association, but significantly, it was used more widely than this. Although the political scientist can isolate four or five types of Chartists, contemporaries usually divided them into 'stalwarts' and 'fair-weather birds'. At Great Horton, near Bradford, at least five key members of the association of 1840 were named in the 1861 list. Their pride in the name Chartist was such that they refused to give it up, even after the national movement collapsed.

Mercifully, there were many colourful characters amongst the 'Old Guard' Chartists. Peter McDouall, the 'little doctor' of Ramsbottom, who wore a flowing cape, sold quack medicines and carried on a tempestuous love affair with his followers, deserves a biography. O'Connor has one, but his charisma and conviction are best caught in his own writings (44). 'I have booked right through for Equality station,' he said in 1847, and few could match his pace or political perception. With him and McDouall in the movement, humour was never far away, but Chartism had its bores – the garrulous antiquarian R.J. Richardson and the terrible twins, letter-writer H.D.Griffiths and that most prolific of journalists, W.H.Clifton.

As Clifton and Griffiths grew old in the movement there were complaints that Chartism in the provinces was no longer attracting young blood as it had done in the early 1840s. Then, Young Men's Charter Associations had been established at Salford, Greenock, Stockport, Lambeth, Birmingham and at least a dozen other towns. These specialized in organizing social events and collecting money, and several of their members became officials in senior branches. An easy optimism runs through many of their discussions and addresses:

BRETHREN, – All you that have arrived at the age of fourteen (the age of discretion), are affectionately entreated, for our mutual good, to come forward and join us in aid of the Chartist cause . . .

Remember the students at Paris – it was to their youthful zeal that the glorious revolution of 1830 was owing. Let us emulate them and the other noble youths who have often played the part of men – better than men themselves – and, be it said, the Charter was gained by the youths – more than by the men of England . . . (Address of the Youths of the National Charter Association residing in the City of London, October 1841).

The excitement of 1848 brought another wave of young people into the radical clubs, yet the general impression is that the Chartist movement continued to rely heavily on veterans like William Hill of Staleybridge, T.M.Wheeler of London and

George Harrison of Nottingham. In weaving villages and some of the larger industrial towns Chartism became a family affair; sons following in fathers' political footsteps and female relations giving active encouragement. This was not accidental, for Chartist leaders believed that the surest way to achieve a 'universal' object was to 'enlist the sympathies and quicken the intellects of our wives and children . . .' At least eighty female Political Unions and Chartist Associations were established between 1837 and 1844, their main function being to support the political ambitions of their husbands and brothers. Chartist marriages and christenings emphasized this much-vaunted familial pattern of early radical politics, and Fanny Amelia Lucy Ann Rebecca Frost O'Connor McDouall Leach Holberry Duffy Oastler Hill, daughter of Richard and Maria Boden, was one of its victims.

At the moment it is impossible to provide a comprehensive account of the occupational structure of known Chartists. Most association minute-books have been lost, and so we must rely on the painstaking research of scholars like Dr Kemnitz. In his close analysis of some forty Brighton radicals he finds that the great majority of them were craftsmen and shopkeepers, only two being described as labourers (167). More impressionistic studies by two Swansea undergraduates of Chartists in the North-east and the South-west indicate the great variety of trades involved in the movement, though mono-occupational localities were fairly common in parts of London and Lancashire. Of the 113 men who entered the Great Horton Chartist Association between November 1840 and July 1842 three out of four were woolcombers and weavers, and most of the remainder (masons, coal-miners, etc.) joined in the cruel winter of 1841–2. The character of the local Chartist leadership is an easier problem because of the nomination lists sent to the national executive in the early 1840s (see Table I, p. 30). Using these as a starting-point it has been calculated that amongst 109 leading popular radicals in industrial South Wales were seventeen miners, eleven boot- and shoe-makers, seven tailors, five or six ministers of religion, four merchants, four cordwainers and four labourers (166). Although labourers, gardeners, engineers and representatives of the higher trades occasionally belonged to Chartist clubs, the most committed and literate members were usually depressed outworkers (weavers, framework knitters, nailers, etc.), artisans (especially shopkeepers, carpenters, masons, shoe-makers and tailors) and professional men (schoolmasters, doctors, surgeons, artists). Shopkeepers occupied a special place in the organization and political strategy of Chartism; and those who were not radical by tradition could be made so by propaganda and exclusive dealing. In Wales, the Black Country and East Anglia there is evidence that in the early years of the movement small businessmen and master craftsmen sometimes withdrew from Chartist committees because of pressure from 'men of inferior status'. The evidence from half a dozen Welsh and English counties suggests that organized Chartism flourished only briefly amongst agricultural workmen. Miners brought their own brand of commitment to the cause in the difficult years of 1839, 1848 and especially 1841–2, when they sometimes clashed with cautious artisans. In some areas the latter were as wary of the industrial proletariat and the unemployed as they were suspicious of the well-to-do. Although comparatively prosperous men like William Gould, the grocer of Merthyr, London publisher George William MacArthur Reynolds and James Williams of Sunderland brought much-needed organizing ability and money to the cause, they were given sharp reminders from time to time that 'Chartism is a movement of the working classes'.

'We are born again' ran the inscription on one radical banner. The ideas of Chartism were old, but the movement was new. Beginning officially with the publication of the Charter in the late spring of 1838, the enthusiasm of its reception surprised its author, William Lovett. The economic crisis, anger over the New Poor Law and an Irish statesman helped to give the movement a mass appeal and a provincial character. Even outlying areas in West Wales and the Scottish Highlands were caught up in the drama. In more independent centres Chartism absorbed other working-class interests in a total and unique way; here for a while everyone literally 'spoke the same language'. The National Convention of 1839 was called in a spirit of euphoria and suspicion, but ironically this soon highlighted the fissures in the movement and shattered its confidence. As 'cautious Scots' and middle-class supporters pulled away,

Chartists like Joseph Linney and James Leach, the Manchester bookseller, thought increasingly in terms of an organized movement on a national scale. In the aftermath of the Newport rising they established the National Charter Association; men of principle and millenial vision now committed themselves to the humdrum world of politics and constitutional action.

The N.C.A. was, together with O'Connor and the *Northern Star*, the chief unifying force in the Chartist movement. In the second wave of popular enthusiasm, from late 1841 to late 1842, the N.C.A. claimed a membership of up to 50,000 in some 400 clubs. 'Success is only a matter of time and numbers,' crowed O'Connor, but the traumatic experience of the Plug Plot, the loss of influential leaders and the rivalry of other movements – notably the Complete Suffrage Union and the Anti-Corn-Law League – proved crippling in some areas. For the next two years many associations were, to use the language of their enemies, no more than 'miserable knots of a dozen or two in each town, meeting generally in some beer house, . . .' Yet Chartism in some areas remained surprisingly strong, as the round of camp meetings in the late summer of 1843 showed, and the revived national organization now moved forward on a wider front. In the winter of 1845 and subsequent months another bout of radical fervour was underpinned by a growing interest in O'Connor's Land Company. Within three years some 70,000 people joined this exciting answer to the Machine Age. Meanwhile, the economic crisis of 1847–8 and international events precipitated the establishment of new and short-lived Chartist localities in areas which had 'long slumbered'. Some of these associations collapsed immediately after the famous National Petition of 1848 was rejected in humiliating fashion by the 'most middle-class Parliament of this or any age'.

It should not surprise us that many accounts of Chartism close with the events of 1848. Contemporary writers and respectable newspapers generally ignored Chartist activities after that date. Ex-members of the N.C.A. spoke of it in the early 1850s as 'all used up', 'a despicable nonentity'. Yet Chartism continued as a minority movement, though the battles which once had been fought with other organizations now raged within. After the terrible fragmentation of 1851, the half-dozen 'revivals' and 'new beginnings' were often simply the triumph of one particular Chartist group. The story ends sadly with the last conference of 1858 and the winding-up of the N.C.A. two years later.

As the map (p. 9) partly indicates, the strongest Chartist areas were South Lancashire, the West Riding of Yorkshire, the East Midlands and London, together with parts of the Black Country, Wales and West Scotland. Professor Asa Briggs's *Chartist Studies* (1959) contains chapters on some of these regions, and this can be supplemented by recent publications. Research has still to be carried out on the North-west, parts of eastern England, the border counties and the South-west. According to John Campbell, the energetic secretary of the N.C.A., the places where organized Chartism made little impact included the counties of Hereford, Hertford, Bedford, Kent, Surrey, Essex, Middlesex, Devon, Cornwall, Gloucester, Worcester, Glamorgan, Flint, Cardigan, Montgomery, Caernarvon, Buckingham, Berkshire, Dorset, Huntingdon, Lincoln, Oxford, Somerset, Suffolk, Cambridge, Denbigh, Anglesey, Hampshire and Pembroke. This list of July 1842 contains a few surprises but it is a useful guide. Within this prospective mission field there were, of course, a few brave clubs and isolated individuals like William Jones of Neath and Stephen Miles of Mere (Wiltshire) who contributed regularly to the *Northern Star* and the Victim Funds. Chartists appeared in other unexpected places – in wealthy deferential communities like Leamington and Bath, and in cathedral cities such as York and Lincoln.

'History is not written for nothing friends . . .' said the *Irishman* in 1848. Chartist leaders always had one eye on history, but unfortunately only one of them wrote a comprehensive account of their movement (26). In a sense they were too aware of the vastness of the task, and besides, sadness and resentment still lingered. Interpretation was another problem; it is fascinating to compare the comments of R.G.Gammage in 1854 with his speeches only ten years previously. 'We no longer think and feel as we thought and felt so many years ago,' wrote Thomas Cooper in 1872. 'We see the past, as it were, through a false glass . . .' (32)

The Marxists and Fabians who began to write about the movement in the late nineteenth century were less inhibited

(28–30, 94). Chartism for them was part of the great Labour tradition; a sophisticated political response to poverty which developed class consciousness and provided men and models for later socialist and international movements. In recent years several historians have reacted sharply against this view, and have studied personalities and trends which ran counter to the Charter–Socialist theme (95–102). This new approach suggests that the temperance Chartists, Henry Vincent and Robert Lowery, were typical of a large group of working-class radicals who moved contentedly into mid Victorian Liberalism.

Meanwhile, 'local historians' continue to emphasize the marked regional differences in the texture and chronology of Chartism (59–75). So much work is now under way that in the near future a definitive study of the movement is a real possibility. In this book I have summarized much recent work and have pointed to the gaps that remain. Throughout, I have kept two considerations in mind. First, what did Chartism mean to its adherents in the mid nineteenth century? For them, it was a heroic struggle calling for prodigious dedication and energy. 'He would not be bullied out of his principles,' said George White at one of his many trials, 'and if any supposed he would do so, he would find that he had got hold of the wrong man.' The death of Samuel Holberry in York gaol and the dismissal of 100 Merthyr Chartists from the ironworks in 1842 give us some idea of the sacrifices involved. One writer has estimated that some 1400 Chartists were arrested and imprisoned between 1839 and 1848, and that another 500 emigrated to America (103). 'Radicals of our own day,' said W. E. Adams in 1903, '. . . can form but a poor conception of the trials, difficulties and privations to which the Radicals of a former generation were exposed' (31). But if we miss this aspect of Chartism, the colour, excitement and optimism are easier to capture. The picture of the adjourned Convention of 1842 busily pasting and folding the massive National Petition is unforgettable; so were the nation-wide green-and-white celebrations to mark O'Connor's election victory five years later. In the final resort, however, it is the language which conveys the psychology of the Chartists and I have used their speeches and poetry extensively. Poetry had a special appeal to Chartists: in the ungodly material world 'Church bells rang not for us. Poets were indeed our Priests . . .' (86–8).

The other theme in this book is of Chartism as a national movement in relation to others. This comparative approach is valuable for, in spite of criticisms from novelists and others, most Chartists never considered franchise reform as sufficient in itself. Lovett and Leach, for instance, were involved in educational and co-operative ventures, and the Chartist press could be extraordinarily catholic. What is interesting, however, is the way in which a political movement was kept alive and intact in the face of much rivalry and opposition, even when, at times, it was reduced to minute proportions. 'Hope on, hope ever' ran a poem by Gerald Massey; and no one in Owen's lunatic-asylum world could offer the working class more.

Table 1. OCCUPATIONS OF PROMINENT CHARTISTS
IN 1841

Weaver	130	Schoolmaster	5
Shoe-maker	97	Twister	5
Tailor	58	Turner	5
Framework knitter	33	Button-maker	4
Cordwainer	30	Carder	4
Labourer	19	Cooper	4
Carpenter	18	Fustian-cutter	4
Joiner	17	Gardener	4
Wool-comber	17	Mechanic	4
Boot- and shoe-maker	13	Moulder	4
Mason	12	Nailer	4
Hatter	12	Needle-finisher	4
Potter	11	Warper	4
Printer	10	Watchmaker	4
Painter	10	Baker	3
Spinner	10	Boot-closer	3
Newsagent	9	Bricklayer	3
Stonemason	9	Brush-maker	3
Pitman	8	Chair-maker	3
Smith	8	Currier	3
Silk-worker	7	Engineer	3
Block-printer	7	Hairdresser	3
Boot-maker	7	Lace-maker	3
Flax-dresser	6	Machine-maker	3
Cabinet-maker	6	Plumber	3
Calico-printer	6	Publican	3
Cloth-dresser	6	Shipwright	3
Dyer	6	Tinman	3
Basket-maker	5	Watch- and clock-maker	3
Bookseller	5	Blacksmith	2
Grocer	5	Brass-founder	2
Glover	5	Carver	2
Linen-weaver	5	China-painter	2
Plasterer	5	China-potter	2

Table 1. (*continued*)

Clothier	2	Carter	1
Confectioner	2	Chartist missionary	1
Dairyman	2	Clerk	1
Farmer	2	Coach-trimmer	1
Fitter	2	Coal-dealer	1
Framesmith	2	Coal-merchant	1
Greengrocer	2	Collier	1
Millwright	2	Dirt-refiner	1
Needle-stamper	2	Draper	1
Pattern-maker	2	Dresser	1
Packer	2	Enamel-fireman	1
Pan-maker	2	Engraver	1
Paper-stainer	2	Fancy-silk hosier	1
Pipe-maker	2	Fancy-weaver	1
Sheet-iron-roller	2	Fish-hook-maker	1
Shopman	2	Fishing-tackle-maker	1
Stationer	2	Forger	1
Tool-maker	2	Foundryman	1
Upholsterer	2	Forgeman	1
Workhouseman	2	Harness-maker	1
Whitesmith	2	Hawker	1
Beer-seller	1	Hinge-maker	1
Besom-maker	1	Horse-shoer	1
Banding-manufacturer	1	House agent	1
Bleacher	1	Leather-cutter	1
Bookbinder	1	Leather-dealer	1
Bodkin-maker	1	Letter-press printer	1
Brewer	1	Locksmith	1
Book-keeper	1	Medicine-dealer	1
Brazier	1	Model-maker	1
Brightsmith	1	Newsvendor	1
Brass-finisher	1	Needle-hardener	1
Brick-maker	1	Needle-maker	1
Butcher	1	Needle-pointer	1
Block-cutter	1	Overlooker	1
Plater	1	Paper-maker	1
Quarryman	1	Porter	1
Reed-maker	1	Rag merchant	1

Table 1. (*continued*)

Salesman	1	Saddler	1
Screw-turner	1	Sawyer	1
Shopkeeper	1	Shipsmith	1
Sign-writer	1	Silk-glover	1
Snaffle-maker	1	Spur-maker	1
Striker	1	Stay-maker	1
Stuff-dresser	1	Stripper	1
Tea-dealer	1	Stuff-presser	1
Tilt-maker	1	Teazle-setter	1
Tinplate-worker	1	Tinner	1
Trunk-maker	1	Tobacconist	1
Twist-hand	1	Twine-spinner	1
Weaver and newsagent	1	Veterinary surgeon	1
Watch-glass-cutter	1	Wheelwright	1
Wire-drawer	1	Wool-sorter	1
		Total	853

Source: Nominations to the General Council in the *Northern Star*, 1841. Where the list for one area was duplicated, the first list has been used.

1. CHARTISM AND SOCIETY, 1836–48

'Chartism, Trade Unionism, and Socialism; or which is the best calculated to produce Permanent Relief to the Working Classes?' (Pamphlet of 1848). In spite of the seemingly endless inventiveness of Victorian reformers those seeking to change society had two main choices. First they could adopt a partial approach, selecting areas or evils for special attention. The attraction of this approach was the prospect of immediate success. In a country where an elected government refused to carry out its 'positive moral duties' much could be done by self-help; vast amounts of money and effort were spent on mechanics institutes, friendly and temperance societies, savings banks, co-operative stores and Sunday Schools. These improvement organizations appealed strongly to the artisan mentality within reforming circles; the enthusiasm of the Scottish editor of the *Chartist Circular* was overwhelming. Radicals sometimes tried to capture these institutions, or to create rival bodies. The Bradford Chartist Temperance Co-operative Society was one of a number of ambitious projects which catch the breath and imagination. Chartist co-operative stores were popular in Yorkshire, South Lancashire, North Cheshire, the North-east, Nottingham and Scotland, and the elected representatives of these regions sometimes tried to make them an integral part of the Chartist fight. A few of these co-operative stores continued to flourish long after the initial enthusiasm of the years 1839–42 had worn off, although one suspects that Ernest Jones was possibly right about the parallel decline in their radical idealism.

The limitations of self-help organizations reinforced the opinion of some reformers that the problems of society required a comprehensive solution. 'We seek the most perfect of all

B

revolutions,' said the *Northern Star* in November 1840, 'the revolving of the whole system.' The starting-point had to be the regeneration of the working class. Only this could prevent the total collapse of a society groaning under the weight of a debauched aristocracy and Church which had monopolized land and education. 'We all bear the mark of the beast . . .' said Walter Currie in his lecture to the Glasgow Chartist Debating Society, but the moral was clear. 'We must think and act for ourselves.'

For these men in the Detroisier mould thought and action were indivisible. Godwin, Paine and Bentham had been right – to achieve a lasting revolution changes were necessary in education and morality as well as politics. 'True freedom is only possible when men lose every vestige of slavery.' William Taunton, a Coventry market collector, personalized this conviction better than most. He was a prominent Chartist and Congregationalist, and an ardent Owenite who managed the first co-operative store in the town (68). In pursuit of the millennium such political reformers used a wide range of religio-educational methods and language. Because of this, Chartism sometimes had the character of a Puritan movement, although in the last analysis it was not a sect nor could it have the values of one. 'We extend our views beyond sectarian notions,' said McDouall in a passage which summed up the Chartist philosophy, 'embracing the whole of society within the sphere of the action of just laws.' And the 'People's Charter' could only be forced through Parliament by mass political action.

CHARTISM
AND
THE EARLY SOCIALISTS

'We welcome them all to the combat . . .' (*The New Moral World*, vol. IV, no. 160). The Chartists and Socialists of the late 1830s and early 1840s were compulsive debaters. In this exciting, even millennial period, both groups stressed the immediacy of their message and were 'confident of ultimate triumph . . .'. Public discussions between political and social reformers were

a regular feature of radical life in London, Yorkshire, Lancashire and certain Midland towns; and there were less-publicized
clashes in places as far afield as Bristol and Sunderland. William
Dean Taylor and James Leach specialized in this form of propaganda. This is Leach in argument with Alexander Campbell at
Stockport:

> Mr CAMPBELL then rose, and observed that the misery and distress of
> this country were to be subjected to four causes. First, want of education;
> second, want of employment; third, low wages; and fourth, competition
> of machinery against manual labour . . . He contended that there was
> no hope for the people, so long as society was carried on under the com-
> petitive system . . . The American records proved this to be the case, and
> it ever would be till competition was put a stop to, and the people turned
> their attention to co-operation . . .
> Mr. LEACH, who gave a clear definition of the Charter, proving it to
> be founded on natural law. He thought Mr. Campbell's argument,
> relative to education did not stand good . . . many of the greatest tyrants
> in existence were the best scholars. He contended that the want of
> political power was the greatest evil to the mass of the people . . . America,
> although a Republic, was not governed by Universal Suffrage . . . Mr.
> Leach then remarked that it was impossible for the people to save
> money to purchase land for a community . . . He would say let the
> people get political power . . . The Charter was only a means to an end.

The early nineteenth-century Socialists were an extremely
varied collection of writers and philosophers (120). What
united them was a common concern about the destruction of
village life, and the divisions and misery of the new capitalist
society:

> of hopes embittered in their birth –
> Of a heart snapped while all its chords were new –
> Of feelings crushed and broken in their youth
> By all the hard machinery of age!
> (*New Moral World*, 14 July 1838)

The Socialist answers to this state of affairs included controlled
industrialization, land and currency reforms and the nationalization of transport and public works. By the 1830s the term
'Socialist' had become synonymous with 'Owenite', for it was
the eclectic Welshman who gathered up various strands of anti-
capitalist thought and sought to translate them into reality. In
the late 1830s Robert Owen concentrated on propaganda; Halls
of Science and Socialist schools were established in many of the

large towns, Social Missionaries were appointed, and millions of tracts found their way into workmen's homes (128). It was almost impossible to escape his influence, and few Chartists even tried. 'No man living has done so much to undermine all [society's] existing Institutions,' said Feargus O'Connor, whose newspaper was staffed with Owenites. Owen gave reformers liberation, insight and hope.

Several themes of the early Socialists had a special appeal to Chartists. The unequal division of Britain's vast wealth, the irresponsibility of machinery, the predictable collapse of unrestricted capitalism, the misuse of talent, the concern for human happiness and the possibility of creating a new world through education – all these ideas merged with the legacies of Cobbett and Paine in the corporate Chartist consciousness. Lovett's autobiography shows what importance his radical friends attached to the notion that society was artificial, dominated by unnatural feelings of selfishness and class antagonism which lowered the cultural, moral and living standards of the poor. Here, Lovett was at one with Oastler and O'Connor (37, 44, 121). The Irishman claimed that the history of the previous sixty years had been the unbinding of ties which held society together. 'Soul is cut off from soul,' echoed the Chartist poets, and the high rate of crime, drunkenness and prostitution was the inevitable and degrading result.

Another popular idea, which Thomas Hodgskin, Owen, Henry Hetherington and a whole battalion of anti-capitalists placed at the centre of their philosophy, was that the distribution of wealth should be regulated by the labour theory of value. This ancient theory, so often quoted by James Leach, had two aspects. First, to obtain the benefits of society, man had to work. The division of the world into 'workers' and 'idlers' was a stock Chartist metaphor; Lovett and his friend, Henry Vincent, had no patience with the shirkers of any class. Secondly, all wealth, property and capital were the offspring of labour; only an unequal system of exchange had created the gulf between rich and poor. The economic machinery necessary to rectify this situation was not the immediate concern of the Chartists, though McDouall believed that their growing interest in such matters during the 1840s was a tribute to Robert Owen's continuing influence on political reformers.

Chartists and Socialists shared so many dreams and ideas that some people chose to belong to both camps (138). Isaac Ironside, teacher, John Goodwyn Barnby, poet and 'communist', and Thomas Livesey, Chartist leader and treasurer of the Rochdale Owenite Institution, were three important examples. They advocated closer ties between reformers, and in the Manchester area, Rochdale, Sheffield and certain Midland towns they had limited success. Socialists lectured to Chartists, allowed them the use of their Halls of Science, collected money for political prisoners, and joined them in co-operative ventures. Reports from certain Chartist localities in the late 1840s anticipate a fusion of committees, and from time to time a national alliance was considered. In 1838 the brilliant Irish lawyer, J. Bronterre O'Brien, suggested that such a union would make them irresistible.

O'Brien, 'the schoolmaster' of Chartism, had an Owenite appreciation of the need for the working class to understand society and its laws (43). In a series of short-lived newspapers and a stream of well-argued articles he propounded the concepts of 'Capital versus Labour' and 'Modern Slavery' which became part of the Chartist intellectual armoury: 'in our United Kingdom, which is accounted the most civilized country in the world, wage-slavery is attended with greater hardships, and subject to more privations and casualties, than anywhere else' (21). His answer to the system of 'legalized plunder' was a collection of primary and secondary socio-economic reforms, but his methods were those of the French Jacobin and not the Owenite communitarian. Although O'Brien worked hard in the early Chartist movement he was soon angered by its policies and lack of democracy. He was later joined by other disillusioned Owenites and Chartists, and out of their discussions the National Reform League of 1849 was born.

Significantly, the O'Brienites became a separate party or sect. As the years passed it was found extremely difficult to retain dual allegiances to both movements. Tension was always present; in the late 1830s and early 1840s Owenites often left the political movement because of its militancy and limited objectives. That versatile reformer, Lloyd Jones, pleaded – tongue in cheek – for his Socialist colleagues to be charitable. The process of dissociation can be seen at Leeds where John

F.Bray and the Owenites withdrew from the Working Men's Association (24). Recent studies of London, Brighton and the Black Country suggest that most reformers belonged exclusively to one party or the other (163, 167, 169). Rivalry and even fierce opposition were common, for in England the Chartist and Owenite movements were often influential in the same areas. From Halifax, Leigh, Bath, Ashton, Hyde and Dunfermline there were complaints that Chartist lecturers distracted people from Socialism, whilst Robert Owen at a rival conference in 1842 cheekily brought forward a nine-point 'Transition Charter'. In some areas – Bradford appears to be a good example – there may well have been an inverse ratio between the success and failure of both movements (62).

The competition and parallel development were perhaps inevitable, for between Chartists and Socialists there were clear differences of emphasis, ideas and methods. Political reformers were generally less adventurous in their analysis of the old society and their vision of the new, though they stoutly denied the suggestion that the Chartist programme was 'crude and undigested'. Artisans like Vincent and Lovett claimed to have a better understanding than Owen of the weaknesses of human nature, and of the value of 'healthy competition' and private property. To them, 'communism', the reduction of mankind 'to one dead level', was a 'dreamy system'. Even worse for some Chartists were the Welshman's views on religion and the family; the Reverend Joseph Barker and the Scottish radical, Abram Duncan, never tired of quoting the Bible at Socialist meetings.

Yet it was over methods that the Chartists were in most disagreement with their fellow reformers. The lines of divergence had been marked out in the early 1830s when Henry Hetherington and his friends complained bitterly of the naïveté of the Owenites – 'dancing jigs at two-shilling hops . . .' – and joined a political pressure group, the National Union of the Working Classes. Their attitude was summed up by Bronterre O'Brien, writing in the *London Mercury* in May 1837:

> The grand error of such men as Mr. ATKINSON (advocate of home colonization), Mr. OASTLER, and Mr. OWEN, is that of supposing that because a plan is good in itself – because it is calculated to produce prosperity and happiness for the masses – it must, therefore, prove accept-

able to the government. No delusion can be more complete. Before a Government will attend to the wants of a people it must be responsible to that people ... That (present) Government represents only the vampires and oppressors of society. As the representative of those classes, its mission is to maintain the existing order of things at any price. It is therefore the *ne plus ultra* of madness to expect any good from that Government.

By rejecting political action and threats of violence Owen was playing into the hands of the ruling classes. Significantly, relations between the two movements were probably at their best when the Chartists took up the land question in earnest, but even here, as the Owenite William Galpin discovered, the strains were still evident.

Although Robert Owen's belief in the power of persuasion and the ultimate acceptance of the Truth had a powerful appeal to educators like Lovett and Isaac Ironside, the process was too slow and the enemy too implacable. 'Knowledge without power is useless,' said O'Connor, who kept a close watch on Chartist reactions to Owenite approaches in the early 1840s; 'only a great political movement can obtain the new moral world.' Land and co-operative experiments, education and temperance reform, and even women's rights must be subordinated to the immediate political goal. The collapse of the Queenwood Community in the mid 1840s and the subsequent lack of community idealism in some of the successful co-operative stores seemed to confirm O'Connor's view. A few disillusioned Owenites turned to Chartist politics and economics – Owen himself was an interested observer at the Chartist land conference of 1847 – but most were unwilling to make such a fundamental change. The political reformers, as we shall see, probably had more ties with other improvement movements of the mid nineteenth century.

CHARTISM
AND
EDUCATION

Chartists and Socialists had a common interest in education; they valued it not only for its own sake but also because it brought consistency and strength to their movements. 'The hoof of despotism could never trample down a nation of thoughtful and virtuous men,' wrote Henry Vincent. Schoolmasters like the poet and scientist William Aitken of Ashton-under-Lyne and David Evans of Merthyr were an important force in the local Chartist leadership, whilst at a higher level, self-confessed educators such as O'Brien and R.J.Richardson constantly encouraged the passion for knowledge and discussion. By 1841 the *Chartist Circular* claimed that working men had crossed the Rubicon: 'they have their own movement – their circulating libraries – a newspaper press they claim as their own. The present age beholds them combining for the education of their own offspring!'

It was a hard struggle. In Chartist memoirs complaints of poor schooling and the lack of suitable cheap literature flew thick and fast. This was the age of G.L.Craik's *Pursuit of Knowledge Under Difficulties*; primary education was narrow and religious, and secondary schools for workmen were virtually non-existent. Edwin Gill, speaking to the famous Fig-Tree Lane Chartists of Sheffield in 1842, considered the purpose and effects of such an education system:

We have Sunday schools, charity schools, Lancastrian schools, and national schools, where orthodoxy and loyalty are crammed into the brain or thrashed into the breeches of the rising generation . . . I ask, have the people been rightly educated? Morality is at an equally low discount, crime is said to be rapidly on the increase. We are told that a great majority of the prisoners tried at the sessions and assizes are not able to read or write, and a reverend divine has said that there are thousands 'living without God, and without hope', how well the instructors of the people have done their duty! Well may they sing their old song over and over again every Sunday, 'We have done the things we ought not to have done, and left undone the things we ought to have done'!

In some areas – witness the remarkable weaving communities in Ayrshire and mid Wales – workmen themselves made strenuous efforts to ward off the threat of 'ignorance' and mass-illiteracy. For such people the concept of an education franchise was doubly insulting. 'As regards intellect, their common sense is more than a match for the book learning of the educated classes' was the angry response.

Government and middle-class philanthropists who sought to perform a rescue operation in the 1830s and 1840s were faced by a wall of suspicion (129). 'Educationalists are still what they were in Cobbett's time – the pretended friends, but the real enemies of the people' (*Northern Star*, 1848). Ernest Jones insisted that the people's education was safe only in the people's hands; and the chequered history of the mechanics' institutes at Greenock, Sheffield and other places illustrates the tension between middle-class founders, with their enthusiasm for Political Economy, and radical working-class members. Mass resignations followed the removal of Chartist newspapers from Institutes at Crewe and Croydon.

Significantly, many Chartist leaders were self-educated. William Lovett's and Thomas Cooper's autobiographies reveal the familiar pattern of astonishing perseverance and proud mothers. After Lovett's fragmentary education in the West Country, the young cabinet-maker moved to London. There he taught himself with the aid of Lindley Murray's *Grammar*, and by discussions at coffee-houses and political societies. 'My mind seemed to be awakened to a new mental existence; new feelings, hopes, and aspirations sprang up within me, and every spare moment was devoted to the acquisition of some kind of useful knowledge' (37). Cooper went further than Lovett in his pursuit of learning, and had several breakdowns as a result. Inspired by the example of Dr S. Lee, he decided to master Latin, Greek, French, Hebrew and a host of other subjects by the age of twenty-four. In the 1840s, like his literary *alter ego*, Alton Locke, Cooper found himself drawn into the maelstrom of radical politics.

So many men followed this path – John C. Farn, a Coventry working man, John Fraser, a teacher from Johnstone, W. E. Adams and Gerald Massey were four others – that Chartist attitudes to education were never in doubt. They supported O'Brien who had insisted, in argument with William Cobbett, that education was a natural right. 'Universal Secular Education' became the radical cry, though, as the Chartist Convention of 1851 made clear, there was some division of opinion over state interference and compulsion.

A few Chartists, like Lovett, O'Brien and John Bainbridge, a Yeovil upholsterer, regarded education with the urgency of

the Owenites; the depressing events of the late 1830s and early
1840s convinced them that men could not develop beyond the
limits of their knowledge. Lovett gathered round him men
who shared his passion for a truly democratic education. The
Bible of their 'Knowledge Chartist' movement was a book
written in gaol by Lovett and John Collins (22). This advocated
comprehensive and scientific state education, with new buildings, new teaching methods, new subjects and a new view of
British history. A National Association was formed in 1841 to
promote these ideas, but in the face of O'Connor's opposition,
Lovett's 'hobby horse... only rocked backwards and forwards...'
(John Watkins).

The Irishman assured the working class that it was already
the most intelligent group in this or any European country,
and that political power and a general improvement in its
conditions were the best schoolmasters. For him, the keen
interest taken by the Chartist rank and file in educational plans,
such as those of Lord John Russell in 1847 and the Secular
School Movement a few years later, had to be balanced by an
awareness that a People's Parliament would give them more.
In the meantime, Chartists should follow the *Northern Star* and
teach 'a knowledge of our rights as men'. Taking their lead
from the London Working Men's Association, many Chartist
organizations held weekly lectures and reading classes. In time,
some of these classes became separate debating societies, whilst
others concentrated on building up extensive libraries and news-
rooms, with the help of donations from ministers, landowners
and M.P.s. At Carlisle, Newcastle, Nottingham and Leicester,
Chartist mutual instruction had a distinctly professional air.
Here the workmen displayed a deep interest in poetry, history
and science, and it is fascinating to see how the Chartist leaders
turned this to political advantage. The popular winter series of
debates included such mind-bending topics as 'Was Christ a
Chartist?' and 'Have the poetical works of Robert Burns, the
Scottish poet, tended to destroy superstition, promote morality,
and forward the cause of public liberty?'

The next step was obvious but difficult. 'Why not Chartist
teachers?' asked the *Chartist Circular*. 'This would be striking
at the root.' Much encouragement was given in the early 1840s
and early 1850s to the establishment of Chartist evening and

Sunday Schools. These were most popular in the factory districts of Yorkshire, in Lancashire, North Cheshire and the Midlands. The *Circular*, somewhat blinkered by the Scottish experience, anticipated the triumph of Chartist education in every British parish. Typical was the Partick Chartist Education Club, which met between 8 and 9 o'clock every evening, and which taught the essentials of writing, reading, arithmetic, geography and grammar. These schools were closely associated with Chartist halls and churches (142). The halls, centres for meetings and learning, existed in London and some of the largest towns in the North and Midlands. At the famous Carpenters' Hall in Manchester several hundred fortunate scholars were visited by O'Connor on the day of their examinations, and were given the kind of instruction which was guaranteed to anger the local dissenting ministers. The first four rules of this school should be set alongside the complaints of Edwin Gill:

1st. That a Sunday School be established at the Carpenters' Hall under the auspices of the National Charter Association of the Manchester locality. To be known and designated by the appellation of the Chartist Sunday School for the children of all denominations.

2nd. That the following branches of education be taught to the children, namely, reading, spelling, writing, arithmetic, and English grammar; also their duties to their Creator, parents, and fellow creatures, with the moral and social requirements of public and private life; to which will be added instructions in and explanations of the principles of democracy as contained in the document called the People's Charter.

3rd. That no sectarian or peculiar dogmas be allowed to be taught to the children under any circumstances.

4th. That no corporeal punishment or particular mark of degradation be allowed to be inflicted on any of the children, for any forwardness or contrariety they may evince during their attendance at school. But instead of the cane or the whip, the more rational means be used – as entreating, mild expostulation, and kindness on the part of the conductors and teachers, shall be substituted, and strictly attended to by them in all cases.

Chartist teachers were anxious to retain the goodwill of women and children on all occasions, for these 'hold the key to the regeneration of society'.

It may well be that at the local level the Lovett–O'Connor controversy over 'Knowledge Chartism' had little relevance. In places like Sheffield and Keighley, Chartism was an experiment in living as much as a political movement. 'Nowhere in England does Chartism stand higher than in Keighley,' said the Scottish protectionist Samuel Kydd in 1848.

The hall – which is an excellent and substantial building – is their own building, to which belongs a committee room and a library; they teach a Sunday School; hold their mutual instruction and reading classes; also classes for instruction in grammar and logic; their orchestra consists of vocal and instrumental music; all their leaders are sober men of known respectability and worth – some of them men of property.

The effect of these schools and societies, aided by the Chartist press, was to raise the standard of thought, literacy and public speaking amongst working men. The spectacular court speeches of George Bartlett and other political prisoners are vivid testimony to their depth of knowledge, range of language and love of words. Many workmen acquired an appealing intellectual pride and arrogance. David Ellis, a Chartist weaver from Merthyr, told his friends that newspapers feared them more than Rebeccaites because 'we are intelligent men'. They also contrasted themselves with the drunken 'fools' at Westminster, the 'stupid' Queen and the 'coarse and vulgar manager of an ironworks'. Morgan Williams, leader of the Merthyr Chartists and a national figure in the early days of the movement, packed his election address so full of statistics that he confused his 'respectable' opponents.

Williams was one of the first group of Chartists who, disillusioned with party politics, left the movement for the wider field of working-class education. Cooper soon followed his example, as did Samuel Kydd some years later. They joined the lucrative lecture circuit. The third quarter of the nineteenth century was, of course, a great age of lectures; Cooper, Vincent and even the old Chartist convicts, John Frost and Robert Peddie, talked for perhaps £2 per evening on a wide range of topics – history, the classics, poetry, foreign affairs, and so on. Old Chartists were also active in the parallel expansion of libraries and educational institutes. Yet the importance of political power was never far from their minds; men like W. E. Adams in the 1850s and 1860s still believed the Chartist adage that 'Education will follow the suffrage as sure as day succeeds night.'

CHARTISM
AND
TEMPERANCE*

Another way of changing society was that advocated by temperance and teetotal reformers. 'I have long seen the necessity of the working classes wiping from their characters the name of "drunken mob" and such like names,' said John Page of Brighton in 1841. John C. Cluer, the Mancunian W. H. Chadwick and many other radicals began their public career in the temperance movement. Chartist leaders like William Ellis of Burslem knew personally the effects of insobriety on family life and the temptation of 'drunken week-ends'. Temperance had, of course, long been an integral part of the radical ethos – 'Drinking radicalism is a contradiction in terms,' said John Fraser, who spent much of his life campaigning against the demon.

The growing popularity of the temperance and total abstinence movements in the 1830s and 1840s encouraged some people to consider 'a grand union' between temperance and political reformers. But the problems were virtually insurmountable. For many, if not most, middle-class Nonconformists, abstinence was a religious and moral question, completely divorced from politics, especially politics of a radical nature (127). 'As an association,' said the *Aberdeen Teetotaller*, 'we have as little to do with Chartism as the man in the moon.' The Chartists replied by accusing teetotallers of narrow-mindedness, naïveté and middle-class pretension. This is George Bartlett, Bath shoe-maker and 'moral politician':

> It is a great mistake to suppose that intemperance has arisen from the want of religious instruction, or that it is the cause of the whole of the distress and poverty of the working classes. Upon inquiry we should find that nearly the whole of our evils, even that of intemperance, are to be attributed to misgovernment. Men are first made poor, and then intemperate –

Amongst temperance circles in Bradford (Wiltshire), Banbury and Rotherham, controversy broke out between middle- and working-class members, and the latter were faced with the

---

* For further detail on this subject, see the new article by B. Harrison, 'Teetotal Chartism', *History*, June 1973.

choice of expulsion or secession. In some areas Chartists and teetotallers competed for recruits. The Chartist delegates Robert Lowery and Abram Duncan found in 1839 that the leaders of Cornwall teetotalism opposed them at every turn. Feelings of jealousy and suspicion continued into the late 1840s and early 1850s, by which time drink reform had developed into a great national movement. In this period, Dr McDouall and the Londoners Child and Stratton refused to condemn either 'wholesome beer' or the publicans on whose goodwill the Chartists frequently depended.Like the Reverend J.R.Stephens, Stratton believed that 'the pot-house [was] a good place to meet in, and that a glass of beer or brandy produced a fine, genial, generous spirit, from which the best Chartism had always come'. Ernest Jones repeatedly emphasized that 'the Charter was not to be found at the bottom of a glass of water'. 'Virtue would bring them nothing,' said Jones. 'Be they as good as the angels in heaven, they would never gain political power or social regeneration.'

Yet from the start of the Chartist movement there were people and institutions committed to both changes in drinking habits and an extension of the franchise. Many Welsh and Scottish Working Men's Associations followed the example of the London organization and denied membership to drunken or 'immoral' men. The National Charter Association consistently recommended sobriety, though it stubbornly refused to make total abstinence part of Chartist policy. This was made plain at the Conference of 1842, where R.K.Philp vainly resorted to blackmail in his effort to give 'a high moral tone to the people':

> Seeing the names of Messrs Leach and Bairstow attached to a paper as pledged teetotallers, he trusted they would support the resolution.
>
> Mr. Leach explained that his name was a forgery.
>
> Mr. Bairstow stated that his name had been sent by a teetotaller, without his consent.

Leaders of the Association were asked to abstain from drink and tobacco – in Scotland, North Lancashire and the West it was almost a condition of office – and meetings in pubs and beer-shops were discouraged. Ernest Jones, when he took over the leadership of the Chartist movement in the 1850s, found it wise to reflect this demand for a 'moral movement'.

A section of the press and a large number of individuals campaigned for both the Chartist and the temperance movements. In 1838 John Fraser gave space to both in his *True Scotsman*, as did the *English Chartist Circular* and the *Udgorn Cymru* ('Trumpet of Wales'). One of the last journals pledged to support Temperance Chartism was the *Edinburgh Weekly Express and Railway and Commercial Courant* (1846–?), edited by the one-legged tailor, Robert Cranston, who was once charged with 'preaching sedition under the guise of temperance'. Some of the teetotal leadership, notably F.R.Lees and the Reverend Joseph Barker, sympathized with Chartism, whilst political radicals like Robert Lowery and W.H.Chadwick became better known perhaps as temperance advocates. Scotland and the North Country provide the best examples of the dual agitator: the list includes Adair, Brophy, Cluer, O'Neill, Cullen, Abram Duncan, Parkes and MacFarlane.

The most famous champion of both causes was young Henry Vincent, deceptively florid and with a voice 'like a whirlwind' (46). He came out of prison early in 1841 like a new man, convinced that 'we have the power of quietly revolutionizing our country, if we will but exercise that power in a proper manner…' He toured the country, calling upon Chartists to sign the pledge and establish democratic teetotal societies. Some of these societies were already in existence, but in the aftermath of the Newport rising there were more reasons and support for a Chartist–Temperance alliance. In the early months of 1841, when enthusiasm was at its height, Teetotal Chartist societies sprang up in London, Scotland, the North and the Midlands, and district associations were formed. Some of these favoured the establishment of a national organization, which would be a fitting climax to 'this year of redemption'. O'Connor, caught by surprise, launched a bitter attack on this deviation from pure Chartism, and after a few 'electric sparks' the new movement collapsed overnight. Only a few societies in London, Yorkshire and Lancashire managed to survive until a smaller revival of democratic teetotalism in the 1850s.

The swift disintegration of Vincent's movement can be deceiving, for in some localities teetotalism remained a powerful adjunct of Chartism. In 1843, for example, when the Sheffield Chartists were only one of a number of associations to sign the pledge, the *Northern Star* called upon all radicals to follow their example. The reasons for the close relationship between certain Chartists and teetotallers tell us much about the quality of their radicalism. Both groups attacked common enemies, the aristocracy and the irresponsible poor. As long as the former could bribe the people with large quantities of beer and money, especially at election times, political progress was impossible. So, in the eyes of these reformers, everything depended on those working men 'who have no aspirations beyond mere sensual enjoyments; who, forgetful of their duties as fathers, husbands and brothers, muddle their understandings and drown their intellect . . .'. 'The most chilling, the most heart-rending view that meets our sight,' said Edinburgh Chartists in 1844, 'is on a Saturday night, when we leave our deliberation, straightened in our means of advancing the regeneration of the people, and behold hundreds, issuing from the pothouses in a state degrading to themselves, and revolting to humanity.' It is significant that as the years passed, Vincent and Lovett grew increasingly bitter in their attacks on these people; 'the lower stratum of the working classes,' wrote Vincent in 1867, has 'no political past – or future.'

Amongst the practical reasons for Chartist support of teetotalism were that it held out the prospect of cheaper bread, produced fitter radicals, brought in more money for the cause and was a method of bringing the government to its knees. 'It is intoxicating drinks that in general supply tyranny with its armed mercenaries,' said the *Chartist Circular*. 'Few sober, well-educated young men enlist.' John Frost, ex-mayor of Newport, wanted a more immediate strategy – 'Our aim should be to cripple the revenue' and to alarm the middle classes. The government raised at least a third of its income from drink; if the working class stopped contributing its share, it would produce chaos. In the event 'universal abstinence' was tried in the summer of 1839 and in 1840, but it received very limited support. Thereafter, only a few hopefuls, like Roger Pindar, the Hull merchant, continued to urge its re-adoption.

After the lessons of 1839–40 many Chartists advocated teetotalism not to embarrass the government, which had proved its strength, but to gain more support for the radical programme. 'Our movement has, in the past, been robbed of its moral stamina by the all-devouring cup,' admitted the Provisional Executive of the N.C.A. in 1852. According to Jonathan Bairstow, one of the greatest of Chartist lecturers and ministers, C.H.Neesom, a key figure in London temperance circles, and Walter Currie, abstinence would improve their image in the eyes of women and take 'from the mouth of the opponent the objection of drunkenness as a proof of unfitness for elective existence . . .' Women's Chartist groups at Bradford and Blackwood (Monmouthshire) were certainly delighted when their menfolk took up temperance, and did their best to publicize its beneficial effect on family life. Vincent, in his moral crusade amongst the working class, always had one eye on his adoring female audience and the other on the middle classes. When he, Lowery, Malcolm McFarlane and others left the N.C.A., and campaigned for 'respectable' temperance organizations, they still hoped, in true Godwinite fashion, to remove the fear of democracy amongst potential middle-class friends.

CHARTISM
AND
RELIGION

'He has been Protestant, Dissenter, and Infidel – Puritan, Saint, and Atheist – total, teetotal, abstemious, and boozy; in fact, he is the very impersonation of trinity in unity. He has been all things to all men, and God only knows what he may be next...' (O'Connor on Thomas Cooper). The radical preachers of the period like Cooper, Abram Duncan, William Hill and Joseph Barker were fascinating and often complex individuals, who personify the vital and organic link between politics and religion in the early Victorian period. This was a religious age when new churches, sects and Sunday Schools sprang up like daisies, and when Protestant evangelical fervour was at its height. Within each sect there was a desire for greater lay control, and for a deeper commitment to social, educational and political reform (25). Primitive Methodism, the working man's denomination, now enjoyed its greatest success.

Chartism was of its age; and outside the world of Leeds and

London secularism, the movement – like so many others – used religious language and religious leaders. Consider the case of George Binns who was, along with James Williams, the dominant Chartist figure on the Durham coalfield in the early years. At his open-air meetings the flags proclaimed 'Who is on the Lord's side?' and 'We are born again' – a sentiment which runs through the popular agitation of the late 1830s and early 1840s. Binns' speeches were full of the need for regeneration, the unchristian behaviour of their opponents, and the ultimate triumph of the numbers and energy of the people – 'they may boast of their Wellingtons, but we have a God'. Gammage tells us that Binn's speeches had a magical effect and were frequently interrupted by the most vociferous cheering. In South Wales and Nottingham Henry Vincent and Dean Taylor had the same impact. These missionaries played a vital role in creating a great popular feeling, and in giving it a Christian rationale. In some cases their peculiar approach was as calculated as that of Owenite organizers, but for others – William Hill's 'true Christian Chartists' – the fusion of politics and religion was instinctive. O'Connor was one of a number of leading Chartists who distrusted this second group, but Hill, the Swedenborgian editor of the *Northern Star*, defended them vigorously. At the start of a lecturing tour in the early summer of 1843 he stated that his purpose was to show that 'every consistent Christian must be a Chartist, and that all will be better Chartists for being Christians ... I believe Christianity to be the soul of which Chartism is the body; and I cannot consent to separate them.' Perhaps historians should pay more attention to such people, and to the religious soil in which they worked.*

The same can be said of ministers who sympathized with the Chartist movement. There were at least forty such clergymen, ranging from Henry Solly and William Linwood, Unitarians of Yeovil and Mansfield, to the Baptist Thomas Davies of Merthyr and the eloquent Alexander Duncanson, a Congregationalist who represented Falkirk at the Chartist Convention of 1851 (38, 75). They supported the movement by lecturing, chairing meetings, loaning chapels and presenting radicals with books and money. Their happiest position was generally on the 'moral

---

* There is a vast amount of untapped material here. See, for example, the excellent accounts of Chartist sermons in the Central Library, Derby.

wing' of the movement, but their chapel invective was fiery enough. This is Patrick Brewster, who was, for a brief period, a prominent Scottish Chartist:

> The Son of God came, especially, to the poor. He came to preach his Gospel to the poor. He came, emphatically – literally as well as figuratively, temporally as well as spiritually – to 'loose the bonds of wickedness, and to undo the heavy burdens'. And the whole of his life on earth corresponds with this character, and the whole of his blessed Gospel tends to this effect. He taught and fed the poor in their ignorance and destitution. He healed their diseases and comforted their sorrows; whilst he directed all the force of his most piercing rebukes against those who deceived and oppressed them – their unfaithful teachers and wicked Rulers – confounding and overawing the hollow-hearted Pharisee and the dishonest Scribe, by tearing off the mask of their hypocrisy; and holding them up to the scorn of the people, by exposing their real character, in all its naked selfishness and deformity.

In some areas the attitude of Church leaders to any form of working-class action appears to have been crucial. The Stroud Chartists dated their successful revival from the 'political conversion' of a local minister. In Wales and Manchester, Chartists bombarded chapels with requests for help, for they realized that ministers could bring an element of respectability and organizing skill to the cause. This clerical support, which was most obvious amongst the oldest and newest branches of Dissent, raised hopes of a general alliance between Chartism and Nonconformity over such issues as education, the relationship between Church and state, and political reform. At a local level there were examples of joint action in the mid and late 1840s – disruption of vestry meetings, the sponsoring of anti-Church-rate candidates, etc. – but amongst the leadership there was too much rivalry and suspicion. Both Vincent and Ernest Jones, two very different radicals, deplored the fact that 'Chartist and Nonconformist looked shyly at each other'.

Suspicion sometimes gave way to outright hostility. The Anglican and orthodox Methodist Churches led the attack on the atheism and violence of working-class radicals. In Cornwall, Denbighshire and Mottram preachers went further than the customary verbal warfare, disrupting political meetings and visiting houses to warn people against signing national petitions (6). The Chartists, raised on Cobbett, replied with a withering combination of anti-clericalism and indifference. 'None of us had any great love for the "cloth",' said the fictional hero of Henry Solly's novel, *James Woodford, Carpenter and Chartist.* 'The same with regard to religion generally . . . We only thought it humbug . . .' When the vicar of St Stephen's in Norwich quoted St Paul – 'I have learned, in whatever station of life, therewith to be content' – at his working-class audience, the Chartists shouted, 'You get £200 a year! Come and weave bombases!' and put out the gas. Nonconformist ministers who organized public protests against the educational clauses of Sir James Graham's Factory Bill in 1843 were frequently surprised by the independence of the Chartist response. Radicals called upon all ministers to return education and money to the people. The provincial Chartist press and the court speeches of 1843 are full of the fiercest denunciations of men who had long forgotten Christ's calling. Nothing angered the Chartists more than being called 'infidels' who broke the Sabbath and who refused to accept the state of affairs which God had created. When they visited churches *en masse* in 1839 and 1842, or walked bravely into 'priest-ridden' towns and villages, it was their proud boast that they were more truly religious than their enemies.

Studies of Chartist leadership and organization give a new dimension to their claim. Lay preachers and Sunday School teachers played an important part in radical activities in Wales, Scotland and certain English towns. John Black, John Barratt, John Harrison and several other preachers in the Nottingham area defied the warnings of their religious superiors. At the weaving village of Arnold the Primitive Methodist chapel appears to have supervised the Chartist movement. In 1841 the weavers opened a 'Chartist chapel' with Sunday School and library attached. Vincent spoke at the opening ceremony. Bradford was another centre of temperance and 'religious Chartism'. Here, where only a small proportion of the population attended church, the radical movement was organized by Methodists, one of whose ministers acted as a Chartist missionary. It seems clear that such people were carrying over their feelings of responsibility, status and power from the religious community to the wider field of local politics.

It was a similar story amongst the Presbyterian Free Church radicals in Scotland who enthusiastically endorsed the advice of John McKerrow, treasurer of the Gorbals Chartist Association, to appoint as officers 'only moral men who have the fear of God before their eyes'. The whole Chartist movement responded to this call in the years 1840–41, when men like Abram Duncan, Unitarian David John of Merthyr, John Skevington, the lame Primitive Methodist preacher from Loughborough, and Charles Clarke of Bath edited provincial Chartist newspapers and were chosen as delegates and election candidates. Their popularity was less obvious during the economic crisis of 1842, but some of them remained important at a local level. In the Manchester area the Reverend James Scholefield and the peripatetic William Jackson did their best to hold the movement together in the difficult mid 1840s, whilst Benjamin Rushton, the veteran lay preacher of Halifax, was the obvious representative of a number of people who were still adding the weight of their Nonconformist conscience to 'the People's Cause' in the 1850s.

These Chartist leaders spread the political message by traditional religious means: preaching in church halls, holding prayer-meetings, love-feasts and camp meetings, and teaching in Sunday Schools. The Sunday School, the vital link between the churches and the working class, was a special target for reformers; and one which clergymen found difficult to defend. When Nonconformist scholars in Lancashire and mid Wales were chastized for 'mixing reform with their religion', they sometimes moved with their teachers to independent premises. Wesleyan leaders were horrified by this turn of events and, like their Anglican brethren, suspected that religious institutions were being used in a purely secular way, especially during the winter of 1839–40 and the autumn of 1842.

Amongst the weaving communities Chartism frequently took on the character of a desperate holy war, with all the trappings of religious revivalism. In some of their famous camp meetings political and religious fervour were deliberately fused. Dr Wearmouth has discovered over 500 camp meetings, most of which occurred in the early years of Chartism and in the later 1840s (152). They were most popular in parts of Lancashire, Yorkshire and the Midlands. In certain villages these gatherings were organized by working-class Methodists, and were usually held on neighbouring hills and moorlands. Families, carrying food and bibles, would walk miles to hear political sermons, accompanied by hymn-singing and bible-readings from lay preachers. These day-long meetings were enthusiastic, and, in the late 1830s, often millennialist in character.

Once the millennial period of Chartism was over, the close relationship between religion and radical politics became institutionalized in the Chartist churches. Although Professor W.R. Ward believes that this development does not compare in scope and energy with the breakaway religious groups formed during the 1790s and the Peterloo period, nevertheless between twenty and thirty Chartist churches have been traced in Scotland, and perhaps twice that number were established in Wales, the West Riding, Lancashire, London and parts of the Midlands and the West Country (75, 151). The most famous Chartist church – that at Birmingham – even had its own missionaries. These churches developed casually from existing working-class congregations, or as breakaway groups from 'respectable' Dissenting chapels. When Joseph Barker was expelled from the Methodist New Connection in 1841 he took with him twenty-nine churches, a good number of which became Chartist in spirit if not in name. Several new Chartist churches were erected, and here the general rule was free seats, unpaid ministers and no denominational theology. A Glasgow congregation took on the offices of chairman and vice-chairman in rotation, and these lay representatives conducted services and performed marriages and baptisms. The religion of these churches was *primitive*, with a strong political and social content. Congregations helped the unemployed, collected money for political prisoners and signed Chartist petitions (25).

Comparisons with Trevor's Labour Churches at the end of the nineteenth century are obvious, but the Chartist variety had a stronger religious character. William Hill delighted in this, and was one of those who believed that such examples of 'true religion' would prove a vital source of commitment and continuity in the Chartist movement. But other pastors, men like Abram Duncan and John Collins, could separate their functions in a way alien to Hill, and in the mid 1840s they repudiated any formal connection with political organizations. In the 1850s and 1860s some of the leaders of Chartist churches appear in the guise of traditional ministers, whilst others toured the country on behalf of religious and temperance organizations. In the meantime, the Birmingham Chartist Church had returned to the Baptist fold.

*

O'Connor had always feared this train of events for he, more than anyone else, saw the appeal which non-political movements had to the working class, especially in times of prosperity or situations of political frustration. Hence his crushing attack in the spring of 1841 on the 'Religious, Knowledge and Temperance Chartism HUMBUG': 'If Chartists you are, Chartists remain; you have work enough without entering into the new maze prepared for you . . . get your Charter, and I will answer for the religion, sobriety, knowledge, and house, and a bit of land into the bargain . . .' The Irishman and the executive tried to contain the moral and self-help fervour of the early 1840s within the confines of the N.C.A. 'Sectional alliances' only narrowed the basis of the movement, and once Chartism was involved with another 'ism' people inevitably became concerned with matters other than universal suffrage. In the early 1850s considerable amounts of money and energy were absorbed in the prohibition movement, the anti-popery scare and the National Public Schools Association. Ernest Jones, who was then struggling to find audiences in the Midlands, understood O'Connor's point.

O'Connor was also wary of the Puritan element in the Chartist 'deviations', and the cultural differences which it might implant into the working class. Politics for Lovett, Abram Duncan and the Christian Chartist, Arthur O'Neill, were about morality, and the American situation was never far from their thoughts. Vincent and James Williams of Sunderland warned the working class that it would not succeed in politics because 'they were too much caught up by mere glitter and show', whilst William Beesley in the moral fastness of North Lancashire was, for a period at least, even critical of the glamour of the Chartist movement and its leadership. Several provincial Chartist secretaries admitted to a deep suspicion of London, with its 'splendid and voluptuous temples of club and political life', and were also critical of the 'ignorance, beer and superstition' of rural areas. A few radicals indulged in long speeches attacking the old rural sports which had been encouraged by squire and parson. Arthur O'Neill and William Thomasson went further, and annoyed some Wednesbury Chartists by protesting against the use of the local People's Hall for dancing one night per week.

In place of this gaudy and immoral existence these reformers offered workmen respectability and the prospect of material success. Daniel Hopkins, a London teetotaller, announced at a public meeting that 'by sobriety and co-operation, he had obtained a house near the White Conduit . . .' Behind this call to morality and respectability was the notion of 'true independence' – that workmen could, and must, stand on their own feet. Those who attacked Lovett and his friends for forgetting the real causes of distress in their anxiety to 'reform men in a middle-class image' never fully appreciated this concept of independence. Vincent gave it an historical dimension:

> The present movement in favour of the Charter differs in character from any preceding movement. Formerly the brute passions of the multitude were appealed to in wicked imitation of our rulers. *Feeling* was roused; but there was neither mind or morality to support it; and when the burst of indignant fury had spent itself, the people again sank into a state of hopeless indifference. The knowledge of past failures is a beacon for the future. We shall henceforth avoid the rocks upon which our former hopes were wrecked. We shall direct our attention not to the mere agitation of the people, *but to their mental and moral improvement* . . .

What was significant about Chartist 'deviations' was not just the obvious working-class interest in self-help, but that it was articulated in a way that ran counter to many middle-class hopes.

Paradoxically one of the desires behind the moves of Vincent, Neesom, Lovett and Collins was to capture a wider section of political support in the country, for they believed the events of 1839 had shown the inability of the Chartists to succeed on their own. Many of the radicals described in this chapter emerged from this crisis as apostles of class co-operation. They denounced intervention in the meetings of other reformers, and tried in 1840 and 1842 to re-establish good relations between the working and 'the industrious middle classes'. The winter of 1842–3 saw the climax and collapse of their hopes. 'As a whole,' reflected Neesom, '[the middle and working classes] were both too ignorant to be in a condition to unite for any common good, but he had expected that a union might have been effected between the honest and intelligent portions of both classes.' The *Nonconformist*, which occupied the shelves of Chartist libraries, praised such efforts, and Edward Miall, Joseph Sturge and Henry Richard were the ultimate beneficiaries. George White, the ferocious enemy of Christian Chartism in Birmingham, bellowed, 'Real Chartism is Labour against Capital,' but many workmen were being guided towards the calculated embrace of Victorian Liberalism.

2. CHARTISM AND POLITICS

TRADITION, ORGANIZATION AND METHODS 1836–51

The Chartists were interested in a wide range of social and economic developments, but their preoccupation was politics. Some became obsessed by it, like R.J.Richardson who combed Puffendorf and the labyrinth of English history to justify the actions of the Convention of 1839. William Rider, whose mind 'cracked,' remembered that assembly as the place where money was 'recklessly expended, and time killed by the reading of Acts of Parliament, culled from some chandler's stock of waste-paper . . .'. Blackstone was cited endlessly, even by George White. It needed an anonymous workman to remind them that much of this was irrelevant because his class was outside the body politic.

This was the problem: how to obtain a revolutionary goal by constitutional means. Most reformers believed that no government could stand against the 'moral tempest' of a hostile public opinion. To create a public opinion favourable to the Charter, a great variety of methods were used in bewildering succession. The famous manifesto which the Chartist Convention submitted to the public on 14 May 1839 was an encyclopedia of traditional forms of radical protest:

We respectfully submit the following propositions for your serious consideration:

That at all the simultaneous public meetings to be held for the purpose of petitioning the Queen to call good men to her councils, as well as at all subsequent meetings of your unions and associations, up to the 1st of July, you submit the following questions to the people there assembled:

1. Whether they will be prepared, *at the request of the Convention*, to withdraw all sums of money they may individually or collectively have placed in savings banks, private banks, or in the hands of any person hostile to their just rights?

2. Whether, at the same request, they will be prepared immediately to convert all their paper money into gold and silver?

3. Whether, *if the Convention shall determine that a sacred month* will be necessary to prepare the millions to secure the charter of their political salvation, they will firmly resolve to abstain from their labours during that period, as well as from the use of *all intoxicating drinks*?

4. Whether, according to their old constitutional right – a right which modern legislators would fain annihilate – they have prepared themselves *with the arms of freemen to defend the laws and constitutional privileges their ancestors bequeathed to them*?

5. Whether they will provide themselves with *chartist candidates*, so as to be prepared to propose them for their representatives at the next general election; and, if returned *by show of hands*, such candidates to consider themselves veritable representatives of the people – to meet in London at a time hereafter to be determined on?

6. Whether they will resolve *to deal exclusively with Chartists*, and in all cases of persecution rally round and protect all those who may suffer in their righteous cause?

7. Whether by all and every means in their power, they will perseveringly contend for the great objects of the People's Charter, and resolve that no counter agitation for a less measure of justice shall divert them from their righteous object?

8. Whether the people will determine to obey all the just and constitutional requests of the majority of the Convention?

A few Chartists, influenced by the campaign for a free press and events in Britain and France in 1830–32 and 1848, believed in the *instant* success of the popular will once mobilized. Others adopted a gradualist approach. 'I love to contemplate the progress these principles are making,' said John McCrae, the Chartist candidate in the Greenock election of 1847, 'even during the last 20 years . . . I can remember full well when we who professed these principles had to run as it were from our homes, and under cloud of night, or before the dawn of day, meet with some kindred spirit to talk over a nation's wrongs...' Optimism was at the heart of the Chartist movement; the future was secure.

What mattered in the short term was the survival of a radical movement committed to universal suffrage. In the difficult years after the passing of the Reform Bill, the *Poor Man's Guardian* and the *True Sun* kept this message alive. One group of reformers, bred on Godwin and Owen, emphasized the quality of conversion; their concern was the individual not numbers. Their politics were élitist; by tracts, propaganda

associations of 'worthy men', and perhaps ties with sympathetic
M.P.s, they hoped to convince both workmen and Parliament
of the need for universal suffrage. Another group of Chartists
placed more trust in 'collision politics'; they wanted a central-
ized people's party to give force to petitions, take advantage
of current events, and compete with the established political
associations. 'Centralization and organization are the weapons
of the government,' said McDouall in 1841, 'and until you can
successfully imitate their tactics, you never can reduce their
power.'

All popular radicals were agreed on the importance of unity
and independence. Men as different as O'Brien, Vincent and
George Loveless, the Tolpuddle Martyr, never forgot the lessons
of the Reform crisis. The N.C.A., which embodied some of their
dreams, stated that 'the people are ready to receive the rights
which have been withheld from them'. In the past the working
class had been tricked on this and other issues by 'Sham
Radicals'. A liberal Whig had turned out to be as bad as a
Tory. 'The difference between them,' said Ebenezer Elliott, the
Sheffield Corn Law Rhymer in 1837, 'is your Whig is dressed
in hen's feathers and has a sheep's heart in his bosom, with a
serpent's cerebellum for a brain.' 'Your Tory is a straight-
forward robber and cut-throat, greedy as a shark, blind as a
bolt!' (71). The Chartist movement was born of suspicion.

THE RADICAL TRADITION: MEN AND IDEAS

'The cry of Reform in this country is not a cry of today or
yesterday,' Julian Harney told his Glasgow audience in 1840.
'It was raised so far back as the time of the great and glorious
American Revolution.' The radical tradition was extraordinarily
rich; Newtown weavers had Voltaire and Volney as their staple
diet. The main ideas of ultra-radicalism had, of course, been
worked out years before the Chartist movement (147). Opposition to a standing army and a large police force, an attack on
land monopoly and primogeniture, and support for religious
freedom and cheap government – these were the principles
around which each group of reformers built their own particular

programme. At the heart of this radicalism was the concept of popular sovereignty, justified by Tom Paine, supported in Parliament by Orator Hunt and sanctified by the martyrdom of Muir and Palmer. 'The People, the source of all legitimate power' was the first toast at Chartist dinners.

Paine and Hunt, together with William Cobbett and Major Cartwright, were perhaps the most venerated of Chartist heroes, taking pride of place over the men of the English and American revolutions. The appeal of Paine was unmistakable: 'he taught so many of us to think.' When the Chartist Philip McGrath in 1846 disputed the Master's definition of government as an evil, some of his London audience were clearly dismayed. For Paine and the early reformers had not only provided Chartism with an ideology but had also defined the political contestants and given radicalism its own version of history. For them, the main conflict in society lay between the 'corrupt rulers' (the 'aristocracy') and the 'ruled' (the 'people'). Although the language of Henry Hetherington and some of the Unstamped Press indicates a search for a new terminology more in keeping with the contemporary power structure, the first generation of Chartists often saw society and class in political rather than economic terms. Much to the annoyance of George White, virtually all the Chartist leaders at one time or another considered forming an alliance with a section of the 'grasping middle classes' against the aristocracy. 'It was not that he placed much reliance on the middle classes,' said McDouall in 1840, 'but still, if their services could be rendered available, they should be accepted.' The radical view of history – with its emphasis on Good King Alfred, the Norman Yoke, the mythical Chartist millennium prior to Henry VI's reign, the Cromwellian triumph and the subsequent aristocratic counter-revolution – sanctioned such a union.

Most Chartists traced the beginnings of the popular reform movement to the second half of the eighteenth century. At a great Wigan demonstration in November 1838 Dr Matthew Fletcher, a surgeon from Bury, produced a cap of liberty which had been exhibited at a similar meeting fifty-two years previously. By the late 1830s there was not one, but several radical traditions, and the representatives of each were eager to claim the Chartist movement as their own. Samuel Smiles's

Leeds Times, the *Nonconformist* and the Metropolitan Reform Association suggested that the six points had been devised by middle-class men like Horne Tooke who had always envisaged a reform movement based on class co-operation. In towns like Bath, Birmingham and Chelmsford there were issues – taxes, church rates, Corn Laws, etc. – over which men of different classes could and did unite, and this was one path into Chartism (97).

Yet even here mutual suspicion was rarely absent. Disappointment over the actions of 'Rational Reforming Whigs' had heightened the differences between middle- and working-class traditions. Not only had many of these Whigs shown a surprising rigidity over taxation, poor-law and franchise reform, but they had also been 'transformed in a trice into sticklers for "law and order"'. Lord John Russell's finality statement of November 1837 was the last 'blow on a cracked whistle'. Julian Harney and a host of enemies to and victims of 'middle-class Reform' in the 1830s saw themselves as heirs to the English and French Jacobins. Respectable Reform Associations were surprised by the intensity of this feeling in the elections of the mid 1830s – 'We don't want any gentlemen to represent us, we can represent ourselves' (170).

This independent strand of popular radicalism merged comfortably into the Chartist movement. 'We must rely on ourselves alone' became, as we have seen, a recurring theme of the years 1838–42. But once the Chartist honeymoon was over, differences within the independent tradition became more obvious. Various groups of Chartists accused one another of deviating from the spirit and methods of the old National Union of the Working Classes (N.U.W.C.). Messrs Stallwood and Stiles did so in the early 1850s and, much earlier, Henry Hetherington and James Watson withdrew from the movement on a similar pretext. The final showdown between these leaders of freethinking radicalism and O'Connor was a ferocious verbal battle in the *Northern Star* over the character and history of the independent working-class movement. The Irishman, who invariably gave Chartism his own pedigree, asserted that *all* agitations before 1835, including those of London 'Philosophical Radicals', had been associated with middle-class figures like Dr Black. Chartism was something new.

As the debate over ideological origins still continues (98, 99) it is perhaps more rewarding to look at the antecedents of Chartism through the political careers of some of its leading adherents. Many of them could echo the words of Samuel Bamford – 'I was born a Radical.' Amongst the most respected men in the movement were those who could trace their interest in politics back to the magical 1790s: Thomas Preston and William George (London), Robert Hames (Oundle), T. R. Smart (Loughborough) and John Allan (Parkhead). Other Chartist veterans still hoping to 'eat of the tree of liberty' included 'Radical John Jackson' (Hull), George Harrison (Nottingham), Archibald McDonald (Aberdeen), James Cuin (Cheltenham), 'Commodore' E. P. Mead (Birmingham) and Mr Rothwell of Manchester whom the Chartists buried under Hunt's monument. Most of this second group emerged as prominent figures during the mass agitation of the postwar years. For Lancashire Chartists like John Knight and James Fenny, the dour shoemaker of Wigan, the new movement was a continuation of a long campaign. 'James Fenny is no Reformer of a day,' said John Taylor in the *Operative*,

He took part in the dangers of 1819, and was present on 16th of August, at the Manchester Massacre; his undeviating consistency has acquired for him a greater influence among the hand-loom weavers of the part he represents than is possessed by any other man, and to mark their sense of his worth, when he set off for the Convention, he was escorted for miles by thousands, with bands and banners, each flag surmounted by a pike . . .

Peterloo survivors were given a special place in the Chartist movement.

In some areas the political experience of Chartist leaders was more limited. On the South Wales coalfield, Zephaniah Williams, Morgan Williams and Matthew John made their first public appearances during the Reform crisis. They *became* Chartists during the next four years. In this crucial period opinions were clarified and politicized by the 'betrayal' of the Whigs and the collapse of national trade unionism. In the remnants of Political Unions and radical periodicals, future Chartist leaders discussed the feasibility of creating a national convention or dreamt of a violent revolution, and gave new life to three old issues – universal suffrage, the Corn Laws and the Stamp Duties (123).

Significantly, Samuel Cook, who was to become the personifica-
tion of Dudley Chartism, chose March 1834 to publish his
political gospel.

Cook's dangerous passion for local politics – he was imprisoned several times – was shared by many other radicals in
the early 1830s. Bailie Hugh Craig, the future chairman of the
first Chartist Convention, and John Frost became magistrates;
Londoners, Harper and Fussey, achieved lesser prominence in
local affairs; and James Taylor, the quiet Rochdale minister,
and the flamboyant Dr John Taylor stood as popular candidates
in general elections. The adoption of Hobhouse's Vestries Bill
and the Municipal Corporations Act of 1835 naturally increased
the interest in local matters, and in certain districts of London,
Brighton and Coventry Chartism was partly an extension of
the conflict over vestry and voting rights.

Such a development was, of course, unlikely in places with
a narrow or rigid structure of government. Here it needed the
case of the Tolpuddle Martyrs to bring disillusioned radicals
back *en masse* into politics, and the campaigns against the
'Taxes on Knowledge' and the Poor Law Amendment Act to
create martyrs, new leaders and a ready-made organization for
the Chartist movement (132, 133, 153). Amongst those trained
and embittered in the battle of the Unstamped Press (1830–36)
were Julian Harney, James Ibbetson of Bradford and Thomas
Powell of mid Wales. Chartism absorbed these people as it did
so many committees, traditions and hopes.

THE CONFLICT OVER ÉLITE POLITICS, AND MOVES TOWARDS A NATIONAL ORGANIZATION

Much of the uniqueness of Chartism lay in its absorbent quality
and popular appeal, yet it began as part of a continuing experiment in élite politics. Lovett and O'Brien compared the latter
to throwing a stone into water; progress had to begin with the
few who would pass on their knowledge to a greater number.
Both men believed that radical politics was an exercise in
discipline and hard work, were critical of leaders who promised
immediate success, and surrounded themselves with intellectual
guarantees against disappointment.

Their attitude was embodied in many of the Radical Associations, Working Men's Associations and Political Unions which appeared in the years 1835–8. There were hundreds of these organizations; by the winter of 1838 there were twelve Radical Associations in the parish of Halifax alone. One would like to know more about their origins and character. Some of those in Scotland and Wales were lineal descendants of Jacobin clubs; others in London and the Midlands were launched by middle-class reformers. Most associations had an unmistakable missionary zeal and passion for education. The London Working Men's Association, an organ of the respectable trades, is the most obvious example. In 1836 Lovett, James Watson, Henry Hetherington and other veterans of London club life decided 'to establish a political school of self-instruction amongst [the working class] in which they should accustom themselves to examine great social and political principles' (37, 40, 42). Their purpose was to create an independent spirit amongst the 'intelligent and influential', and to give them an accompanying 'moral stamina'. This was élitism of a special kind; a method of guiding a popular movement away from the snares of 'false friends' and unprofitable temptations to the ultimate embracing reward of universal suffrage (see Appendix 1).

The work of this Association reflected the belief that ignorance was the greatest evil. Its many committees supported the campaign for 'a cheap and honest press', and encouraged the establishment of libraries and the collection of social statistics. Through pamphlets such as the famous 'Rotten House of Commons', and through petitions and addresses, the L.W.M.A. reached a national audience. Lovett even drafted appeals to the people of America and Western Europe – here the message was consistently democratic and the tone schoolmasterly. These calls for reform were interwoven with practical advice: '*With Union* everything will be achieved; *without Union* nothing.' In 1837 the L.W.M.A. took its first hesitant steps towards creating an organized national movement. Excursions by its missionaries (James Watson, Hetherington, Vincent, John Cleave and John Hartwell) into Wales and the North produced an associated membership of some 136 clubs.

O'Connor ridiculed their achievement. In later years both he and Ernest Jones claimed that his contribution towards the

c

birth of Chartism had never received its due reward. In 1835 the Irishman lost his parliamentary seat and took up the mantles of Hunt and Cobbett. The failure of the Great Marylebone Radical Association deprived him of an early London base, but his provincial tours of 1835–7 were singularly impressive. It is probably impossible to estimate the number of Radical Associations which he established, but in the North of England and western Scotland he found a keen response to his campaign for 'a new radical party'.

The case of the Glasgow cotton-spinners, whose trial occupied the attention of radicals and unionists in the winter of 1837–8, brought the animosity between O'Connor and Lovett's men into the open, and several northern W.M.A.s changed their allegiance. The delighted Irishman chose Leeds as the base from which to launch a second front, and the publication of the *Northern Star* was followed, in April 1838, by the setting up of the Great Northern Union. George White, its secretary, William Rider, Abram Hanson and others worked hard to attach associations to this new body, and by the summer of that year O'Connor could say, with an element of truth, that 'London, Birmingham, Sheffield, Manchester, Leeds, Newcastle, Carlisle, Glasgow and Edinburgh, had now become forged as it were together . . .'

Almost at this very moment the L.W.M.A. chose to publish their People's Charter. According to Lovett this document grew out of a prayer accompanying a petition of 1837. Its final character was decided after discussions with Francis Place, and J.A.Roebuck and other interested parties. The immediate response to its publication was probably disappointing – Radical M.P.s held back and O'Connor ignored it – but in the late summer of 1838 even branches of the Great Northern Union were discussing its contents. The spectacular breakthrough came in August of that year, when the Charter was taken up by the Birmingham Political Union.

The B.P.U. was the first of the Political Unions to be revived after the collapse in the early 1830s. These organizations had provided Samuel Cook, Peter Bussey, R.J.Richardson and Bailie Craig with their first schooling in radical politics. The B.P.U. was reformed in April 1837, as a result of financial and popular pressure, and it quickly drew up a National Petition calling for sweeping changes in the economy and system of

parliamentary representation. The history and methods of the
B.P.U. inspired and required optimism. 'It is only necessary,'
said Thomas Attwood, 'to exhibit the public will well combined
and acting simultaneously with one heart and one hand to
ensure instant success in any right and just cause' (56).
Missionaries were sent to encourage Political Unions in Wales
and the North, and plans were made for a great delegate
meeting to sanction the Birmingham programme. Attwood,
R. K. Douglas and John Collins received a tumultuous welcome
in Scotland, especially from the angry workmen of Glasgow (75).

At one of the monster Glasgow demonstrations two rival
delegates from the L.W.M.A. introduced the People's Charter.
It was later discussed by the Council of the B.P.U., and was
formally adopted at a mass public meeting on 6 August 1838.
R. J. Richardson, O'Connor, Hetherington and other leading
radicals were present at this assembly which Mark Howell
described as 'the official beginning of the Chartist movement'
(28). Attwood later claimed, with some chagrin, that the
Birmingham reformers gave Chartism a new impetus and
strategy; the National Petition, the National Rent and even
the National Convention were 'set . . . in motion' by them.

Tensions were present from the earliest days of the merger
between these two movements. The B.P.U. was faced by the
growing confidence of its own working-class members. O'Connor,
sure of the North and hungry for the South, exploited these
divisions in the winter of 1838–9. The founders of the B.P.U.
were alarmed by his presence, promises and language (2). In
one of their many acrimonious council meetings, Douglas
pleaded the virtues of gradualism – 'for saying this his friend
Collins was laughing at him . . .' In the Convention which met
a few months later the laughter reached a crescendo. Gradually,
and perhaps inevitably, the 'old women' of Birmingham withdrew from the popular movement.

The collapse of the dialogue between Birmingham reformers
was typical of the process of secession and separation in the
years 1838–9. 'These were not,' as one commentator put it, 'the
times for well-meaning men to play the moth around the flame
of revolution.' On their tour of Scotland, missionaries of the
B.P.U. commented on the absence of important middle-class
reformers at public meetings. O'Connor and Dr John Taylor

were always willing to take their places. At Bolton Messrs
Lloyd, Warden and Gillespie replaced Naisby and Thomasson
at the head of the popular movement. It was a similar story
at Leamington, Brighton and Bath. 'Respectable' reformers no
longer found it possible to contain both their own doubts and
the independent feelings of working men. Significantly, Political
Unions and Associations were rent in the winter of 1838–9 by
the first of many Chartist debates over the integrity of middle-
class reformers. As always on such occasions, questions of
history and confidence rose to the surface:

> Mr. James Ayr said, that he would suspect any man who proposed
> such a discussion [with the middle classes] of impure motives, the French
> working people had gained a revolution, and the middle classes came in
> and deprived them of the fruits, such he doubted not, was the intention
> of the middle classes of England. Mr. Mason said, that Mr. Ayr was
> mistaken as to matter of fact and history, the French Revolution was
> a revolution of the middle classes into which the people were merely
> brought as assistants. Therefore it was that the middle classes were able
> to take all the fruits to themselves, it would be very different in England
> ... Mr. Devyr said ... If they considered that the Whigs were more
> intelligent and could cajole or bamboozle [their] leaders, then were the
> people perfectly right in avoiding discussion, but if they considered that
> there could be found men as intelligent as the Whigs, then ought they
> to meet them at once, they having everything to gain and nothing to
> lose by the discussion. (Council of the Northern Political Union at
> Newcastle in April 1839)

In 1838 and 1839 joint middle- and working-class Reform
Associations in some of the larger towns were dissolved in
favour of working-class Radical Associations, and to these
were added militant Democratic Associations.

The London Democratic Association was the model for some
of these new societies. Like the L.W.M.A. it developed out of
the National Union of the Working Classes and was formally
established as the East London Democratic Association in
January 1837 (164). For a time relations with the L.W.M.A.
were amicable, though their social composition and areas of
support were different. The turning-point appears to have been
the Glasgow cotton-spinners' strike, over which O'Connor and
his *Star* sided with the L.D.A. against Daniel O'Connell and the
L.W.M.A. In March 1838 Harney, Neesom and Tom Ireland
resigned from the older institution, denouncing Lovett and his
friends as 'sham patriots'.

The appeal of the L.D.A. to a man like Harney was obvious – 'the Jacobin club again lives and flourishes . . .' 'Your whole social system requires "revolution"' was the message in their news-sheet, 'your commercial system requires "revolution" and nothing short of actual convulsion will effect a cure...Establish the People's Charter tomorrow, and the working man will not have one difficulty the less to contend with' (3). In the 'Objects of the L.D.A.' an attempt was made to identify the areas of economic exploitation:

First. – the objects of the Democratic Association are, to avail itself of every opportunity in the progress of society, for practically establishing the principles of Social, Political and Universal Equality.

Second. – To this end, they desire to unite the unrepresented of all classes into one bond of fraternity, for the attainment of Universal Suffrage: this Association being convinced that, until the proletarian classes are fully and faithfully represented, justice in legislation will never be rendered unto them.

Third. – To obtain, in addition to the extension of the Suffrage to every adult male: that the country be divided, according to the population, into equal electoral districts. That the elections of the Legislative Assembly to be taken annually: the Legislators to receive wages of attendance: and the only qualification required, to be the confidence of the electors . . .

Fourth. – To devise every possible means and to make every exertion to remove those oppressive, odious, and unjust enactments that prevent the free circulation of thought through the medium of an untaxed and honest press.

Fifth. – To procure the total and unqualified repeal of the infamous New Poor Law Act, and a restoration of the spirit of the 43d. of Elizabeth, with such improvements as the circumstances of the country may require.

Six. – To promote the abridgement of the hours of labour in factories and workshops, and the total abolition of infant labour altogether. Even in the present artificial state of society no adult person should be *required* to work more than eight hours per day, especially while so many thousands are without employment at all.

Seven. – To support, as circumstances may determine, by all available means, every rational opposition made by working men against the combination and tyranny of capitalists, wherever the latter shall seek to reduce the wages of labour, extend the hours of toil, or institute proceedings against the labourer, the character of which proceedings in the estimation of the association shall be deemed vexatious and oppressive.

Eight. – To promote public instruction and the diffusion of sound political knowledge.

And finally, the great object, end, and aim, of this association is the destruction of inequality and the establishment of general happiness.

The L.D.A. attacked contemporary examples of collaboration with 'Malthusian radicals'; why repeat the blunder of 1832?

Perhaps the main concern of the Association in the first half of 1839 was to 'stiffen the resolve' of the Chartist Convention. It was a difficult task; those representing the views of the L.D.A. gained little support and only encouraged a flurry of resignations. Undaunted by the failure of an intended May rising, Major Beniowski and other disillusioned members of the L.D.A. made preparations for a rebellion. The Newport affair galvanized them into action, but the government swooped on two key men – Neesom and Joseph Williams. It was a body-blow to an organization already torn by dissension. The L.D.A. continued to function for another year, but an increasing number of its supporters were attracted by Chartist societies associated with O'Connor and by the National Charter Association.

THE
NATIONAL CHARTER
ASSOCIATION

The origins of this important Chartist body are fairly obscure. James Leach claimed responsibility for the original idea, but in the aftermath of the Newport rising there were many individuals and groups calling for a national organization. The collapse of pressure politics in the face of stern government opposition had shown the need for a permanent leadership to guide a united popular movement. Hetherington's Metropolitan Charter Union, formed in April 1840, was one of several regional attempts to bring together those associations which had survived the difficult winter of 1839–40. In July a further step was taken; Chartist delegates meeting at Manchester decided to create a national political party and appoint a provisional executive. From the outset this National Charter Association had a bureaucratic spirit and a determined policy of centralization. In regions like South Lancashire and the West Riding, Working Men's Associations quickly joined the N.C.A., but

Chartists in Scotland and the Midlands were suspicious of its powers, professionalism and legality. In Birmingham George White failed to persuade John Collins and members of the Chartist churches to join the national body. Even in the autumn of 1842, when the N.C.A. claimed 400 localities, certain Chartist groups remained outside its authority.

The strikes of 1842, during which prominent radicals were arrested, emphasized the N.C.A.'s problems of leadership and co-ordination; local branches drifted away. But demands for united action persisted, and for the first of many occasions, London leaders and the *Northern Star* took over functions of the executive. Since the beginning of the N.C.A. O'Connor and his newspaper had held an ambivalent relationship with that organization. Although the Irishman was accountable to its members, he held a position of enviable independence. His problems really began in the winter of 1842, when rival reform movements gathered strength and when prominent Chartists like William Hill launched an assault on an expensive and irresponsible executive. During subsequent months Thomas Cooper and district bodies like the Birmingham and Midland Counties Charter Association widened the debate, and proposed sweeping changes in the near-lifeless N.C.A. O'Connor and the executive responded to the challenge, and from their new London base tried to bring more unity and efficiency into the organization.

After the important Convention of 1844 the main topics of discussion within the N.C.A. were the Land Plan and local politics. Directors of O'Connor's Land Company controlled the executive, and were accused of sacrificing the interests of one movement for the other. Criticisms of their power and inactivity reached a peak in the spring of 1848 when the Convention and National Assembly tried to give the N.C.A. an infusion of democracy and missionary zeal. A few delegates wanted to change its name, and most supported London's demands for reorganization. The next three years saw a bewildering debate over the nature and spirit of the N.C.A., which ended in a degrading stand-up fight between London and Manchester Chartists. For months the argument ran like an electric current between rival executives and conferences, and the Manchester Council even established a breakaway organization known as the National Charter League. Many provincial localities retired in confusion, still pleading for guidance and consultation. The N.C.A., which had once claimed a membership of over 50,000, seemed in 1851 to be on the verge of extinction.

The nature of the constitution of the N.C.A. can be seen in Appendix II. The most controversial feature of the constitution was the executive. Its purpose was to give continuity and direction to the Chartist movement, especially at times of political crisis or when threatened by rival movements like the Anti-Corn-Law League. Through its addresses and circulars the executive laid down a national policy. The following recommendations were issued in the spring of 1842, after several localities had expressed uncertainty about how they should react to successful initiatives by middle-class reformers:

1st. Every Corn Law Repealer or middle class professor of Chartism, should make a public and unreserved declaration and attachment to the whole principle of the Charter, before he can take part with us in the agitation, or co-operate with us. 2nd. The Corn Law party or middle class agitators desiring to co-operate with us, should be called upon to agree to the unqualified right of speech for all our leaders at all political meetings, and the full privilege of moving amendments to all motions, whenever it may appear to the people or their advisers to be necessary.

Without the first unreserved admission, we can have no security for the sincerity of their professions, and consistency of conduct.

Without the second all important provision we can have no effective check upon the guidance of public opinion . . .

Another primary function of the executive was the co-ordination of fund-raising, petitioning and lecturing; and here the 'servants of the People' sometimes exceeded their authority. Throughout the life of the N.C.A. there was a continual debate over the composition and powers of the executive, the method of its election, and its finances. Radicals' instinctive distrust of a small, salaried body had to be balanced against the advantages of single-minded professionalism.

For almost a decade O'Connor dominated the N.C.A. This self-styled successor to Orator Hunt imposed his will, men, money and policies on the organization. He popularized the Association, personalized its unity and gave it direction. Above all, O'Connor made the N.C.A. into a viable political party. He understood as well as anyone the weaknesses of the movement, and demanded from the Chartists a policy of realism and flexibility. 'We must take advantage of every passing event' was a creed not an apology, and helps to explain his balancing act between Whigs and Tories.

On one thing O'Connor would brook no opposition – the 'Chartists must retain their own organization'. 'One party, one programme' was an old radical cry but the Irishman took it to new lengths. In print and in speeches, his constant themes were unsophisticated 'out and out Chartism' and the importance of an independent national party. 'United we stand, divided we fall' was perhaps his most famous motto, and was applicable to the N.C.A. in both good and bad times.

In carrying out this policy O'Connor denounced 'traitors' and attacked rival organizations. Nothing incensed his critics so much as this. W.P.Roberts, the legal adviser of the N.C.A., local branches and even conventions called for harmony; and generations of writers have blamed O'Connor for dividing the movement. Denunciation certainly split some associations and kept others on the fringes of the N.C.A., yet it had its own *sans-culotte* logic. Harney and O'Connor claimed that it purified the movement and left it stronger; the fomenters of discord had been consigned to retirement by 'sound public opinion'. Amongst the most famous victims of O'Connor's incredible abuse were Hetherington, Dr Fletcher and O'Brien. The charges were almost incidental; 'middle-class', 'Whig' and 'spy' were some of the epithets commonly attached to these people. Radicals, of course, revelled in verbal battles, but for deserters like Neesom, the 'little renegade' Vincent and John Fraser (Tower Hamlets) who joined rival movements, there was also physical intimidation from O'Connor's supporters.

Personal denunciation was accompanied by a deep suspicion of alternative reform programmes and organizations. We have seen how O'Connor reacted in the spring of 1841 to various Chartist 'mutations', and with what justification and effect. Local radical mavericks like the Reverend Patrick Brewster soon discovered the power of the Irishman's hold on the rank and file. The attack on Lovett's National Association brought a flurry of resignations and public apologies. Here, as always, the touchstone of criticism was – 'Why do we need a National Association when we have one already?' A similar attitude was

adopted towards middle-class attempts in the 1840s to get up
a popular reform movement:

'Why all this scheming, planning and capering?
First, Household Suffrage;
Second, Education Suffrage;
Third, Complete Suffrage;
Fourth, Twenty-five years' Suffrage;
Fifth, the Charter Suffrage and Vote by Ballot.
Why simply and truly because you (Chartists) are determined not to
budge from the Charter – . . .' (South Lancashire Address, February
1842)

Chartists were encouraged to pursue the old radical policy of
obstruction. They held conferences at the same time as their
rivals, invaded their meetings, and refused to allow public
meetings for less than the six points.

The closest rival to Chartism in the early 1840s was the
Complete Suffrage movement. Its appeal was obvious and
calculated; besides supporting the six points of the Charter,
honest Joseph Sturge proclaimed the virtues of peace, class
co-operation and voluntary subscription (50). The strikes of
1842 gave point to his message, and many Chartists turned
their heads. Part of the executive of the N.C.A., and even
hardened radicals in London and industrial South Wales, gave
the Complete Suffrage Union qualified support. O'Connor, in a
difficult situation, remained suspicious of the success and
divisive nature of a rival organization which acted as a haven
for old enemies like O'Brien, Vincent and Lovett. He advised
members of the N.C.A. to test the programme and sincerity of
the Complete Suffrage leaders on every possible occasion.
Ironically, it was Lovett who provided the final test at the
second Complete Suffrage Conference in December 1842. Sturge
and his friends could accept the principles of the Charter but
not its name nor its organization. The C.S.U. collapsed like a
balloon in most areas south of the Scottish border, and subsequent attempts by Sturge, Vincent and Thomas Duncombe,
M.P., to establish a People's Party received only limited
support.

The integrity of the N.C.A. was ensured. 'Those who are not
for us are against us,' sang a jubilant O'Connor. But the
Chartist party had its own problems, and chief amongst these
was finance. Several thousand pounds were raised for the

National Rent and for subsequent funds to help the Chartist agitation and the army of veterans, victims and 'widows'. Preston forwarded £95 for the John Frost Fund in one week, and the people of Nottingham could be relied upon to give more than was asked. James Sweet, a shopkeeper of that town, was one of the great collectors; others were Harney, Thomas Cooper, Thomas Brown, Mrs Heath and Thomas Ingram of Abergavenny. They organized concerts, plays and raffles, and established permanent fund-raising bodies like the Stockport Chartist Singers. With so many demands on Chartist purses, it was hardly surprising that N.C.A. subscriptions were paid irregularly, and that the executive received only a fraction of the money to which it was entitled. Lecturers could not be paid and conferences were cancelled for lack of money. Various expedients were adopted like the National Tribute and the Liberty Fund, and businessmen contributed a percentage of their income to the Association, but expectation always exceeded the response. In hard times Chartists could pay only district expenses, and the executive was forced to reduce its activities to a minimum. The income of the N.C.A. in 1851 barely covered the secretary's salary.

Much of the blame fell inevitably on the intermediate officials, the 'casual councillors' and the 'slack sub-secretaries'. Communication was a major problem in the N.C.A.; the *Northern Star* regularly printed lists of towns which had not sent in returns and subscriptions. Certain branches just disappeared from the records. Their commitment to the central body was to some extent a reflection of the vigour of the district councils, for these were intended to supervise matters such as elections, lecturing, demonstrations and the collection of money. South Lancashire and West Riding delegate meetings were the dynamo of Chartism in the early 1840s, and proved extremely effective in carrying out the orders of the executive, but in areas like North Lancashire, the Midlands and the West Country experiments in 'regional Chartism' were usually short-lived.

Chartist leaders could be peculiarly insensitive to the problems of local associations. In years like 1850 district meetings *had* to take over the functions of the executive. Many radicals, of course, preferred it this way; Scotland and the North-east, for instance, were areas with a strong independent tradition. During the later years of Chartism two prominent regional bodies even tried to impose their schemes and views on the N.C.A. The South Lancashire delegate meeting in the years 1848–51 criticized the executive, modified the constitution and initiated policy. Its opposite number, the Metropolitan Delegate Council, was also *de facto* an autonomous institution. This address of September 1844 conveys something of its growing stature:

FELLOW MEN, – The Council being about to resign its trust into the hands of those you may think proper to elect under the New Organisation, drawn up by the Executive Committee, at the request of this Council, they are desirous of rendering an account of their stewardship. They, therefore, with much deference, submit the following: –

Firstly – They obtained, and kept in existence, an efficient corps of unpaid local Lecturers.

Secondly – They organised and conducted the various aggregate meetings held in the several districts of the Metropolis, with good effect to the Chartist cause.

Thirdly – They were the humble instruments in meeting, discussing with, and exposing the League and Anti-League humbugs, once so prevalent in London.

Fourthly – They brought forward the subject of registering compound householders and lodgers in favour of the 'Charter', causing it to be noticed in the Metropolitan portion of the Liberal daily and weekly press, until at length, from the information from time to time afforded by our sub-committee and secretary, thousands are placed on the ratebooks, and are at this moment in possession of local power; and after the registration of July, 1845, will be in a position to exercise their votes in favour of the People's Charter.

Fifthly – Active steps were taken by this Council, in conjunction with the Trades, that led to the final defeat and total overthrow of the ever hateful Master and Servants' Bill.

> Faithfully yours,
> John Simpson, Treasurer,
> Edmund Stallwood, Secretary.

Regular members of this Council included the writer T.M. Wheeler and the black tailor, William Cuffay. They organized radical meetings in the capital, and sometimes acted as a provisional executive. After the disintegration of organized Chartism in 1850–51 O'Connor's successors used the M.D.C. as a platform for reviving the national movement.

CLUB, MEETING
AND DEMONSTRATION

The monthly, weekly and sometimes daily meeting of the
Chartist Club constituted the basic machinery of the movement. Associations usually met in homes, schoolrooms, church
halls, coffee houses and inns. In South Wales the Chartist public
houses stretched in a long, inviting line from Newport to
Swansea. Some of them, like the Three Horse Shoes (Merthyr),
the Three Tuns (Newcastle upon Tyne) and the Cap of Liberty
(Brighton) were famous, and were decorated in the style of
Disraeli's Cat and Fiddle with portraits, posters, banners, caps
of liberty and tricolour lanterns. Accommodation was always
a problem for radical workmen, especially in rural areas. Some
associations changed their venue six or seven times. Chartists
were allowed the use of institutes and halls in certain towns,
but friction between them and the middle classes in 1839, 1842
and 1848 underlined the value of securing their own buildings.
London Chartists took over old radical institutions like the
Rotunda; in the North and the Potteries they were more
adventurous and erected 'Chartist Halls'. Some of these were
very temporary indeed, and floors collapsed under the excitement of the first mass meeting. Those at Oldham (1845–),
Manchester (1846–) and Mottram (1847–) were grander
affairs, consecrated by Chartist leaders and held up as shining
examples of what could be done 'by the zeal, the confidence,
and the pence of working men alone' (142).

The constitutions of local associations were highly democratic, with a rapid turnover of officers. 'The business of the
Association is managed by weekly meetings of its members,'
ran a report on the durable Dumfries and Maxwelltown W.M.A.,

and in accordance with a provision of its constitution, which declares
that there shall be no presidents, vice-presidents, or leaders of any
description, a chairman is elected at each meeting from the members
present; but special committees are occasionally appointed, and a
secretary, treasurer, &c. with special and strictly defined powers, every
three months.

To this involvement of members was attributed the success of
Chartist associations and the fact that so few of their officers
disappeared with the account books.

The openness of the Chartist clubs was important. 'We have no secrets and admit anybody' was a necessary preface to a range of near-seditious activities. Yet within this legal fiction it was possible for some associations in parts of Bristol and Glasgow to develop a reputation for exclusiveness. By contrast, clubs in Merthyr, Bilston and Brighton promoted recruiting drives and established sister associations in the surrounding districts. The quality of Bilston Chartism is conveyed by the enthusiasm of lecturer Duffy who at one meeting 'took his pen in his hand and never stirred while an unenrolled person stood' (163). The colourful Shakespearian Chartists of Leicester claimed a membership of well over 2000. When political fever ran high, halls and rooms were packed to overflowing, and associations were divided into classes, but the average attendance was possibly no more than twenty or thirty. In bad times, members were content to be 'all alive here and out of debt'.

The Chartist club had its own cycle of activities. The Wednesday evening class, the Saturday lecture and the Sunday sermon were regular weekly events, and to these were added annual celebrations to commemorate the births of Hunt and Paine, local radical festivals and the round of spectacular Chartist funerals. One feature of these celebrations was the inordinate number of toasts and songs. This account comes from Ashton-under-Lyne in November 1840:

On Saturday evening, a large number of the disciples of the lamented Henry Hunt, met at the house of Mr. Abraham Matley, Charlestown, to commemorate the birthday of that great man. The room was tastefully hung with the portraits of political characters, at the head of which was a large painting of Peterloo, with the black flag waving over it, and this inscription in characters of blood:– 'Ashton demands Universal Suffrage, or Universal Vengeance.' After the cloth was withdrawn, Mr. Ralph Clough, an operative, was unanimously called upon to preside. After opening the business he concluded a very neat address by calling on all present to follow the dictates of our late departed friend. The Chairman gave 'The people, the only source of power' . . . Song by Mr. Andrew – 'Peterloo'. The chairman then gave 'The immortal memory of Henry Hunt, the man who never deceived the people', which was drunk in solemn silence, the company up-standing and uncovered . . . Song, 'The Life and death of Henry Hunt', by John Stafford, the Charlestown poet. The Chairman next gave 'the Plaintiffs in Prison, and Defendants at Large.' Here the Chairman read an address from our townsman, William Aitken, in Kirkdale gaol, approving the object of our meeting. Song by

Mr. James Howcourt, 'Rights and liberty we'll have'. The next toast was, 'The People's Charter, and may it soon become the law of the land'; . . . Song by Mr. John Shane, 'Duffy's lament'. The Chairman next gave, 'The healths of Frost, Williams, and Jones, and may they soon be restored to their country and families'. Recitation, by the Chairman, on the principles of the Charter. Song, 'Exile of Erin', by Mr. John Shaw. The next toast was, 'The Radical Press'; responded to by a shareholder of the *Star*. Song by Samuel Walker, 'Ye wealth producers' . . . Song by Mr. Andrew Grime, 'Famed Peterloo', in which all the company joined chorus. The evening getting very late, the Chairman next proposed, 'The immortal memory of Thomas Paine, Robert Emmett, William Cobbett, Cartwright, Sydney, Tyler, Hampden, Elihu Palmer, the blind philosopher, Volney, Voltaire, Mirabeau, Muir, Washington, Tell, Hofer (sic), Wallace, Joshua Hobson, and all the illustrious dead of every nation, who by their acts or deeds have contributed to the cause of freedom'. Mr. Abraham Matley, an old Republican, passed a high eulogium on all their characters; and John Shaw, in his usual style, sung 'My Emmett's no more'. A vote of thanks being given to the Chairman, and three cheers for Feargus O'Connor, three for Frost, Williams and Jones, three groans for the Whigs, and Peterloo butchers, and three times three for the Charter, the meeting broke up at a very late hour, all present being highly gratified with the evening's entertainment.

For loyal Chartists the club was the centre of political and social life. A plethora of sub-committees organized a full range of family activities, from public breakfasts, tea-parties and dinners to dramatic productions, poetry-readings, oratorios and balls. This celebration dinner at the village of Calverton, near Nottingham, was fairly typical:

This dinner was got up by, and at the house of, Mr. George Harrison, and consisted of roast beef, etc. Ale had been brewed at the farm-house, for the occasion, and at two o'clock the party sat down. Mr. Russell, of Nottingham, was appointed to the chair. The afternoon was spent in the greatest good humour and conviviality; a choice selection of Chartist songs were given and responded to, with other patriotic sentiments . . .

The meeting closed 'at a late hour'. Whilst O'Connor theorized about this evidence of 'social progress' amongst the people, the ordinary member was perhaps more concerned that 'means should be adopted to make their society as interesting and attractive as possible' in the face of competition from benefit clubs and Halls of Science. After considerable discussion, the Dumfries W.M.A. introduced chess and draughts into their club room. The Stockport youths who brought laughing-gas to a

Christmas concert went a little too far, but the spirit was right.
Dancing classes were always popular; cricket matches and
pleasure trips became increasingly so.

Chartist associations, of course, always had a serious purpose,
and one of their main functions was to organize public meetings
and demonstrations. The right to hold such meetings had been
won after a long struggle, and the Chartists defended it vigorously. George White played a special part here, defying policemen to interrupt his speeches, and taking the numbers of those
who tried. When clubs were prevented from publicizing their
demonstrations by poster or town crier, they paraded the
streets behind drummer and fife. Government and local pro-
hibitions on public meetings in 1839–40, 1842 and 1848 were
deeply resented. Chief Justice Wilde's declaration in 1848 that
certain open-air meetings amounted to intimidation produced
a spasm of indignation; Richard Marsden talked darkly of a
return to the bad old days.

The public meeting was *the* Chartist experience, and some
associations held regular weekly assemblies in the market place
as well as fortnightly camp meetings on the neighbouring hills.
From hustings decorated with evergreens, flags and lamps,
radical leaders called on the local population to be firm and
'come on like men', and made fun of the inevitable group of
police and 'respectables'. Visiting speakers were usually very
welcome; at Blackwood in Monmouthshire they were met a
mile outside the town by girls dressed in white. In the early
days of the movement, associations frequently got together and
arranged splendid regional demonstrations of numerical power
(6). Whole towns turned out to watch the procession of bands
and the flag-bearing representatives of working-men's societies
marching through the streets. It brought humour, colour and
a sense of community to their lives, as we can see from this
report of a joint Chartist-and-trades demonstration at Aberdeen:

> Thursday, October the 8th, 1840, was a glorious day in the annals of
> Northern Chartism. The day had been fixed upon for the meetings of
> the Scottish Agricultural and Highland Societies, when a great show of
> prize cattle was to take place; in addition to these the city authorities
> had ordered a grand (?) procession upon the occasion of laying the
> foundation stone of the intended new market; all the grand doings
> were to 'come off' on the 8th, but the Chartists, nothing daunted, deter-
> mined to have a finger in the pie with the rest; accordingly, much to

the annoyance of 'the powers that be', large placards were posted a few days previous, announcing that a great Chartist procession of the trades and inhabitants of Aberdeen would take place on the 8th, where a public meeting would be held to petition Parliament in favour of the People's Charter . . . The following was the order of procession:—

The Convener of the Trades, on horseback.

1. Tailors.
2. Weavers.
3. Machine Makers.
4. Moulders.
5. Flax-dressers.
6. Sawyers.
7. Auchmill District.
8. Boiler Makers.
9. Woolcombers.
10. Slaters.
11. Tanners and Curriers, with Gilcomston District.
12. Carpet Weavers.
13. Messrs Julian Harney, Duncan and O'Neill.
14. Chairman and Council of the Union.
15. The Charter Union.

The following are a few – and but a few – of the mottos displayed on the flags, banners and emblematical devices carried in the procession . . .

Flag, with figure of Justice holding the balance.
Motto, 'Ten Pounders found wanting Universal Suffrage, Union, Peace.'
Reverse – Full-Length portrait of Feargus O'Connor, holding a scroll, inscribed, 'People's Charter'.
Motto – 'Let all govern, and all obey'.
Flag, Motto – 'It is the right of man to be free'.
Reverse – 'Universal Suffrage, and No Surrender'.
Blue Flag – motto, 'Dr. McDouall, the tyrant's foe, and hand-loom weavers' friend'.
Reverse – 'May the British Constitution be thoroughly repaired' . . .

A living fox was carried in a cage borne high upon poles. Over the cage was inscribed on the one side –

> 'Inspector-spy Fox Maule,
> Little Finality's jackall'.

Reverse – 'A hen-house Conservative'.
Wherever this appeared it excited shouts of laughter among all spectators.

A demonstration such as this probably attracted little comment outside its own area, but the rallies at Peep Green, Kersal Moor and Glasgow in the late 1830s were of a different order and these passed quickly into Chartist folklore. Chartist and trade-union committees spent months in organizing these rallies, and the result was some of the largest public meetings of the nineteenth century. However peaceful their intent, such massive gatherings of angry men brought back memories of the Reform crisis and Peterloo. As the light faded on the northern moors, the staves and intimidation of the crowds seemed to grow, and a worried government decided in the winter and spring of 1838–9 to place a ban on all torchlight and armed meetings. The events of the following year were partly responsible for a change in the attitude of certain Chartist leaders, who later denounced the popular rituals of the past as expensive charades. Still, the camp meetings and welcoming demonstrations for political prisoners continued to be held well into the 1850s. They were a particular favourite of the Chartists of the West Riding and South Lancashire, who yearly met together in a great festival at Blackstone Edge.

The preparations for and cost of these meetings were enormous, but the return was obvious. In some areas they were the best legal means of breaking new ground and expanding the size of the Chartist organization. The Colne Chartists claimed that within two months of a demonstration on 22 October 1838, at least four associations were established in neighbouring villages. Whenever the movement suffered a setback, as in the winters of 1840, 1842 and 1850, delegate committees used public meetings to launch a revival. London Chartists, rightly concerned about the state of the movement in the early months of 1843, divided the metropolis into parliamentary and borough districts and began to hold regular public meetings in each of them. Once enthusiasm had been rekindled, mass rallies and demonstrations followed; witness the famous Kersal Moor and Blackstone Edge meetings in 1846 and 1847:

> Then every eye grew keen and bright,
> And every pulse was dancing light,
> For every heart had felt its might
> The might of labour's chivalry. (Ernest Jones)

Here the Chartists came face-to-face with their claim to be the greatest popular movement, and the squabble over numbers was an index of the tension involved.

These public displays of power were intended to 'paralyse

our enemies' and they certainly proved that Chartism had a large army of non-enrolled adherents. 'In Aberdeen,' said James Shirron at the Convention of 1848, 'the Chartists were not well organized, but on great occasions like the present, the people had always come out in great numbers.' When a national petition was about to be presented, or when leaders needed support, public meetings were a way of showing Chartist strength. The Conventions of 1839 and 1848 recommended the holding of simultaneous demonstrations as a means of placing pressure on the government. Associations responded enthusiastically, but the results were disappointing.

PETITIONS
AND
CONVENTIONS

Chartism was remembered for its petitions and conventions. Both were traditional, even 'sacred' weapons, and both could be justified by history. 'Daddy' John Richards of the Potteries claimed that petitioning had been responsible for the passing of a series of important reform measures. In the later 1830s he and other Chartist leaders had been involved in successful campaigns on behalf of the Tolpuddle Martyrs and the Glasgow cotton-spinners. Yet a few reformers objected to petitioning on principle, and there were times when disillusionment with such a peaceful form of protest was general. 'The truth is,' said O'Brien, 'there will be no need of petitioning whenever the people are determined to do their duty; but until they are so determined, neither prayers nor petitions nor God Almighty's self can do them any good.' In the spring of 1840 a good many English Chartists shared this view; at a Manchester conference David Roberts of Liverpool attacked John Richards, insisting that the Reform Act and Catholic Relief Act had been obtained only by threats of violence. A spectator at the meeting denounced petitioning as 'the most abject of things – the prostration of manhood', a sentiment reiterated in 1842 and 1848. Even so, the voting was 2 to 1 in favour of the constitutional method. Chartists were always reluctant to abandon petitioning. 'By that means,' said the *Chartist Circular* in December 1839, 'you will unite public opinion in your favour, and effect a more widespread and complete organization than you have yet accomplished.' Petitioning was an effective and legal way of drawing attention to their cause in both Press and Parliament. Whether it ever worried the upper classes was a different matter; at the very least, it deprived 'our opponents of a pretence against us'.

The Chartists adopted a wide variety of petitions. Some, such as that of 1841 asking the Queen to dismiss her ministers, were sponsored by the Chartist leadership; others sprang from the local situation. Scotland had its own 'Petitioning Movement' which began officially on 2 March 1840 (75). Such was the trade in petitions that a London committee was established to prepare them for individuals and private bodies. The idea of swamping Parliament with individual petitions was considered – on one occasion Thomas Duncombe, M.P., received 407 from Leicester – but few English and Welsh radicals took it up. For them the most popular addresses were undoubtedly the national ones on behalf of the Charter and its martyrs.

Chartist victims had an important place in the organization and propaganda of the movement, and John Cleave, the book-seller friend of O'Connor and Lovett, brought years of experience and compassion to this work. Chartist 'widows' received weekly grants whilst their husbands were in gaol, or were helped to set up in business (Table 2, opposite, provides us with a typical illustration of this work). At the same time, restoration com-mittees, taking a lead from enthusiasts in London and Birming-ham, armed themselves with stickers and collecting sheets in the cause of those men sentenced to transportation. Chartist leaders, who already knew the publicity value of political prisoners, quickly realized that concern for them could also be a useful source of unity and continuity. Within days of the Newport rising, O'Connor had identified himself with John Frost and called upon radicals to make his safety the 'all-absorbing question'. Thereafter, national petitioning cam-paigns on behalf of Frost, Williams, and Jones became a regular Chartist weapon, especially useful – as in the winter of 1846–7 – when political protest had lost some of its steam.

The most famous petitions were, however, those calling for the Charter, the first of which was drafted and presented by Birmingham radicals. According to Thomas Attwood it was

Table 2. BALANCE SHEET
OF THE NATIONAL VICTIM FUND COMMITTEE
28 August 1841 to 2 February 1842*

Receipts		£	s	d
Aug. 28	Cash in Mr. Heywood's hands as treasurer	10	8	0
	From Carlisle, per J.West		2	6
	From Newton Heath, per E.Travis		4	0
Sept. 11	From Sowerby, per J.Crolly to Mr. Campbell		12	0
	From Soyland Mills, do., do.,		9	0
	From Edinburgh, N.C.A. do.,	1	0	0
	Ditto, the readers of the *Northern Star*		10	0
Sept. 14	From the Tower Hamlets N.C.A. per Charles Johns	1	0	0
	From Handley and Shelton N.C.A. per Henry Sharp		10	0
	After a lecture by Mr. Leach, per Mr. Ralton			10
	East Manchester Joint Stock Company, per Mr. James Cartledge		5	0
Sept. 20	From Wellington, Newcastle-upon-Tyne, per Arthur	1	0	0
	From Newcastle-upon-Tyne N.C.A., per I.Bruce		3	0
Oct. 20	From Brighton N.C.A., per W.Flowers	1	0	0
	From Mr. Ruffy Ridley of London, per Heywood		10	0
Dec. 20	From Mr. Buckley, of Doncaster, per Mr. Campbell		5	0
Jan. 22	From the *Northern Star*, per Mr. Ardhill	27	4	4
	Total received by committee	45	3	8
	Total money paid by do.	33	15	0
	Balance in hand, 2 Feb. 1842	11	8	8

Expenditure				
Aug. 28	Mr. Potts, of Bath	2	0	0
	Mrs. Peddie, of Edinburgh	1	0	0
	Mrs. Foden, of Sheffield	1	0	0
	Mrs. Marshall, do.	1	0	0
	Mrs. Holberry, do.	1	0	0
	Mrs Penthorpe, do.	1	0	0
Sept. 12	Mrs. Carrier, of Trowbridge	1	0	0
	Mrs. Jones, of Monmouthshire	1	0	0
Sept. 27	Mr. O'Brien, on his liberation from Lancaster	1	0	0
(Aug. 30)	Mrs. O'Brien	1	0	0
Sept. 27	Mrs. Ashton, of Burnley	1	0	0
	Mrs. Crabtree, do.	1	0	0
	Mrs. Walker, of Bradford	1	0	0
	Mrs. Brooks, do.	1	0	0
	Mrs. Roberts, of Birmingham	1	0	0
Jan. 25	Mrs. Foden, of Sheffield	1	0	0
	Mrs. Marshall, do.	1	0	0
	Mrs. Holberry, do.	1	0	0
	Mrs. Walker, of Bradford	1	0	0
	Mrs. Brooks, do.	1	0	0
	Mrs. Peddie, of Edinburgh	1	0	0
	Mrs. Dawson, of Oldham	1	0	0
	Mrs. Brooks, of Leigh	1	0	0
	Mrs. Emanuel Evans, of Breconshire	1	0	0
	Mr. James Goodwin, do.	1	0	0
	Mrs. Meredith, do.	1	0	0
	Mrs. Price, do.	1	0	0
	Mrs. Elizabeth Jones, of Monmouthshire	1	0	0
	Mr. Penthorpe, of Sheffield	1	0	0
	Mrs. Ashton, of Barnsley	1	0	0
	Mrs. Crabtree, do.	1	0	0
	Mrs. Roberts, of Birmingham	1	0	0
	Expenses of the Committee in stamps, Rent, etc.		15	0
		33	15	0

* *Northern Star.*

signed by 1,280,000 people, and was the result of over 500 meetings. After the bleak rejection of this petition by Parliament in July 1839 it was some time before enthusiasm revived. In the next monster petition, democratic demands were fused with the issue of political prisoners and exiles. The spontaneous support for this – at Paisley almost 15,000 people signed the petition in fourteen hours – may well have startled some of those who waited at the Chartist headquarters in 55 Old Bailey:

Previous to the appointed day, roll after roll arrived and were added to the parent sheet. There seemed to prevail a universal enthusiasm throughout the nation, and when the numbers were proclaimed, 1,300,000 signatures, on the morning of the 25th [May], the cheers resounded, through the Old Bailey, and rolled away in its granite recesses. Eighteen stone-masons, principally from the New Houses of Lords and Commons volunteered to carry the mass down, and preparatory to the march a meeting was held in an adjoining tavern. The men were in high spirits, and on eight names being called out they filed out like soldiers, and capital ones they would have made. Our little room, 55, Old Bailey, was crowded to suffocation, and the street blocked up. With some difficulty the eight masons, attired in clean white fustian jackets, got admission, and the place being cleared of the strangers, a large frame was brought in, composed of two long beams of wood, supporting a cup like a socket the size of the immense roll. It was like the end of a tun sawed off, into which the equally tun-like petition was placed, then completing the resemblance. At quarter-past-three we got under weigh, the Members of the Convention marching three abreast in front, and a vast procession three and three in the rear . . .

The spectacle attracted great attention, from the ragged street sweeper to the duchess with the golden eye glass. The city police behaved very favourably, but the metropolitan blues were very indifferent. The omnibus drivers were very rough and violent. We marched down, slow march, through Fleet-Street, the Strand, past Charing Cross, the Horse Guards, and to the Parliament House. The windows of the public offices were particularly crowded, and great curiosity seemed to prevail. The door of the house was finally reached, and around it there was an immense crowd awaiting. Then, but not until then, did the cheering commence. It began in front and rolled back along the line, and swelled louder and louder, until the thunder reached the inner House. Horses pranced and galloped off, carriages clanked together in confusion, and the astonished police ran together to defend the entrance to the house . . .

A message arrived for the petition to be carried into the lobby, and consequently the fustian jackets moved up the matted stairs, and along the entrance, through a line of strangers and Members of Parliament. In the lobby the usual order was upset and a great crowd besieged the door of the house itself, the great petition seeming like the head of a battering ram against the green base doorway. Presently Mr. Duncombe appeared, and the mass being lowered and turned on its side, it was rolled on to the floor of the house like a mighty snow ball, bearing with it the good wishes of all around, and 1,300,000 people's blessings. The door closed, order was restored, and the fustian jackets were ushered into the gallery. The petition was presented, the debate began, finally a bell rang, and the Speaker cried out, clear the gallery. All strangers rushed out, the doors were bolted, and whilst murmers of anxiety filled the passages the bolts creaked again, and out rushed the members. 'How has it gone sir?' 'Votes equal, 58 and 58.' 'How has the Speaker given it?' 'Against.' 'Damn him.' (Report in *McDouall's Chartist and Republican Journal*, No. 12)

This close voting encouraged plans for an even greater petition. In 1842 the collection of signatures was systematized; towns were divided into districts, and groups of Chartist men and women made house-to-house calls. South Lancashire was particularly well canvassed, as we can see from this list of petition-sheets which James Leach delivered to the National Convention, showing the number of signatures obtained in each town:

Middleton	3,200	Ashton	14,200
Leigh	8,400	Manchester	92,280
Ratcliffe	2,000	North Lancashire	52,000
Chowbent	2,200	Newton Heath	1,900
Heywood	6,400	Wilmslow	1,200
Oldham	9,970	Hyde	7,000
Droyslden	2,600	Hazelgrove	1,600
Falmouth	1,200	New Mills	1,400
Eccles	2,600	Congleton	2,400
Hollis Green	800	Chester	2,374
Bolton	18,500	Glossop	5,600
Rochdale	19,600	Leicester	15,600
Astley	3,000	Loughborough	7,600
Pilkington	3,368	Derby	3,700
Prestwich	1,200	Burton-upon-Trent	3,400
Wigan	8,500	Dukinfield	3,600
Salford	19,600		

The result of all this activity was over three million signatures, and a petition which needed sixteen men to carry it into the House of Commons. Thomas Duncombe, M.P., presented the Chartist address to his colleagues, and received their sympathy but little else. Macaulay attacked the concept of democracy, Roebuck remained stoutly independent and Russell offered his 'direct negative'. The voting was 287–49 against the motion; 'the lads and the lasses walked thoughtfully away'.

The manner of defeat was as important as the voting, and for several years frustrated leaders 'racked our brains for other methods'; without success. By 1845 the idea of a genuinely *national* petition had formulated in their minds. Christopher Doyle mentioned the magic figure of 5,000,000. When Chartism began to revive as a mass political movement late in 1847, it was identified with the National Petition. Inspired by the French example the mood was: 'with five million signatures, and a huge demonstration who can refuse us?' A British Parliament could; and fire a broadside about forged signatures. O'Connor tried to salvage something from the wreck, but the message was clear. No one would be involved in such a 'farce' again; at the 1851 convention D. W. Ruffy spoke accusingly of men 'sacrificed' for the last petition. But what was the alternative? Ernest Jones, one of Ruffy's heroes, ultimately accepted O'Connor's pragmatism. 'Do not object to petitioning,' he said, in 1858. 'It is an old prejudice, but a foolish one.'

The supervision of national petitions was usually performed by conventions working in close touch with interested M.P.s. Although some Chartists had scruples about the legality of conventions, they had good historical precedents. Richard Carlile, caustic as ever, called that of 1839 the 'third "abortion"', but for many people Chartist conferences were the nearest approximation to the ideal of a People's Parliament. 'Parliament does not represent me, and I will not obey its laws,' said Edward Charlton at a Newcastle meeting in 1839, 'but I second this resolution to support my own Parliament, as the most likely means of securing justice to my family.' The Convention of 1839 had some of the nomenclature and ritual of the Westminster body. Predictably, O'Brien had the clearest conception of an alternative political system, with people's candidates being chosen at election hustings by a show of hands – 'as in the time of Henry VI' – and descending upon London as the true representatives of the people.* Ironically, the one Chartist

---

* T. M. Parssinen discusses the history of, and differences within, the anti-Parliament ideal, in a new article, 'Association, convention and anti-parliament in British radical politics, 1771–1848', *English Historical Review*, LXXXVII, July 1973.

assembly intended to be permanent was accused of being the least representative. 'He had sat disgusted with the (National) Assembly,' said James Leach in May 1848. With the dissolution of this body, hopes first awakened in 1839 collapsed.

The functions of the other Chartist conventions were of a more limited and temporary nature: to change the constitution of the N.C.A.; to decide on tactics, policy, and finance; and to oversee the presentation of addresses to Queen and Parliament. The most famous conventions were those of 1839, 1842, 1848, 1851 and 1858, and some idea of their work can be gained from the collections of documents which have appeared in recent years (3, 4, 5, 6). With the obvious exception of 1851, they were primarily concerned with action and organization. Debates on their effectiveness were common, especially during difficult times, and there was always a running battle over the power and independence of delegates. O'Connor, one of the keenest advocates of conventions, believed, with some justification, that they were an invaluable method of stimulating interest in the Chartist movement and of keeping the executive up to the mark. Others, unable to recover from the disappointment of 1839, called them divisive and 'expensive parades' of professional politicians. South Lancashire Chartists, of course, and Merthyr radicals could allow these debates to float over their heads; 'if petitioning would do, they would do that,' said the Welshman David John in March 1840, 'if a Convention were recommended, they would support that.' One suspects that the size of their representation at the last Chartist conference was a testimony to their pride rather than to their finances.

Many localities, however, never sent delegates to Chartist conventions, and resented paying a share of the costs. Although some of the conventions were fairly representative of the country as a whole, most had fewer than thirty delegates. Conferences in the mid 1840s were, much to the regret of Robert Lowery and Thomas Cooper, little more than O'Connorite show-pieces. Continuity was provided by a small group of 'regulars', men like James Leach, Samuel Kydd, James Sweet and T.M. Wheeler, who represented London in every convention between 1839 and 1852. They brought experience to the delegate hall, an awareness of what Chartists could and could not do. They generally tried to moderate the tone and policy of angry militants, believing, after the disasters of 1839, that a primary role of conventions was to unify the movement. The calling of two rival conferences in 1851 signified their failure.

CHARTISM AND LOCAL POLITICS

'Above all we impress upon you the absolute necessity of attending to local and parochial affairs' (Chartist Convention, 1844). When petitions and conventions failed, the reflex action of many Chartist leaders was to turn to local politics. 'You must conquer locally before you can conquer nationally' had a comforting logic. By the mid 1840s this advice had become an integral part of Chartist policy, a development which invited comparisons with the Anti-Corn-Law movement. If they willed it, said O'Connor, the people already had enough political power to change the system; and his great election victory at Nottingham in 1847 seemed to confirm the thesis.

The real pioneers of 'local Chartism' were such varied characters as John Fraser, Stallwood, Vincent, R. G. Gammage, William Brook of Leeds and Isaac Ironside. Many of them shared Nonconformist and Godwinite suspicions of national government; Ironside, with his belief in the sovereignty of local direct democracy, went one stage further (171). For these reformers participation in local affairs not only brought the prospect of power and established Chartism as an independent political party, but it also had important social and educational effects. It brought them face-to-face with the electors and demonstrated to the world that Chartists were respectable politicians. Vincent, a candidate in the notoriously corrupt Ipswich elections, must have felt like Daniel in the lion's den.

Radicals had, for many years, taken an interest in parliamentary elections. In places with a large electorate, like Carmarthen, Coventry and Tower Hamlets, working-class electoral and registration committees were fairly common. These, as we have seen, sometimes sponsored their own M.P.s. Chartists continued this activity, but gave it greater centralization and direction. Here the N.C.A. assumed the role of a traditional party; under pressure from London, national and regional electioneering committees were set up in the mid 1840s to supervise local agitation. Some attempt was made to place Chartist leaders like Samuel Kydd, McGrath and Ernest Jones, and to concentrate money and energy in those areas where radical candidates stood the best chance of success (see Appendix IV). Nottingham, Halifax, Blackburn, Carlisle and Greenock were amongst the constituencies selected. Benjamin Wilson remembers the excitement of Halifax in 1846:

> Meetings were held nightly, excitement was very great, and party feeling ran very high. Exclusive dealing became very common, and was never known to be so extensively carried out as at this election. Mr. Boddy, a grocer in Northgate and a supporter of Messrs. Jones and Miall, became very popular; I have seen his shop many times crowded with customers, and considerable numbers of people in the street opposite . . . The bulk of the publicans voted in favour of Wood and Edwards, but those who voted for Jones and Miall did a roaring business. The Queen Inn became one of the most noted and popular public houses in the town . . . (39).

If Halifax broke Chartist hearts, Nottingham was their great success story; here the continuous application of James Sweet, George Harrison and non-electors' committees complemented the temporary exertions of a bevy of national figures. O'Connor got home in 1847 by over 200 votes. Elsewhere, the opposition was too strong, and arrangements made too late. In 1841, for example, when at least twenty popular radicals stood at the elections, the results included McGrath (Derby) 216 votes, Charles Brooker (Brighton) 19 and William Edwards (Newport) nil! Preparations seem to have improved for the elections of 1847 and 1852, and several hundred pounds were expended, but O'Connor's dream of a dozen Chartist M.P.s was never realized.

Where constituencies had no radical candidates, Chartist electors were placed in a dilemma. All they could do was to subject the Whig or Tory politician to public examination, hoping to obtain from him a promise of support for their views. If he were not an advocate of universal suffrage, he might nevertheless be a working man's friend over such matters as the poor laws and the Ten Hours Act. In this difficult situation O'Connor and the N.C.A. executive were inclined to waive doubts over men like Sturge and Miall, and even to enumerate the good points of 'Sham Radical' M.P.s. A parliamentary friend had his value. Where there was no significant difference between candidates, O'Connor's policy was one of balance, depending on the state of politics. In 1841 O'Connor, McDouall and others advised Chartists in this position to support the Tories against the 'cruel Whigs', and applauded their victory. O'Brien, a keen advocate of independent Chartist election clubs, was one of those who took a different line: 'a Chartist who votes for a Tory, unless that Tory votes for him, is either a fool or a traitor.' 'Down with both factions!' The 'Schoolmaster' wanted an independent policy, with each Chartist association sending a representative to the hustings in order to advertise the movement. Publicity was certainly achieved, as Harney proved at Tiverton in 1847, and non-electors' associations once established could be permanent. Gammage and Stallwood carried the message into the early 1850s.

Even so, parliamentary politics always contained an element of frustration for working-class radicals, and this was possibly why many of them chose to narrow their sights. Benjamin Wilson and L. T. Clancy maintained that participation in local affairs was on a small scale, but presumably they were talking of formal politics. In towns like Paisley, Carlisle, Glasgow, Dundee and Merthyr Tydfil, whenever matters such as the New Poor Law, Church rates and the appointment of additional magistrates and policemen were considered in public, the Chartist-led workmen attempted to take over these meetings and prevent action being taken (73, 75). Radicals used public meetings, mock trials and history to assert the principle of local democracy, and in this campaign even George White and John Collins worked side by side. After one notable Scottish triumph in 1841, a jubilant reporter exclaimed: 'Henceforth, there will be no politics in Dundee but the politics of Chartism.' William Hill and many of his friends believed that this determination to dominate the arena of popular politics was a surer guide to the progress of the working classes than the condition of their Chartist clubs. Workmen became proudly conscious of the power that they could wield, and the Chartists established observation committees to monitor the necessity for calling it into action. 'Local warfare' – a happy phrase coined by the radicals of Penzance – also included the invasion of select vestry meetings and exclusive dealing. George White, J. Stirran of Bilston and Mr Cudlippe of Swansea specialized in this branch of Chartist activity: the first was carried, still talking, out of a meeting to elect churchwardens; and the last, when imprisoned, threatened to turn the gaol into a Chartist establishment!

The next step was to infiltrate the posts and councils of local government. Here the Chartists were provided with examples from other movements, and with advice from enthusiasts like Peter Bussey. The positions of overseer, churchwarden, constable and surveyor were the obvious targets, and after hard struggles successes were registered in Lancashire, Yorkshire, the Potteries, the Nottingham area, Glasgow and South Wales. The events at Arnold in May 1843 may be taken as typical of at least sixty cases recorded in the *Northern Star*. The resignation of the assistant overseer provided the Arnold Chartists with the opportunity to put forward their own candidate. He was nominated at a public meeting called by the town crier, and then put before the voters at a vestry meeting. Here there was much jostling and the inevitable disagreement over the show of hands, but at a subsequent poll the Chartist scraped home by twenty-five votes. Encouraged by the executive, the *Northern Star* and conventions, Chartists also became town councillors in Merthyr, Newport, Nottingham, Penzance and parts of Scotland, Lancashire and Yorkshire. In this capacity they supported efficient government, popular education, urban improvements and other matters of working-class interest.

Perhaps the most famous areas of 'Municipal Chartism' were Sheffield and Leeds (24, 171). Isaac Ironside, elected to the Sheffield council in 1846, led the attack in that town. By November 1849, there were twenty-two Chartist-sponsored candidates on the council. 'Victory! Victory! Victory! Victory! Over the Borough Goths and Vandals by the British Iron Steam Ship Labour!' ran the triumphant posters. At Leeds some twenty-five Chartist candidates stood for election to the council between 1843 and 1853, and eighteen were successful. But their slide into 'establishment radicalism' confirmed O'Connor's warnings against 'the sectional use of democratic power'.

TRACT
AND
NEWSPAPER

For some people disillusionment with political action went hand-in-hand with a feeling that Chartism should widen the base of its support. This was Vincent, writing in 1841:

> It is a fact – and we must not shut our eyes to the fact – that thousands upon thousands of *our own class* are heavy drags upon the wheel of improvement . . . while I would recommend that we should resort to every constitutional mode of pressing our claims upon our rulers, I implore all true Chartists, at the same time, to endeavour by tracts, by papers, by books, by lectures, by conversations, to rouse from the slumber of ignorance their less-instructed fellow men.

Vincent, like many other Chartists, was impressed by the propaganda efforts of religious and rival organizations; workmen in this period were bombarded with literature from Christian Socialists, Owenites, teetotallers, Complete Suffragists, Corn Law Repealers, and Factory and Financial reformers. This was paralleled in the 1840s by an enormous growth in cheap publications – magazines, pamphlets of 'useful knowledge', novels, etc. – directed primarily at the working-class market. Surveys of homes in industrial South Wales and East London at this time revealed that whereas religious and popular journals were fairly common, political publications were comparatively rare. Yet in some of the radical weaving communities the reverse seems to have been true; here workmen sometimes collected impressive personal libraries of political tracts and unstamped newspapers.

Chartism was in part an extension of the moral fight for a free press. 'When the Press is free, the people will know their rights' had been the dominant radical cry of the mid 1830s. Edmund Stallwood, John Cleave and most of the other prominent Chartist journalists had been involved in the struggle for the Unstamped Press, and they continued to use the vigorous style and content of these earlier papers, as well as the old distribution centres (132, 153). Their enthusiasm for a free Press never faltered, though for a time it was submerged under the demand for universal suffrage. Only at the very end of the 1840s and in the early 1850s when political reformers were looking for allies, excuses and new methods, did the Chartist executive and its editors recommit themselves to the national campaign for the removal of all newspaper taxes. This is Harney, one of the keenest supporters of the new move:

> Consider the importance of this question . . . The repeal of those taxes is the only way through which the press can be purified, and made the promoter, instead of the opponent, of Progress . . . With a Free Press, the Charter would be easy of obtainment; and, better still, the enactment of that Charter would find the people educated in a knowledge of their rights. (February 1850)

From the outset the problems of disseminating radicalism through the newspaper press had been obvious, and some Chartists turned instead to the popular pastime of printing and selling cheap books, tracts and broadsheets (125). A good number of Chartist leaders – James Williams, George Binns, James Leach are three examples – were booksellers. In fact in some localities it was policy to set up promising ‘factory slaves’ and favourite lecturers as booksellers or newsagents. The radical movement in London grew around the premises of men such as Hetherington, Cleave, Watson and the luckless John Watkins – ‘God Almighty never intended me to be a bookseller, and God knows I never intended it myself.’ All four of them advertised their wares in Chartist newspapers. This list was placed by Cleave in the *Northern Star* of 27 February 1841:

What is a Chartist? – Answered. – 5 for 1d., or 1s. 6d. per 100.
The New Black List (comparative table of allowances given to rich and poor paupers) – Broadsheet – 1d.
R. Lowery, *Address to the Fathers and Mothers, Sons and Daughters of the Working Classes on the System of Exclusive Dealing, and the Formation of Joint Stock Companies* – 1d.
T. Paine, *Dissertation on First Principles of Government* – 2d.
T. Paine, *Common Sense* – 6d.
R. Southey, *Wat Tyler; a Dramatic Poem* – 2d.
Lord Byron, *The Vision of Judgement* – 3d.
The Life, Conversations and Trial of Robert Emmett – 1s. 0d.
Emmett’s *Celebrated Speech* – 1d.
The Law-Endowed Churches – 1s. 6d.
An Abridgement of Howitt’s Popular History of Priestcraft – 1s. 6d.
J. Collins and W. Lovett, *Chartism: a New Organisation of the People* – 1s. 0d.
J. Milton, *Considerations Touching the Likeliest Means to Remove Hirelings out of the Church* – 6d.

J.Milton, *A Speech for the Liberty of Unlicensed Printing* – 6d.
The Cobbett Club Petition – 1d.
E.Moore, *An Address to the Working Men of New York* – 2d.

The Dumfries and Maxwelltown W.M.A. was one of a number of clubs to buy these publications; in this instance the younger members insisted that 'nobody can learn politics from newspapers alone' and formed a library of some fifty books. Other Chartist libraries were larger than this, with extensive runs of Parliamentary Papers, popular newspapers and the complete works of Tom Paine, Voltaire, Volney, William Carpenter, Cobbett, Lemennais and many others. Some of the associations which were reformed in the early 1850s made the collection of books and the distribution of tracts their first priority, 'for by this means we think more can be done than by any other' (Barnsley N.C.A.).

These sentiments had been voiced in the early years of the movement by Chartists in Yeovil and other rural areas. When the radicals of Banbury invaded neighbouring villages they took with them armfuls of tracts and addresses. The most famous tract – 'What is a Chartist? – Answered' – was distributed in tens of thousands, and translated into Welsh and Gaelic. This pamphlet, and half-a-dozen others with similar titles, were sold in shops, churches and public houses, and handed out free at meetings and demonstrations. It was customary for clubs to exchange books and pamphlets, and to send unwanted literature to the more remote areas of the Chartist world. In the autumn of 1842 Sheffield Chartists sent the Irish Universal Suffrage Association a huge parcel containing 250 copies of 'What is a Chartist?', 250 copies of No. 25 of the *Chartist Circular*, 250 copies of 'Hints about the Army', 1000 copies of John Watkin's 'Address to the Women of England', and two complete sets of the *English Chartist Circular*. Some Chartist publications were sent to America in exchange for papers like the *Philadelphia National Laborer* and the *Working Man's Advocate* of New York.

Such was the demand for radical literature that the N.C.A. promised to publish a regular magazine, but in the event it did little more than act as a clearing-house for the publications of individuals and local groups. R.J.Richardson, who had his own Popular Library, Joshua Hobson and Joseph Barker wrote and edited cheap political almanacs and the famous Red, Blue and

Black Books which provided the vital statistics for Chartist lecturers. For their part, Chartist associations, both male and female, published long addresses, as well as the poems, court speeches and lectures of almost every major Chartist figure. All these were a source of revenue as well as propaganda. In this period it was fairly easy to obtain a cheap printing press; it enabled Morgan Williams to forge his moral revolution west of Merthyr, and the Darlington tailor, John Stephen Metcalfe (editor of the *People's Friend*) to instruct his readers – and Lord John Russell – on the thoughts and problems of local working men (see overleaf). Several pioneer associations in Edinburgh, London and Yorkshire established Tract Loan Societies to distribute the fruits of this work. Stimulated by the events of 1848, the Metropolitan Delegate Council took up the question in earnest, and tried – with some success – to convince the N.C.A. of the urgent necessity of publishing tracts on a national scale. The executive agreed to sponsor a Tract Fund as it had done a Missionary Fund, but the response was disappointing.

Perhaps the average Chartist attached greater importance to the radical newspapers. When the previously sympathetic Whig editors of the *Birmingham Journal* and the South Wales *Cambrian* turned violently against Chartism in 1839, workmen knew in their bones that the survival of their movement depended on the popular Press. 'If they exist not,' said a Dundee Chartist in 1841, 'we doubt it will die.' The most vital function of the Chartist Press was to keep radicals in touch with what was happening in other regions. Lecturers visiting Cornish seaside villages or isolated areas of Wales and Scotland frequently made for the house of a local correspondent. Elsewhere, too, the newspapers did the work of a weak organization; imposing a unity on the movement, publicizing leaders, nationalizing problems and keeping a few issues constantly in the front of the popular mind. Partly for these reasons 'the Chartist Press' was honoured in poetry, toasted at radical dinners and praised in innumerable lectures. Yet it was never simply a political weapon; it promised, in an age of neglect, to be the working man's 'greatest schoolmaster'. Apart from receiving political instruction from such able teachers as Vincent and O'Brien, readers also obtained information on a great variety of topics: religion, poetry,

D

My Lord,

I take the liberty of sending the inclosed copy of a letter (an extract from *The People's Friend*) which I have addressed to you. Judging from the reports of your speeches as given in newspapers, I infer that you like to think for yourself, and consequently hope that you are too liberal to be offended with others because they think for themselves.

I humbly yet boldly stand forward as the advocate of the *masses*, whose real character I am confident that those of your lordship's rank know next to nothing about. At least *strange words*, and sundry quite a few *strange actions* oblige one to adopt this, as the most charitable conclusion which can be come to after a consideration of them.

Legislators ought to know the *real* character, spirit, and circumstances of those for whom they legislate. Were this the case, what heart-burnings might we escape! And what impositions would both legislators, and the legislated for, be freed from!

Sept. 3rd 1838.   Your lordship's
                                        Very respectfully,
                                        Tho. S. Metcalfe.
                                  Tailor, High Row, Darlington.

(Public Record Office, H.O. 40/36, folio 221)

history, temperance, gardening, dieting and legal matters. For those who could not read there were always friends to help out, or professional readers who toured public houses.

Altogether, at least fifty Chartist newspapers appeared in this period, though most of them reached only a local audience. Circulation figures were minute by modern standards; a report in the winter of 1839–40 stated that of the twelve or thirteen unstamped papers advertised in Manchester shops, the two native publications, the *Political Register* and the *Regenerator and Chartist Circular*, were purchased by only 500 people. Districts, even small provincial towns, loved to have their own organ of radical news, but still-births were common. Newcastle, Sheffield, Cheltenham, Leicester and Nottingham had one or more Chartist journals, a few of which, like the *Northern Liberator*, had a regional character and popularity. In the early years of the movement the virile Scottish radical Press, which ranged from the obscure *Clachnacuddin Record* to the quietly impressive *Chartist Circular* (its circulation was over 20,000 for a time), was the envy of many south of the border. By 1842 it was virtually dead (75). The Welsh Chartist Press, by contrast, did not get under way until 1840. It was constantly monitored by the authorities who suspected sedition in every Welsh line and their harassment helped to bring about its collapse two years later. Thereafter, the Welsh Chartists relied solely on English papers for news of the radical movement, and appointed committees to raise money for, and to sell, the publications of O'Connor, Harney and Ernest Jones.

The papers with a national reputation were established in two periods of intense activity, in the late 1830s and early 1840s, and in the exciting aftermath of the French Revolution of 1848 (125). The key figures in the early years were experienced journalists such as O'Brien (*Operative*), William Carpenter (*Charter*), John Bell (*London Mercury*) and Hetherington (*London Dispatch*). Some of these papers were started without optimism by men 'who had good reason to be sick of politics', and 'without capital, and [were] too dear for the class of readers by which alone they could be supported'. They had little sale outside London, and never really caught the rising tide of Chartist fervour. By the early 1840s they had been replaced by the *Northern Star*, the educative *English Chartist Circular*, and its Scottish counterpart. The *English Chartist Circular*, a weekly which originally cost a halfpenny, was aimed at workmen who could not afford the price of other Chartist papers. It eventually failed, much to the astonishment of its editor, James Harris, as did several attempts to establish a cheap daily newspaper. O'Brien and O'Connor told their supporters in 1838 that, with a daily paper, 'there is, at once, an end to the long reign of usurpation'.

The most successful of all Chartist journals was undoubtedly the *Northern Star* (20). At its height it sold some 50,000 copies. 'Never was a journal started more opportunely,' wrote Gammage. 'It caught and reflected the spirit of the times.' It also reflected O'Connor's belief that publicity could carry the Charter, and his determination, in the face of many doubts, that the enemy must be attacked with their own weapons. Launched in the winter of 1837–8, this Yorkshire journal soon became, in the words of its proprietor, 'a national organ, devoted to the interests of Democracy in the fullest and most definite sense of the word'. Although the *Star* embraced many issues – the poor law, trade unionism, Irish affairs, etc. – its main achievement was to run local grievances, leaders and opinions 'into a mighty ocean', and its main concern was to direct the course of this united democracy. From its columns, critics and even the N.C.A. executive accused it of 'dictatorship', but with its large staff and wide coverage of events at home and abroad it set an enviable standard of radical journalism. Writing in 1903, W.E.Adams could still remember the excitement and humour which it brought to the life of a crippled Cheltenham shoemaker.

The gradual collapse of the *Northern Star* in the late 1840s and early 1850s coincided with an explosion of publishing ventures by socialist, republican and 'Old Guard' Chartists. The list of new papers seemed endless; it included W.J.Linton's *Republican*, Gammage's *Progressionist*, Goodwyn Barmby's *Apostle and Chronicle of the Communist Church*, Joseph Barker's *The People*, Leno and Massey's *Spirit of Freedom* and *Reynold's Political Instructor*. There were also a few short-lived regional publications: McDouall's *Manchester Journal*, the *Edinburgh Weekly Express*, Staleybridge's *Truth Teller*, and the *English Patriot and Irish Repealer*, printed at Liverpool. For Chartist historians the most interesting periodicals of this period have been those of rivals Harney and Ernest Jones (8, 15, 18), but their appeal was deliberately limited to an élite of serious men holding 'ultra opinions'. The repeated calls from the provinces for a popular weekly in the last years of Chartism was never fully met. Jones's *People's Paper* (1852–8) had the right title, but its circulation figure never reached more than 3000–5000, and its price went up and up.

From the beginning of the Chartist movement its newspapers and periodicals had been plagued by financial difficulties. 'We need hardly inform [our readers],' said the *True Scotsman* in March 1841, 'that no Chartist papers in Scotland are paying their current expenses . . . Our own loss has been too heavy to be borne . . .' Ernest Jones made constant changes in the price and size of his newspaper, and even introduced romance stories and free portraits. Some editors made public appeals for money to keep them going, or looked to middle-class and trade-union friends, but they were rarely out of debt. Cleave, the most generous of proprietors, was bedevilled by unscrupulous agents. To avoid paying stamp duties O'Brien and others published papers from the Isle of Man, until the government tightened this loophole. It was a matter of considerable annoyance to Chartists that whereas they were struggling to bring politics to the people, others were able to make good profits from selling 'useful knowledge' and 'vicious literature'. Gammage and Jones railed against the 'sloughs of obscenity contained among the weekly penny press . . .'

Chartist editors were made even more angry by the comprehensive opposition to their heroic efforts. With the help of stamp duties, censorship laws and imprisonment the authorities were able to shorten the lives of papers like the *Southern Star* and the *Western Vindicator*. Shopkeepers and publicans in Bath and Merthyr were warned not to sell these journals. The 'respectable' newspapers, 'the most vile and lying press in Europe', naturally supported anything which embarrassed their Chartist counterparts. Radical speakers, who were always complaining of incorrect reporting, sometimes pointedly ushered 'respectable' journalists to seats in front of the platform. O'Connor took legal action against some of the newspaper critics of his Land Company, and Chartist members refused to deal with publicans and shopkeepers who sold such 'trash'. The relationship between the two groups of newspapers reached its nadir in 1848, when Harney thundered against the 'Press-gang conspiracy' of men who accused Chartists of militancy and cowardice in the same breath, and later pretended that they no longer existed.

But the vigour of the Chartist protest disguised a more domestic problem, the rivalry amongst radical journalists. Chartist associations pleaded with their leaders to combine their talents and interests in a true people's paper, and the *Northern Star*, the nearest equivalent to this ideal, proved adept at warning workmen away from rivals with 'unsound principles'. But the battle for circulation between John Fraser's *True Scotsman* and Glasgow's *Scottish Patriot* in the late 1830s was paralleled a decade later by that between London and Manchester papers. Each Chartist leader wanted his own mouthpiece, and some of them had enough admirers to fund their brief experiments. For those radicals, like Thomas Cooper, John Watkins and Lovett, who were unable to run popular weeklies, the temptation was to use journals such as the *Leeds Times*, *Lloyd's Weekly Chronicle* and *Reynold's News* to voice their opinions and anger. The dangers of this were obvious; many of these newspapers advertised Chartism only to devalue it, and for this reason Ernest Jones fought desperately to keep the last *People's Paper* out of the hands of middle-class friends.

LECTURER
AND
MISSIONARY

'We know not a more decidedly useful and patriotic body of men at the present time than this' (*Northern Star* editorial, 26 February 1842). Many of the Chartist leaders believed that lecturers produced infinitely better results than tracts or conventions. The names of famous lecturers flash through the pages of the radical press – Deegan, Kydd, Gammage, Millsom, who travelled 1500 miles at his own expense, Dickenson, the Manchester packer, Black, the lady-killer from Arnold, and many others. Their role was not unprecedented in the history of working-class movements, but their importance probably was.

Frightened magistrates, radical poets and disparaging novelists highlighted the contribution which these 'agitators' made to Chartist organization and propaganda. The frenzied orator became the archetypal Chartist figure, and the N.C.A. was sometimes remembered as 'the old lecturing association'.

The character and work of popular lecturers varied enormously. Some, like Thomas Jenkins of Carmarthen, Abraham Hanson of Elland and James Williams of Sunderland, were dedicated Sunday lecturers, amateurs who explained the six points to local meetings. Associations in Merthyr and Sutton-in-Ashfield made group sorties into the surrounding countryside. Other lecturers were paid professionals. They were a motley crew; handloom weavers seeking employment, misfits, academics, ex-political prisoners recalling their sufferings and ordinary workmen convinced that they had 'been sent into the world as a means of working out the liberty of the people'. They tramped the country under their own steam, or worked as 'missionaries' under the auspices of conventions and radical organizations.

Stamina was the first requirement of a radical lecturer. 'My friends I feel somewhat fatigued, having spoken every day for the last fortnight . . .' Vincent told a Manchester audience in August 1838, and seven months later he returned to Bath in a state of complete exhaustion. This was Bairstow's programme for 3–28 January 1841:

3 – Manchester	15 – Warrington
4 – Newton Heath	18 – Warrington
5 – Sheffield	19 – Ashton
6 – Sheffield	20 – Manchester
7 – Staleybridge	21 – Salford
8 – Stockport	22 – Radcliffe Bridge
10 – Newton Heath and Failsworth	24 – Rochdale
	25 – Oldham
11 – Hunsworth and Bolton	26 – Droylsden
12 – Preston	27 – Middleton
13 – Wigan	28 – Mottram
14 – Liverpool	

No wonder this exciting young lecturer was sometimes late for meetings! Apart from travelling through rain and snow, the physical strain of the expected long speeches was acute. Laryngitis was a constant companion. Missionaries were expected to give a fine speech, and some of them, like Vincent, Dean Taylor and John West, rarely disappointed. It was O'Connor's proud boast that he could appeal to every type of audience. George Weerth, a young German exile, captured some of his magic:

After listening attentively for half an hour there gradually arose a visible restlessness among the whole mass. O'Connor had reported on this and that, and then there followed his disquisition, and he was advancing into the heart of his subject. He had already several times audibly slammed the edge of the rostrum with his right hand, several times he had stamped his foot more and more angrily and shaken his head more wildly. He made preparation to attack the enemy – the meeting noticed this and spurred him on by loud clapping – it was as a red rag to a bull. Then the Titan had gripped his victim! The voice took on a fuller sound, the sentences became shorter, they were wrung in spasms from his seething breast, the fist drummed more wildly against the edge of the rostrum, the face of the orator became pale, his limbs trembled, the cataract of his rage had flooded over the last barrier, and onwards thundered the floodtide of his eloquence, throwing down all before it, breaking up and smashing everything in its way – and I do believe that the man would have talked himself to death if he had not been interrupted by an applause which shook the whole house and set it vibrating. (109)

A lecturer's career might well depend upon the impact made; initial appointments were for a few weeks, and only the lucky ones were re-engaged in a particular area. Nottingham hung on to Dean Taylor for almost a year, and Bairstow spent thirteen months in Derbyshire.

Some lecturers became famous because of their specialized knowledge and interests. McDouall was an acknowledged master of the statistics of the factory system, whilst James Leach and Charles Connor studied the intricacies of the Corn Laws. These men usually had an area of influence or were attracted to one occupational group. 'Commodore' E.P.Mead, for example, had a special relationship with radicals in Nottingham, the Birmingham districts and the south-west, whilst Harney cultivated his Scottish circuit. Over the years the turnover of lecturers was high; to remain successful required considerable intellectual and mental flexibility together with an extraordinary capacity for hard work.

Competition and temptations were often fierce. Some unlucky

Table 3. CHARTIST PLAN OF LECTURERS FOR SOUTH LANCASHIRE, 1841*

PLACES	Time of Meeting	January.					February.				March.			
		3	10	17	24	31	7	14	21	28	7	14	21	28
Tib-street, Manchester, Sunday	6	8	2	5	13	14	3	6	5	4	2	12	3	9
Brown-street, Do.	6	6	3	9	8	11	17	2	7	5	6	10	14	4
Salford, Do.	6½	2	7	17	10	6	8	3	9	2	4	5	6	11
Oldham, Do.	2	13	11	2	14	3	13	14	11	6	5	2	13	14
Do. Do.	6	12	14	2	11	3	12	11	13	6	5	2	12	15
Middleton, Do.	6	9	17	3	6	4	8	5	4	7	3	9	8	10
Ashton, Do.	2½	3	8	10	7	6	10	4	13	8	9	4	7	3
Newton Heath Do.	2½	1					6				8			
Do. Saturday	7				4			7					6	
Bolton, Monday Evening.........	8	16	15	16	2	15	16	11	15	16	15	16	2	16
Mottram, Thursday Evening ...	8				3			2					11	
Droylsden, Tuesday	8	3	5	2	6	7	3	8	10	11	4	9	3	2
Failsworth, Sunday	6		1		9		17		14		10		5	
Rochdale, Do.	2	14	5	11	3	2	12	11	17	9	14	3	16	6
Do. Do.	6	14	5	11	3	2	12	11	17	9	14	3	16	6

LECTURERS
1. James Leech, Manchester
2. William Tillman, Do.
3. Charles Conner, Do.
4. Joseph Linney, Do.
5. Edward Curran, Do.
6. James Cartledge, Do.
7. William Shearer, Do.
8. John Campbell, Salford
9. William Bell, Do.
10. Richard Littler, Do.
11. James Greaves, Austerlands
12. John Greaves, Shaw
13. Francis Lowes, Oldham
14. Henry Smethurst, Do.
15. Richard Marsden, Bolton
16. John Gardiner, Do.
17. Edward Clark, Manchester

* P.R.O. H.O. 45/46.

lecturers found that their arrival in a town coincided with fairs and races, and there were suggestions that local authorities deliberately encouraged popular entertainment such as circuses at times of political tension – a nice twist on a Dickens theme. But it was the rivalry of other propagandists that caused most anguish; Arthur O'Neill, lecturing to hundreds on 'The Anatomy of the Human Frame' with magic-lantern slides, and millennialists and mesmerists packing adjacent rooms. Every Sunday in the summer of 1842 James Williams and dissenting ministers played cat-and-mouse with one another on the Sunderland moor. Harney was one of a select band of Chartist missionaries who managed to draw a congregation out of a church, but on a long tour even he sometimes found the pressures too great. When the accommodation was bad and the rain poured down, as it often seemed to do at camp meetings, the natural reaction was to accept too much hospitality from sympathetic friends. In 1843 O'Connor launched a muted attack on the 'beastly habits of some of our district lecturers', and Dean Taylor ended a spell of lecturing in Leeds by running away with the wife of a Chartist friend. Dean Taylor, Thomas Dickenson and James Williams were just a few of the many Chartist lecturers who were obliged to undergo a public trial during their political careers. Williams was accused, along with others, of having exploited their talents for money; they 'had been made valuable by the poor Chartists, and had since joined the ranks of our enemies' (Samuel Kydd).

Of all the problems facing lecturers none was greater than finance. The large sums spent on missionary activities by the Convention of 1839 was quite exceptional. A good speaker might expect to earn up to £2 weekly, but payment was uncertain as Gammage recalls with some bitterness. District secretaries made constant appeals for localities to pay their quota of the Lecturers Fund. Realizing these problems, the famous often preferred to take an established circuit where attendances and expenses could be guaranteed. In virgin territory like North Wales and the Highlands the reception was very different; here it was sometimes impossible to hire a room or even find an audience. This account of part of McDouall's Midlands tour of January 1842 captures some of the apathy and prejudice which confronted the visiting lecturer:

I next marched, escorted as usual, through the snow to Pitchford, and was received by a joyful peal of bells rung for the occasion. I lectured in a barn where there were two pigs outside and two policemen inside. The pigs grunted, the police grumbled, and the people were satisfied. The police were sent for by an old lady, who either imagined we were going to storm her house, or steal the pigs. The pigs remained unmolested to digest the first Chartist lecture ever addressed to the swinish multitude, and the police, like all watchful guardians on a frosty night, repaired to the public house, for the purpose of drinking the old lady's health, at her especial expense.

On the following evening I lectured in the Town Hall, which was filled to overflowing by my constituents, and were, by all accounts, satisfied that free trade was good enough abstractly, but likely to be ruinous, under present circumstances, if practically enforced, without the People's Charter.

I proceeded to Wellingborough, where I delivered two lectures, in a coach-maker's shop, and, enrolled twenty-five new members, which fact is the best illustration of the effect of the lecture.

At Kettering I lectured twice, and attended a very large tea-party, given by the ladies. Thirty cards were taken at Kettering, which, I am happy to say, is very likely to take a leading part in the movement. I proceeded onwards to Weldon-in-the-Woods, where I found but few Chartists to begin with; they were, however, of the right sort, and the agricultural labourers were very attentive.

Oundle was the last place in Northampton which I visited, and I had much pleasure in meeting with a venerable and respected old gentleman, of the name of Hames, who has distributed an immense number of tracts of all kinds, who contributed largely to the old Convention, and who provided a place of meeting. Chartism is much indebted to Mr. Hames, and he has my thanks, as one of the party, for his unequalled exertions in the cause, surrounded as he is by prejudice and hostile interests.

At Blandford (Dorset), Colchester and other southern 'parson-ridden' towns, the clergy and gentry used every means to prevent lecturers from holding meetings. Thomas Clark braved stones, turnips and potatoes at Ravensthorpe (Northampton-shire), and Vincent was knocked unconscious at Devizes. Arbitrary arrest was another possibility, especially during the strikes of 1842.

In spite of frequent complaints that lecturers were late for, or even missed, public meetings, their usefulness was hardly questioned. William Jones, the marvellously articulate Liverpool Chartist, claimed 100 new members for the N.C.A. as a result of his meetings at Todmorden. In the more difficult

Cornwall terrain, Abram Duncan held twenty-four meetings in the spring of 1839 and helped to establish three associations. E.P.Mead and N.Powell continued his work in the West Country, 'uncurling the hedgehog' of public apathy. Chartist revivals in outlying areas were closely related to lecturing tours; hence the desperate appeals for help and the subsequent gifts of ties and plaids. 'Associations . . . were almost politically dead for the want of lecturers,' ran a recurring complaint, 'a talented lecturer would bring out the whole district in a few weeks.' Kelso and Yarmouth associations highlighted the difficulty of confronting visiting politicians like Cobden and Hume without comparable public speakers of their own. Ironically, the fortunate localities became more selective in their demand for lecturers, sometimes describing the style of oratory required, and occasionally begging the executive to send some new faces. The last point was important; tours by O'Connor and McDouall in the mid 1840s produced a good response from Scottish associations which had, according to William Hill, grown tired of hearing the same 'old story over and over again'. Towards the end of the decade there was a growing realization that Chartism had prematurely deserted its missionary role, and that more care should be taken over a lecturer's appointment, pay and area of work.

The need to organize lecturing had been obvious at an early date, and it formed one of the main points of discussion in the first three conventions. By 1842 the circuits had become overloaded. Towns refused to pay unexpected visitors and the convention of that year passed a motion:

> That those persons who go from town to town calling themselves Chartist lecturers receive their credentials from the sub-secretary of the association to which they belong, certifying that they are of good moral character, sober, and qualified to undertake such an important mission, and that the various associations be requested not to countenance any one who cannot produce such requisite credentials, there being persons out at present who, however enthusiastic they might be, would do well to retire until time and experience had better qualified them for such an arduous and responsible calling.

Behind this resolution was a fear that certain workmen had insufficient knowledge of the sedition laws, and a concern that others were addressing trade societies and mass meetings as self-appointed representatives of the Chartist movement. There was also a reluctance on the part of some localities to allow outsiders to influence the character of their particular brand of Chartism. Districts were formed to draw up local lecturers' plans (see Table 3, p. 105). It was common practice for counties like Nottingham and Derby to join forces and exchange lecturers. Inevitably, friction developed between these supervisory bodies and the executive of the N.C.A. who wanted to control missionaries sent into the provinces. It was a measure of the movement's decline that in the later years the executive was little more than a lecturing body, answering desperate appeals from associations which had once been stoutly independent.

*

The pull between local and national activity was a central feature of Chartist politics. Although some associations like those at Merthyr and Brighton followed the directives of the N.C.A. executive with remarkable equanimity, others complained of neglect or interference. The Dumfries and Maxwelltown W.M.A., an outpost of Chartism in southern Scotland, kept going for ten or eleven years with hardly a visit from a national figure. In this situation associations were often very dependent on local heroes like Matthew Fletcher, William Beesley, Martin Jude, J.B.Hanson (Carlisle) and Stephen Tudgey (Monckton-Deverill). James Williams, under attack for being a member of both the N.C.A. and the Complete Suffrage Union, reminded O'Connor that he was responsible only to his Sunderland constituency. Some regions strongly resented any interference with local leadership, agitation and finances. Many Chartists in Scotland refused to acknowledge the N.C.A. or the National Petition of 1842; instead, they joined Birmingham in a vigorous campaign for a return to the days of federalist Chartism.

This localism merged at times with a demand for democracy in all things. Some radicals were highly suspicious of leaders in general, kept the closest watch on the distribution of effort and money on behalf of political prisoners, and insisted that executives and conventions should be representative and democratically elected. Those individuals who were criticized by Chartist organizations should, it was felt, have the right of public trial. One of the more fascinating aspects of the movement was the open debates and pamphlets on the merits of its officials, and the rule that the general body was more important than any leader or executive. In O'Connor's own account of his triumphant leadership of the movement it is easy to miss the questions and criticisms – 'with all due deference' – from friends, females and ordinary workmen. 'Watch us [the leaders] well,' he told a questioner at a Nottingham meeting, 'it is the only way to keep us honest.' It brought a laugh, of course, but the joke was ultimately on O'Connor; in the late 1840s this elected representative found it very hard to keep ahead of the swiftly flowing currents of opinion in the N.C.A. The *Northern Star* now proved its worth. Significantly, one consistent strand in Chartist thought was that the media should be open to all, and that members of the executive should be prohibited from editing newspapers. After all – so the argument ran – Chartism was a composite movement of individuals, views and prejudices. Thomas Cooper, who tried unsuccessfully to establish a viable Midlands newspaper, personalized this fight for individualism, though his touching interview with prisoner W.S.Ellis has a measure of double think:

> We talked of the great cause in which we had mutually embarked, and of the suicidal quarrels of its leaders. Our hearts beat fully in unison here. 'What might not have been accomplished by this time', was the real language of both our bosoms, 'if the right feeling had possessed each leading spirit in Chartism! O'Connor, O'Brien, Lovett, Vincent, McDouall, Richardson, Leach, Hill, Lowery, Carpenter, Collins, Binns, Williams, Bairstow, West, White, Harney, Doyle, what an endless list of energy, intelligence, knowledge, and eloquence, commingled! all could not 'speak with the tongues of angels', but each and all had some endowment of high value in conducting our high empire to its destined end. How irresistibly mighty would the host have become, if the union and co-working of its leaders had been preserved! (*English Chartist Circular*, No. 147)

Cooper wrote a pamphlet entitled 'The Right of Free Discussion' and attended the Convention of 1846 to plead for charity and tolerance.

He was ejected on O'Connor's orders. O'Connor had, of course, an enormous influence on Chartist politics, being leader, prophet, teacher and treasurer of the movement. His favourite maxim was that 'in every political movement there were three requisites – firstly, the creation of public opinion; secondly, the organization of public opinion; and thirdly, the direction of public opinion'. The sudden popularity of Chartism disposed of the first, so that almost from the beginning 'the great desideratum of our party [was] organization'. 'Action not words' was the cry; a blazing professional approach, and not the suspicious local amateurism of old radicals. However, organization did not bring unity – to this extent O'Brien and Vincent's judgement had been sound; and between 1848 and 1851 O'Connor threshed about, trying to rediscover himself and his old following. The old and the new finally combined against him and he was led bemused into a lunatic asylum.

One of the problems which O'Connor faced was that of continued élitism within the movement. After periods of excitement there was a natural tendency amongst disappointed radicals to turn in on themselves; a few wanted stricter controls over the admission, education and expulsion of Chartist members in order to rebuild the movement on a surer base. In August 1848 the executive warned members of the N.C.A. against teaching 'the doctrines of Chartism as the doctrines of a sect, and only fitted for a section of men'. There was a feeling in the provinces that London radicals 'met and lectured to the same Chartist audience in the fumes of liquor and smoke', and that their publications had only a narrow appeal. After 1842 Chartism had neither the drive nor finances to reach new people and new areas, but O'Connor was determined to retain the image of a people's movement. His calculated optimism must have convinced a few stalwarts. Meanwhile, Vincent, Lowery and Sturge waited in the wings.

It was a hard struggle. Competition increased all the time as rival reformers and wealthy Nonconformists tried to catch the working-class market in politics and publications. Chartist lecturers found themselves working alongside representatives of other popular organizations, and Chartist conventions were dwarfed in size by those of trade union and co-operative movements. Alternative political movements were more serious; the Complete Suffrage Union and its successors caused a fraying at the edges and induced splits in Chartist associations at Bath, Bristol, Newcastle and a dozen other towns. In such a volatile situation it was important for Chartists to have their own organization, active and intent on 'singing only one song'. The N.C.A. showed its value here and at elections, though in the

latter case it sometimes had less appeal to the working class
than older parties. Still, it could face competition; the worst
indignity was to be ignored. In later years complaints mounted
against the 'Silent Enemy' who preferred the world of bad
literature and the 'games of the upper classes' to the serious
world of politics. In 1851, when the N.C.A. membership
numbered only a few thousand, Chartist leaders probably felt
like Church dignitaries after the religious census of that year.

At such times the relationship between middle- and working-
class reformers assumed a new importance. 'The working class
could not obtain their rights without that [middle-class]
assistance,' said Edmund Jones at the Convention of 1848.
'We can, we can,' was the reply. 'Then why have you not done
it?' asked Jones. 'They have been trying for twenty years . . .'
Most delegates disagreed, but they still passed the traditional
'final address' to the middle classes. In the world of parliamentary politics Chartist leaders needed the help of Radical
M.P.s like Thomas Wakley and Sir William Molesworth, and
there were occasions, especially in the early 1840s, when middle-
class reformers courted popular support (101). In some places –
Birmingham and Newcastle are obvious examples – the latter
claimed permanent successes. O'Connor looked on suspiciously:

> If the middle classes wished to join the people, they must not expect
> to lead, they must go into the shafts together; but the moment they
> got to Whig Cross, they flashed the dark lantern in your face, and said
> 'Good-night, Mr. Chartist', leaving you to grope your way along as well
> as you could.

'Be strong and independent' *because* 'they need you' was
O'Connor's advice to the Chartists. He tried in the 1840s to
give working-class radicals their own values and history, and
constantly emphasized the economic differences between them
and their middle-class 'friends'.

3. CHARTISM AND THE ECONOMY, 1839-48

Before the Pen, the Press, the Rail,
Must old opinions fall;
        (Chartist poem of 1851)

The second quarter of the nineteenth century was a time of great economic development; 'mines were opened, canals dug, railways projected, all old things were swept away, and all things became new' (*McDouall's Chartist and Republican Journal*, No. 3). Amongst many people there was a strong feeling that politics, like religion, must adapt to the new situation. Richard Needham, veteran Bolton weaver, said in 1834 that steam-power rather than ideas was 'causing all the revolutions on the continent and in England, and all the reforms' (118). O'Connor took the point, and warned his political enemies that the Charter was the first carriage behind the railway engine.

Reactions to economic change varied enormously, though anger was always near the surface. 'We are the Conservatives; they are the Destructives,' bellowed free-trader George Thompson at a Manchester meeting. 'It is the spirit of monopoly which has (created poverty) . . . political power is monopolized and we are in chains. The green earth around us is monopolized, and we are turned into a desert.' His opponents used similar invective, but they sought to control the worst effects of industrialism and urbanization by legislation, Christian paternalism, land reforms and experiments in primitive communism. At the heart of this response was a vision of a natural society where land formed the main source of wealth and where the inhabitants were mutually dependent. Working-class poets, who shared this dream, wrote of King Alfred and Queen Elizabeth's 'earthly paradise', in which the natural rhythms of work and play had encouraged manliness and freedom (87).

By comparison, the economic structure of the mid nineteenth century was artificial. Britain's commercial greatness depended for its existence on favourable foreign markets, the exploitation of textile workers and a large reservoir of unemployed. Working-class reformers insisted that the result was unprecedented inequality and 'white slavery'. Political Economy, the gospel of the 'cannibal system', offered its casualties a choice of emigration or population control. Some Chartists found it hard to escape the logic of this contemporary religion, though others recoiled from it with Oastlerite ferocity. O'Brien, one of the second group, emphasized the importance of economic knowledge and the concept of 'capitalist warfare'; and like Samuel Kydd, James Leach and R.J.Richardson, he publicized radical ideas on trade, currency, taxation, banking and the national debt. These ideas reinforced the experience and hopes of men living in the new industrial world. O'Connor once said that the appalling conditions in northern England could be almost justified if they led workmen to discover their true situation and their power to change it. In 1847 Thomas Clark claimed that the people 'were learning a political economy of their own'. But, significantly, the Chartist movement never adopted a comprehensive economic plan. 'All they seem to exert themselves for,' wrote a naïve Birmingham correspondent of the *Morning Chronicle*, 'is, some ill-defined notion of getting "a fair day's wage for a fair day's work". . . .' Instead, most Chartists busied themselves with political reform, confident that without universal suffrage the artificial society would collapse under the weight of corruption, taxation, commercial greed and the national debt, that 'old and faithful ally'.

'THIS MAD WORLD'
THE MACHINE AND DISTRESS

> 'From the loom, the factory, and the mine,
> Good Lord deliver us.' (Chartist prayer)

Radical artisans feared change; their poetry speaks of the disruption of old communities and the black horror of the new towns – 'Fire vomits darkness, where the lime-trees grew.' James Leach, who had escaped from the 'murderous manufacturing system', and doctors McDouall and Matthew Fletcher of Bury were determined to place their experience at the centre of the Chartist movement. Other reformers could be more detached about economic progress. One of the favourite debates at the first Working Men's Associations was 'Whether machinery has helped the working classes.' By the mid 1840s the Chartist leadership had few doubts. 'The evils of (uncontrolled) machinery' was now a standard lecture for northern and Midland audiences.

What were these evils? Although the terrible physical conditions in manufacturing towns formed part of the Chartist indictment, the main theme of these lectures was 'Man versus Machine' and the loss of individual status. In the northern industrial unit or Mayhew's over-competitive London, man no longer controlled the price of his labour, but was dependent on mechanical production and the whims of masters (143, 148). The machine even invaded his home. 'We have stood coldly and apathetically by,' said William Dixon at a Middleton camp meeting,

whilst the ruthless hand of the oppressor has dragged our wives and little ones into the factory or loathsome mine, completely reversing the order of nature, making the wives and children toil, whilst the father and the husband is an unwilling idler and a pauper, living upon the blood and vitals of those he loves.

In this situation men became 'mere exotics, acting in the extreme of remorse or grief, or in the reverse state, of lunacy, drunken and unreasonable delirium' (*Labourer*). To prove their case, Chartists used a wealth of statistics relating to crime, pauperism, prostitution and life-expectancy. Samuel Kydd, who constantly sought to turn Chartist conferences into discussions on distress, conveys the bitter irony which accompanied the facts and figures: 'What matter if a hundred colliers be buried in the coalmine? . . . Half the children born in Bradford die before they are seven years of age. What matter?' The events of 1848 provided an answer, and Ernest Jones never let the ruling classes forget it.

Jones took a prominent part in the standard of living debate, so popular in the mid 1840s and in the aftermath of the French Revolution. Many Chartists claimed that the astonishing rise in productivity in the first half of the nineteenth century had been accompanied by greater despair and dislocation. The handloom weavers, woolcombers and framework knitters could certainly remember better times (148). These craftsmen resisted desperately, exhausting the possibilities of trade unionism, political agitation, co-operative production and violence:

> For twenty years we have petitioned and implored, but in vain – first, for a removal of the Corn Laws, then for Boards of Trade, and a diminution of the taxes; and the only way in which Government has acted in reference to us, has been by an endeavour to silence our complaints in dungeons and bastiles, and getting rid of us by emigration. Our prospects are now gloomy in the extreme. Nothing now presents itself but starving to death on our native soil – the soil which our sires so nobly defended. We are now become convinced that appeals to you are useless; you have destroyed our confidence; the hopes so long and fondly cherished are for ever blasted. Henceforth, on our own strength, and the justice of our own cause, we shall rely; and look within ourselves for the elements of another and better state of things. (Richard Marsden, at Clitheroe in the summer of 1842)

Their last request was put in the 1850s by William Stott, President of the Bradford Woolcombers' Society: 'If the mass of us are not required, then we appeal to the justice of the manufacturers and merchants to enable the able-bodied to emigrate. We ask neither pity nor compassion; we require justice.'

The level of distress in the country can be gauged from the bare statistics compiled by economic historians (131, 135, 140). Regional variations were important. Some Chartist centres like Paisley, Bradford and Sunderland were areas of almost continuously high unemployment; others, such as Brighton, South Shields and Merthyr Tydfil, admitted their relative prosperity. Workmen in parts of industrial South Wales said that they could afford to be Chartists only when wages were good and their bargaining power strong. In certain years regional differences vanished. The depression of the late 1830s hit both factory and domestic workers. Circulars sent out by Lovett and local Working Men's Associations revealed the extent of unemployment and low wages. The people 'are neither ignorant of their condition,' said Francis Place, 'nor reconciled to it' (57). In 1842 they took to the streets. There were protest marches by the unemployed in scores of northern and Midland towns. Gangs of beggars rifled provisions stores and mills, and a wave of strikes culminated in the massive Plug Plot. William Bairstow sketches the background to this unrest:

... notwithstanding the sad and deplorable condition of the working classes, the manufacturers are determined to make it worse, for in Stockport last night [early July] the cotton spinners received notice of a further reduction of fifteen per cent. in their wages ... In Bolton there are eight thousand out of employment; and in Wigan the state of the people is dreadful ...

1848 proved to be a lighter copy of 1842. London had, it was claimed, at least 60,000 people out of work, and the spirit of anger and frustration flashed through a dozen Scottish and northern towns. 'You can form no conception of the state of things here,' wrote Richard Marsden from Blackburn. 'Emigration clubs are the principal topic, which is scarcely interrupted by the exciting rumours of the French Revolution.' Ironically, this Revolution made the British Labour problem fashionable. Novelists and philanthropists now rushed to capture the misery of the working class. 'Their pictures serve only to nauseate the truly humane with the details of vice and misery consequent upon poverty and oppression,' said one radical critic in 1851, 'or to provide a vicious mental excitement for the idle and the careless, but not to point out the causes of the evils they pourtray, or devise remedies.'

This is where the Chartists stepped in. As a general rule they distrusted partial and romantic solutions: the Convention of 1842 refused to debate the question of distress. O'Connor saw little point in such a discussion: 'Your complaint is MACHINERY, and the remedy is the Charter.' Certain occupational groups like the handloom weavers and the block-printers instinctively accepted this analysis, as Cooke Taylor found on his tour of the North country (144). Henry Mayhew, in his articles for the *Morning Chronicle*, describes how London artisans had been brought to a similar conclusion by their work-situation, their depressing industrial record and their feelings of deprivation and loss of status (148). The stonemasons of the capital claimed to be the first trade to take up Chartism, and the under- and unemployed tailors and shoe-makers were not far behind. Regional studies of these 'political' trades show the extent to which their response to Chartism varied according to area and leadership. O'Connor called the handloom weavers of North Lancashire 'his eldest sons', and their early if short-lived attachment to his cause was quite astonishing.

Other depressed sections of society had to be educated in radical politics. Chartists like James Williams (Sunderland), J. B. Hanson and W. H. Chadwick canvassed the unemployed, trying to wean them from their traditional reliance on charity and violence. One would like to know more about the relationship between popular radicals and the committees of the unemployed. In certain towns Chartists drew up memorials for them, led deputations and offered workmen the use of Chartist rooms and banners. Strikers were another target for radicals. In 1842, for example, Chartists addressed large meetings all over Britain, and the radical newspapers enthusiastically chronicled their success. George White, the bravest of Chartists, was said to have enrolled several hundred colliery workers at Dudley, Cradley, Stourbridge and Netherton.

This response appeared to vindicate O'Connor's claim that poverty was 'the parent of Chartism'. Of course, there was no direct line from Professor Rostow's index of social tension to organized Chartism; paternal masters and poor-law officers or sheer exhaustion could interrupt the process (140). Still, distress provided much of the dynamism which turned Chartism into a mass movement. In years like 1842 such disparate groups as rural labourers, lower-middle-class shopkeepers and 'aristocratic' trades saw in the six points 'their only hope of a change for the better'. The loaf stuck on the Chartist pole at Padiham in the summer of 1842 indicates the quality of their radicalism. At such times women underpinned the movement, the language of Chartism took on the quality of a J. R. Stephen's sermon and militants like Peter Bussey found their audience. But as the economy revived, members of the N.C.A. fell away like leaves. Other movements now captured the attention of many workmen in Bury, Bacup and Bolton. 'We must realize,' said a philosophical William Bairstow, 'that the working classes are political only under economic pressure,' and Harney wrote of the cyclical nature of popular interests, but O'Connor and George White were not amused. Their greatest abuse was reserved for those Chartists who 'disappeared into higher society' in the years of prosperity.

PATERNALISM
AND PROTECTION

'Steam, the Poor Law Amendment Act and a Rural Police constitute a trinity of villainy, complete and indivisible' (Feargus O'Connor). The collation is significant; fears of Whig intrusion into community and family life mirrored attitudes to the Machine. After William Cobbett's death in 1835, newspapers like the *Manchester and Salford Advertizer* and the *Northern Star* took up his theme of a 'dangerous government conspiracy'. This had a special appeal to the depressed trades, and their Chartist representatives often supported the inchoate demands for some defence against the rigours and politicians of the 'New Economy'. 'Regulation was the great characteristic of Nature,' Philip McGrath told his Oldham audience in 1846, 'and as the laws of Nature are the surest basis for human law, regulations should not be repudiated in regard to labour.' Samuel Kydd, the leading Chartist protectionist, became Richard Oastler's secretary, and helped to publicize his campaigns in the early 1850s (150).

The protectionist debate of the second quarter of the nineteenth century revolved around the issues of free trade, factory reform and the Poor Law. 'All had a good pedigree. 'The Short-Time committees were in existence before the name of Socialist was known,' Alexander Fleming reminded his colleagues in 1842, 'the Short-Time committees were in existence before the great Reform Bill humbug was introduced . . . they had been composed of all parties in politics and of all sects in religion . . .' But the relationship between factory reformers had never been as harmonious as he suggested, and the cruel disappointments of the early 1830s had highlighted divisions. When their movement revived in 1835–6 as a result of grass-roots pressure, 'King' Oastler, the Reverend J. R. Stephens and John Fielden tried to build up a great non-party organization with a distinct Christian–Tory hue, but Liberal* invective, working-class independence and radical competition proved too strong. O'Connor and the other radical orators who appeared on the Ten Hours platform, gave a new proportion to the

---

*The term 'Liberal' is used here and later in this book to convey a particular mentality which was in existence long before the formation of a party.

discussions. In 1838 Factory Reform officials like Mark Crabtree and William Rider endorsed the Great Northern Union, and many Short Time committees were swallowed up in the wider political campaign.

In some northern areas the relationship between the two movements was very close, and certain men played an important role in both. The Chartist stalwarts James Leach, Benjamin Rushton, Richard Pilling (Ashton), David Weatherhead (Keighley), Allan McFadyen (Glasgow) and George Harrison were always Ten Hours men at heart, and some of these led the protectionist revival of the early 1850s in their localities. Others, such as James Cobbett and Matthew Fletcher, left the radical movement at an early date to concentrate on social reform. O'Connor distrusted this second group, though he appreciated their anxiety; and even such a respected figure as John Doherty suffered the indignity of Chartist amendments at some of his meetings.

In 1844, when the revived Ten Hours movement over-shadowed that for the Charter, Samuel Kydd, James Leach, Harney and many lesser-known radicals put their full weight behind it. But the subsequent parliamentary débâcle appeared to justify Liberal suspicions. 'We call upon all good Chartists to rally around Richard Oastler,' said the *Northern Star* at the beginning of his next major campaign, 'to rid themselves of their false leaders and inefficient committee-men, to elect their own officers, to do their own work, and prepare for a short struggle and a decisive victory, under Duncombe and Fielden, that is, provided the operatives are themselves in earnest.' The sequel to the victory of 1847 underlined this message, though some Chartists chose to ignore it.

The Chartist order of priorities was particularly strained where the Short Time movement became united with the agitation against the New Poor Law. John Fielden saw in this merger the opportunity to create a great national protest move-ment across rural and industrial England. The initial outlook seemed promising; Alfred Power, the Assistant Poor Law Commissioner, faced united resistance on his visit to the northern districts in 1836. Within a year R. J. Richardson had established the great South Lancashire Anti-Poor Law Union, and ranged alongside this were a battery of ministers and newspaper editors. The fiercest opposition came from the small industrial towns and out-townships of larger conurbations where sympathy and financial self-interest walked hand-in-hand. Here various strategies of resistance were adopted until the comprehensive defeat of Fielden's parliamentary resolution in March 1838 reduced the spectrum of hope and action (122).

Already, under the apocalyptic prompting of Stephens and Oastler, opponents of Westminster bureaucracy had turned to violence. In parts of the North and in the factory towns of mid Wales the movement caught fire. But the anger signified frustration, and the Oastlerites began to lose ground to those seeking a more ambitious political solution. From the spring of 1837 onwards the radical bombardment took its effect. Anti-Poor-Law meetings passed motions for universal suffrage, and John Collins, George White, J. B. Hanson and Henry Hetherington persuaded key figures in Wales, the Midlands and the North to commit themselves to the Charter. Significantly, all the northern delegates to the Convention of 1839 had been trained in the Anti-Poor-Law and Ten Hours movements.

O'Connor was the chief architect of this transformation. The decisive breakthrough came in the summer of 1838 when his newspaper openly expressed some of the doubts of London and Scottish radicals over 'Tory Reform', and when universal suffrage became 'as it should, the body and the essence of toasts, pledges, and resolutions'. Stephens, his only rival on the other side, tried desperately to make Chartism a simple 'knife-and-fork question . . . a bread and cheese question', but his disappearance from the Convention of 1839 and subsequent speeches reduced his credibility in radical eyes. Like his friend, Matthew Fletcher, Stephens later accused O'Connor of leading a Whig plot to divert people's attention from the urgent problems of the day, and sponsored a vigorous local campaign against the evils of Political Economy. Much to his delight Chartism in Ashton, as in Todmorden, Ipswich, Nottingham, Llanidloes and Oldham, remained closely identified with the Poor Law question. But the Chartist leaders no longer regarded it as a central issue. Although Chartist press and poetry still featured workhouse atrocities and 'social murders' after 1842, the N.C.A. Executive held firm to its belief that only a People's Parliament could establish a fair relief system. O'Connor and

Ernest Jones's successful intervention at a large London meeting addressed by Oastler and W. B. Ferrand in the summer of 1847 was a sharp reminder of the Chartist order of priorities.

The Tory–Radical alliance, the political front of the Anti-Poor-Law and Factory Reform movements, floundered on the rock of this precedence. There was a strong tradition of popular Toryism in the North, especially in Yorkshire, where the 'old-fashioned, Church and Queen, ultra Tory', Richard Oastler, urged workmen to resist the cruel police state of Edward Baines and Lord John Russell (69, 121). Oastler, James Bernard, John Walter and a number of northern M.P.s sought to recapture that 'fellow feeling' which had once existed between rich and poor. The Poor Law controversy provided an excellent opportunity to bring Tories and radicals closer together, and alliances were forged in a score of Welsh and northern factory towns. Although the frightening events of 1838–9 drove a wedge between them, the prospect of defeat for Frost's persecutors reopened negotiations. In the 1841 elections, a furious *Morning Chronicle* claimed, with understandable exaggeration, that 'the Chartists, such as are voters, have almost to a man supported the Tories'. A delighted Oastler tried, along with Disraeli and W. B. Ferrand, to give a philosophy to this marriage of convenience; and Peel's 'betrayals', economic distress and free-trade victories underlined the urgency of their task (156).

O'Connor, an acknowledged disciple of William Cobbett, was suitably impressed by their calls to paternalism and counter-culture. 'Let us not lose their sympathy, their countenance, their knowledge, and their support as far as it goes.' After the Repeal of the Corn Laws in 1846, O'Connor's opportunist courting of the Tories looked suspiciously like policy. 'The two ends of the trodden worm must get together' was his message, and the Nottingham election victory raised hopes of a national Tory–Radical alliance. But mutual suspicion proved too strong. 'How far can a Radical go with a Tory?' asked W.M.A. debaters in 1838 – not far, if the election experiences of 1837, 1841 and 1842 were anything to go by. Tories offered sympathy and support for 'practical remedies', but never accepted the 'rigmarole' or 'Dissenting heart' of Chartism. And Ferrand showed at Bingley in 1848, when he took the lead in arresting Chartist militants, that most Tories placed order before justice. For their part, the Chartists accused Young Englanders of being romantics, and at the Convention of 1845 reaffirmed the independence of their movement, and universal suffrage as the only effective form of protection.

CHARTISM AND THE REPEAL OF THE CORN LAWS

'He was a Corn Law Repealer; so were all Chartists . . .' (Dean Taylor, 1842). Not all Chartists supported Repeal, but the exaggeration was pardonable. Free trade had been part of the radical programme since 1815; in subsequent depressions the working class and its trade unions imbibed a deep suspicion of all forms of indirect taxation. When the movement for free trade revived in the early 1830s, workmen signed petitions in large numbers and even established their own Anti-Corn-Law Associations. In London and parts of Scotland, the Midlands and South Wales, radical leaders like Dr John Taylor were appointed to the committees of such organizations. Although many of these people turned in disillusionment to Chartism in 1837–8, Repeal still held a double attraction for them; it formed part of the attack on 'Old Corruption', and it promised cheap bread and prosperity. Ebenezer Elliott, the Sheffield manufacturer and reformer, expressed a common attitude when, in September 1838, he came out 'for the Charter, but not for being starved first'. When commercial and harvest crises coincided, Chartists, Protectionists and Owenites found it hard to match the popularity of the free-trade question.

Some Chartists bravely disputed the Repealers' case. 'He was against the repeal,' said Jonathan Bairstow, 'because the party which held this was against an equitable adjustment of the other burdens of the country, and against all those other measures which would be found necessary to enable it to be of any avail.' Armed with impressive statistics and a new radical version of economic history, Bairstow, John West and James Leach toured the North and Midlands during the early 1840s. In numerous public meetings they contested two free-trade premises – that Repeal would improve workmen's standard of living, and that open foreign markets were an essential part of

Britain's economic survival. This is James Leach at the Mechanics Institute, Birmingham:

> He would, therefore, show them in the first place, that a repeal of the Corn laws would not increase the wages of the workman; for although the export trade of the country was rapidly increasing from the year 1793 to 1815, yet within that period the wages of manufacturing operatives had sunk from 33s. 3d. to 14s., and at that period the present Corn laws were not in existence. What, then of the argument that the Corn laws were the sole cause of low wages? From the year 1815 to 1842 trade had increased to a very great extent, and still the wages of the operative were reduced to an alarming extent . . .

Leach and his friends believed that employers were playing a dangerous game, for ultimately Britain would both lose her colonies and face the economic power of America and the developing European countries. These Chartists claimed that free traders exaggerated the extent of the population dependent on industry and the size of the manufacturing exports necessary for economic progress. When employers talked of the national interest, MacDouall reminded his readers that the 'capitalist belongs to no nation'.

John Campbell, secretary of the N.C.A. and author of *An Examination of the Corn and Provision Laws* (1841), gave the debate a new twist. He insisted that free trade would cripple British agriculture and extend 'still further the curse of the factory system' and the machine. His answer to the crisis of the early 1840s was one which became increasingly popular in working-class circles – to develop domestic resources and markets to their full potential. In this ideal situation, free trade would hold no fears for workmen. In public discussions with Leaguers, Chartists usually reiterated their hatred of Monopoly; their target was 'Whig Repeal'. O'Connor confidently predicted ruin and chaos should Repeal precede the granting of universal suffrage.

The Anti-Corn-Law League took a directly opposite line (24, 136). This enthusiastic organization was founded at Manchester in 1839, with the support of the middle-class Dissenting press and pulpit. In spite of its wealth and impressive propaganda, the League only narrowly survived the first years of its existence. Defeats in Parliament and the Tory election victory of 1841 pushed it towards the popular radicals. Lovett had long advocated such a union, and there were already workmen – like

Buckney and Taunton of Coventry – sitting on the local committees of both Chartist and League associations. In the winter of 1841 and the first half of 1842, when hungry workmen burnt Peel in effigy, agreements between the two parties were reached at Preston, Oxford, Stockport, Rochdale, Kendal and several Scottish towns. But the N.C.A. executive and the central committee of the League still eyed each other suspiciously.

The events at Coventry in February 1842 show why this was so. Peter Hoy, a ribbon-printer, on arriving at a public meeting to seal the local pact between reformers, found that the middle classes had welched on their promises over franchise reform, and so he led a Chartist revolt (68). Hoy placed himself alongside George White and Samuel Kydd, two of the most famous League-baiters. These exposed the 'hypocrisy' of 'Gregs and Cobdens' who sought the insurance of low wages, yet denied any protection to their workmen. In the prosperity of the mid 1830s these employers had been quiet enough; now they sponsored Repeal – and a few contemplated extending the suffrage – only out of self-interest. In some areas of Lancashire and Yorkshire the Chartist distrust of local manufacturers was total. Even the Fieldens did not escape the censure of proud working men. Certain Leaguers, 'black-hearted murderers,' were reminded of their behaviour at the time of Peterloo and during subsequent strikes. Chartist workmen in towns like Huddersfield took the Ten Hours and Poor Law questions as their standard; quoted James Leach's *Stubborn Facts from the Factories* (1844); and protested to the *Northern Star* about workmen being forced to attend League meetings. O'Connor proved a ready listener. His attitude to the Leaguers was the same as that towards Complete Suffrageists; 'they offer you the minimum necessary to gain their ends'. The patronage of O'Connell was proof enough.

The Chartist and Anti-Corn-Law movements found it difficult to live together. In the winter and spring of 1838–9 O'Brien, O'Connor and the Chartist Convention made it clear that they were not prepared to accept a secondary role in popular agitation. In these early years the League was unable to establish associations in certain Chartist strongholds. Walter Griffith, on his free-trade tour of 1840, found that the Welsh tolerance which he met during his first weeks in the Principality stopped at Merthyr and Aberdare. In parts of Scotland, East Anglia and London it was a similar story, and Francis Place snarled his disapproval. This action on the part of the Chartists was a mixture of principle and pride, strategy and malice. 'Public meetings are the parliaments of the working-men,' said one anonymous workman at a Corn Law meeting, 'their speakers are their representatives, and in their name I come here to demand attention to the charter; I have a right to be here and to discuss with you our grievances.' 'You can grant the charter if you please,' he continued, 'you refuse: then I tell you, that whether your object is a selfish or a just one, I care not.' This kind of logic brought the best and worst out of League speakers. When Neesom led a Chartist invasion into the White Swan Assembly Rooms, Deptford, in March 1841, Sidney Smith's anger boiled over:

> He did not intend to answer any questions put by men who, by their extreme conduct, had placed themselves out of the pale of political society. He considered them a public nuisance, and as such ought to be excluded from all orderly assemblies. Their interruptions only tended to hinder the efforts being made to obtain cheap bread for the poor. They had put down others in the same way, who were endeavouring to procure a mitigation of the rigours of the New Poor Law; after this they reproached the middle classes with the creation of those evils which [the Chartists] prevented others from putting an end to.

Even in Manchester, Cobden could not hold public meetings without interference; workmen from surrounding districts turned them into Chartist festivals. Demands for cheap bread were drowned by shouts of 'Cabbage! Cabbage!' and Chartist hecklers followed League speakers from area to area. In retaliation Cobden encouraged Operative Anti-Corn-Law Associations and employed workmen to fight Chartists on their own ground. With the help of 'Irish Giants' the League gained a bloody but decisive victory at Stevenson Square, Manchester, on 8 June 1841.

The bad feeling between the two movements came to a head in the second half of 1842, with the collapse of the Complete Suffrage Union and the events known as the Plug Plot (23). Publicly, each side blamed its reverses on the militants in the opposite camp, and thereafter they were more inclined to go their own ways. Where organized Chartism receded quickly, as at Plymouth, the revitalized League professionals marched forward with greater confidence. Although the League increasingly disclaimed any interest in working-class support, preferring the world of parliamentary politics and electoral registers, they were surely delighted when no one seconded Charles Bolwell's Chartist amendment at a Bath Anti-Corn-Law meeting. At Walsall it was, apparently, a similar story, whilst in the *Northern Star* O'Connor listed Scottish Chartists who now preferred the company of Complete Suffrage Leaguers. It is easy to read too much into this kind of evidence. In the first half of 1843 some dispirited Chartist associations, whilst retaining their opposition to Whig Repeal, decided to give up their policy of interfering in the meetings of other reformers; but the subsequent revival of popular radicalism, and the League's paraphernalia of provocative placards, ticket meetings and police bodyguards sometimes proved too much. In some Scottish, northern and Midland towns the argument over support for the respective movements continued as strongly as ever, and there were frequent challenges to discuss their rival claims in public. In 1844, when Samuel Kydd, William Dixon and John West fought some exhausting battles with the League, Cobden finally met O'Connor in public debate and won his grudging admiration. The Stockport M.P. replied with a sneer at the size of the Chartist movement. The Convention of 1845 took his point, and abandoned outright opposition to the League. Not all Chartists accepted this view that it was irresponsible to fight the public will; O'Brien, Jonathan Bairstow and James Leach made a last desperate bid to get 'equitable adjustments' in the field of taxation, poor relief and hours of work, but on their tour of the North they faced hostility from old and young friends.

Repeal came on with an intriguing inevitability. Thomas Cooper and O'Connor prophesied dire results, and the economic state of Britain in the late 1840s appeared to justify their claims. Wages remained low and industrial tension high. Samuel Kydd and James Leach, who continued to invade meetings of Leaguers after 1846, emphasized the need for new solutions. Ex-Repealers in Edinburgh, Merthyr and Rochdale publicly announced that franchise reform was now their primary objective, thus proving Hetherington's long-held conviction that a repeal of the Corn Laws would only push people nearer to Chartism. But O'Connor, who never forgave Cobden and his friends, buried himself in the Land Plan.

THE CHARTIST LAND PLAN

'Robert, I think of the land by day, and I dream of it by night. My mind is set upon it. My every thought is occupied with it, because through its just application I see the enfranchisement of man – the freedom of man – and the independence of man' (O'Connor to R. Burrell, August 1845). O'Connor's alternative to the unrestricted growth of commercialism and industrialism, and the associated problem of surplus labour, was a rapid expansion of peasant proprietorship. His view ran parallel to, and sometimes merged with, a generation of radical notions derived from Paine, Thomas Spence and others, and with instinctive working-class feelings about the expropriation and use of land. 'God never made an Aristocracy of land,' the Irish radical, Christopher Doyle, told his Brighton audience in 1847. 'God gave the land to the whole human family, and first force, and then fraud, by Act of Parliament, made this land the possession of the few.' Such expressions became an important part of the Chartist language in the 1840s and 1850s. For many radicals, especially those with an Irish background, the land had a mystical quality; it was equated with the natural life, with independence, security, happiness and freedom. The moving fictional story of William Wright, a Stockport mechanic, captures the vision. Will, who was given a Chartist allotment, woke early on his first day in the 'Holy Land':

Will's cottage was close to the school-house, and just as the loud bell summoned the youngsters to school, Will returned to his home, when he thought he heard his wife call, and as he opened the bed-room door, he heard her call, angrily – 'Tom, thou varmint, and Betsy – thou b—h, dusn't hear factory bell, eh! – thou'lt be fined, and I'll smack they — for thee; here, suck, wench, or thou mun do without it.' Will stood before her, she rubbed her eyes, looked around, and asked – 'Where-ever am I?' 'In thy own castle, lass,' responded Will, with a triumphant laugh – 'yon is school-bell for youngsters to go to school; turn on t'other side, wench, and tak another snooze and I'll wake thee up, for breakfast –

what dost say to Charter now? Why, if thou wasn't going to pitch little lass out on floor.' 'Nay, Will,' said she, 'I was afeard we mun all be fined and starve – I thought it was factory bell.' 'DAMN THE FACTORY BELL,' roared Will, with all his heart – 'sleep! lass, sleep! and I'll call thee' (*Labourer*, vol. I)

Will's pleasure was no doubt shared by his friends in Stockport. According to O'Connor, the triumph of 'free labour' had a beneficial effect on 'artificial labour', reducing competition for jobs and establishing a standard of fair wages.

None of these ideas was new; some were borrowed from agrarian reformers like William Ogilvie and Cobbett, who stressed the productive possibilities of land, and others were the legacy of O'Connor's family and Irish background. But the Chartist leader gave them an exciting immediacy. His Land Plan was a practical solution to the problems of the age, a model which he hoped Parliament would take up. And the timing was right. For many workers in the 1840s home colonization or emigration seemed the only avenues of escape. Radical newspapers of this period were full of the dark emigration schemes of Whig politicians, and of warning letters from workmen who had crossed the seas. Chartists, who often took enthusiasm for emigration as the standard by which to judge Whig friends, increasingly turned to the old question of the better use of land, especially waste land. Certain paternal landowners had encouraged the development of allotments at various periods during the early nineteenth century, and in the early 1840s Ferrand and Lord John Manners once again brought up the matter in Parliament. Local authorities, worried about soaring poor rates, took more than a passing interest in the debate. The Owenites, of course, had already established several expensive villages of co-operation, and from the directors of the last of these came advice for the Chartists on how to proceed with their own schemes. O'Connor seems to have been more interested in the agricultural experiments of farmers like James Marshall of Leeds, for he was determined to offer his supporters a practical dream at a realistic price.

Peasant proprietorship had long been part of O'Connor's thinking, though perhaps its relevance to the English situation only crystallized in the difficult years of the early 1840s when even government seemed a victim of economic forces. At such

E

a time the Irish leader admitted that 'it was tiresome, and very repulsive, to hear nothing, night after night, but "you are the producers of all wealth, and are entitled to a voice in its representations; once get the Charter, and then you will destroy the power of your enemies"'. Chartist lectures on the Repeal of the Corn Laws and machinery were now given an extra dimension; 'if they would take away all chance of a working man being enabled to live by his labour as a mechanic, they ought, at least, to give him the means of falling back on the land as a security for liberty and life' (James Leach). Lectures on home colonization, whether from Owenites or Chartists, attracted large audiences in this period and, significantly, groups of workmen in Chartist strongholds in the Nottingham area and in parts of Lancashire and Yorkshire had established allotment societies as a defence against poverty. By the beginning of 1842 O'Connor, in typical fashion, claimed to have 'knocked the land' into people's heads. The second stage was to convince them of the feasibility of a return to the land, a task which William Beesley and several other Chartists had already begun. O'Connor's pamphlet, 'A Practical Work on the Management of Small Farms' (1843), supplied the facts and figures of spade husbandry. To this he added his Plan – workmen should club together to buy property which would then be allotted to fortunate subscribers. The Chartist conference of 1843 approved it in outline.

Launching the Plan proved more difficult, and it was two years before the Chartist Land Society was established. O'Connor later bemoaned this fact, but suspicion of such schemes was part of the Chartist psychology. This report of a Newcastle meeting of 1843 identifies two common areas of criticism:

Mr. Swallow then rose to show the impracticability of the people in their present oppressed condition to procure the means of purchasing the land and contended that we should endeavour to get the Charter at any cost, first, and the means of locating the people on the soil would soon follow, and full protection in the enjoyment of it. Mr. Beesley having replied to Mr. Swallow, Mr. Sinclair next rose and said, that the only objections that he had to directing the minds of the people to the possession of the soil was, that he was afraid that it would impede the acquirement of the Charter ... He believed that as people were advanced to comfortable circumstances in life they would perhaps forget the declarations that they had made when pinched by hunger, 'that they would have the Charter or die in the attempt'. . .

There was a constant stream of questions in the *Northern Star* about the details of O'Connor's scheme. But in spite of these, and more serious doubts about the legality of the Plan, the Irishman pressed on, encouraged by American developments and the current British 'rage for land'. For two years lecturers toured the country on behalf of the society, sometimes taking a perverse delight in speaking at the traditional centres of emigration. The Society was firmly launched at the Convention of 1845; in the winter of 1846–7 it changed its name to the National Co-operative Land Company, and began to publicize its activities in a new journal called the *Labourer* (see Appendix III).

From its inception the Chartist Land Plan was dogged by an army of critics. Thomas Cooper, Bronterre O'Brien and John Mason were a triumvirate of doubters, questioning figures and denouncing its naïveté and the power of its directors. Reforming newspapers like the *Dispatch*, *Lloyd's Newspaper* and the *Leeds Mercury* added their weight to the attack. 'Go to the devil,' shouted O'Connor, but some of the mud stuck. People were reluctant to put their money into a scheme which might go bankrupt. 'If those with money would lend it at three-and-a half per cent, on the best security in the world,' wrote O'Connor in the spring of 1847, 'I would change the whole face of society in TWELVE MONTHS from this day . . .' To remedy this situation the Directors established a Land and Labour Bank, which offered workmen the only 'real security' for their savings in a world of speculation.

For a while support for the Land Company seemed lacking; its secretary, Thomas Wheeler, reported that in the first eighteen months of its existence only 13,000 members joined and only £20,000 was subscribed. In 1847 the situation changed dramatically. Signs of the coming economic crisis, in particular the famine and violence in Ireland and Scotland, were matched by improved prospects for the registration and success of O'Connor's Company. Heronsgate was opened in May and the purchase of other Chartist estates was expected. Now 'a mania – if we may call it – seized upon tens of thousands of persons, who eagerly pressed forward to enrol themselves as shareholders'

(*Labourer*). The following table charts the temperature of activity:

RECEIPTS OF THE NATIONAL CO-OPERATIVE LAND COMPANY IN 1847*

2 –30 January	£ 953		–31 July	£13,960
–27 February	£2566		–26 August	£11,762
–27 March	£3312		–30 September	£ 6252
– 1 May	£7015		–28 October	£ 8682
–29 May	£3549		– 2 December	£ 6980
–26 June	£5287		–30 December	£ 6158

Such was the enthusiasm that many subscribers were, by their own admission, men who 'had lost hope in other movements', even in the Chartist agitation. Their interest in this enterprise was stimulated by visitors to the Chartist estates, and by newspaper accounts of the public send-offs for lucky allottees, and the bewildered delight of women and children on seeing their new homes. In dismal Barnsley all things suddenly became possible:

By half-past four o'clock, the capacious new street was filled, but at the departure of Mr. Acklam and family [the successful shareholders] it was literally crowded from top to bottom. To show to the world the estimation in which Mr. and Mrs. Acklam were held, all parties, high and low (so called), offered to him, and his amiable wife and family, their congratulations; but when the open carriage, with four beautiful greys, and two postillions, made its appearance, decorated with the Chartist evergreen rosettes and ribbons, the acclamations were deafening. The church bells announced in merry peals for hours, the first fruits of the Chartist Land Redemption Society.

The Acklams' arrival at Lowbands in August 1847 coincided with the holding of a conference, which in some ways marked the climax of the Chartist land fever. 'Mr O'Connor has proved the greatest wonder of the age,' said Samuel Kydd at this time, and Feargus, now resident in 'Paradise', agreed. Chartists like Kydd and Thomas Frost of Croydon, who had been critical of some of the competitive elements in the Land Plan up to this point, were hoping to use it as a stepping-stone to a new world of co-operation in agriculture, trade and industry.

At the time of the Lowbands conference there were some

* Land contributions, expense fund, money for rules and the Bank. *Northern Star*, 4 September 1847 – 1 January 1848.

eighty-six branches of the Land Company in the North, forty-eight in the Midlands, eighty-nine in the South and twenty-four in London (see map, p. 10). O'Connor had correctly anticipated that the initial support for his Plan would come from the cotton towns of the North, but interest quickly spread southwards. It is interesting to compare the range of working-class support for the N.C.A. with that for the Land Company. The latter had perhaps a greater proportion of labourers, miners and gardeners amongst its registered membership (see Table overleaf). In Wales, once thought to have been immune from the 'land madness', enthusiasm for the Land Plan was strongest in communities on the edge of major coalfields, where branch members read and re-read pamphlets by Cobbett and O'Connor. Although every land branch was different, the history of that at Kidderminster may be taken as fairly representative. In November 1847 it had 260 members who had subscribed over £370 for shares. Two members were awarded allotments, one of whom 'was in weak state of health and was so overjoyed that he took to his bed and died'. The *Labourer* claimed that the allottees were respectable people from 'nearly every class of mechanics', and the studies of Joy MacAskill and Mrs A.M.Hadfield bear this out (24, 106). Labourers, craftsmen and factory victims lived side by side in their sturdy 'Chartist villas'.

Altogether some 250 people were settled at Heronsgate, Lowbands, Snigs End, Minster Lovell and Great Dodford. Flushed with their success the Directors decided to close the Company at the end of 1847, and replace it with a larger one. But the winter of 1847–8 was full of surprises. O'Connor found himself surrounded by a carping press and snapping creditors. And worse, some of the allottees joined the attack, demanding security and compensation. Sir Benjamin 'Backbite' Hall, M.P. for Marylebone, proved a ready listener, and he demanded a government inquiry into the Land Company's affairs. The Select Committee found that the Company was illegal, that its management was chaotic and that it was on the brink of insolvency. O'Connor, writing in the *Labourer*, made light of the Select Committee's most damaging conclusions, and chided the working class for ever doubting his honesty. But the subscriptions stopped, and the complaints flooded in. A few shareholders and allottees toured Chartist localities, proclaiming their

Table 4. OCCUPATIONS OF REGISTERED MEMBERS
OF THE NATIONAL LAND COMPANY*

Weaver	344	Clerk	10
Labourer	334	Dyer	10
Shoe-maker	139	Nailer	10
Cordwainer	92	Sawyer	10
Tailor	91	Servant	10
Stockinger	87	Turner	9
Woolcomber	87	Blacksmith	9
Spinner	63	Brush-maker	8
Miner	55	Cutler	8
Smith	43	Grinder	8
Lace-maker	34	Twister (in)	8
Mason	33	Brick-maker	7
Calico-printer	30	Carder	7
Carpenter	29	Mariner	7
Gardener	29	Schoolmaster	7
Clothier	21	Block-printer	6
Dresser	19	Domestic	6
Hatter	19	Miller	6
Joiner	19	Printer	6
Mechanic	19	Shopkeeper	6
Cabinet-maker	18	Collier	5
Bricklayer	16	Housekeeper	5
Painter	16	Piecer	5
Baker	15	Plumber	5
Engineer	15	Cloth-dresser	4
Farmer	15	Comber	4
Potter	14	Glover(ess)	4
Butcher	13	Hairdresser	4
Flax-dresser	13	Millwright	4
Overlooker	13	Skinner	4
Seamstress	13	Sweep	4
Plasterer	12	Watchmaker	4
Grocer	11	Bleacher	3
Moulder	11	Brass-founder	3

* Occupations of those with surnames beginning with A, B and C, registered by 1 May 1847 (Public Record Office, B.T. 41/474). In an article to be published shortly the author discusses the difficulties in using such evidence, and presents a detailed analysis of the membership of the Land Company in 1847 and 1848.

Table 4. (*continued*)

Brick-burner	3	Furnish man	2
Butler	3	Fustian-cutter	2
Card-room hand	3	Greengrocer	2
Comb-maker	3	Hawker	2
Cooper	3	Japanner	2
Designer	3	Jeweller	2
Fitter (up)	3	Jobber	2
Fulling miller	3	Lace-mender	2
General dealer	3	Leather-dyer	2
Innkeeper	3	Lime-weaver	2
Leather-dresser	3	Loom-jobber	2
Merchant	3	Pipe-maker	2
Musician	3	Porter	2
Shuttle-maker	3	Rope-maker	2
Thatcher	3	Slater	2
Victualler	3	Spinster	2
Architect	2	Spirit dealer	2
Bailiff	2	Stonemason	2
Boiler-maker	2	Striker	2
Button-maker	2	Tinplate worker	2
Carter	2	Toll-collector	2
Chair-maker	2	Trunk-maker	2
Clogger	2	Vice-maker	2
Coal-miner	2	Warehouseman	2
Coal-dealer	2	Waterman	2
Coachman	2	Wire-weaver	2
Coach-maker	2	Wool-stapler	2
Coach-trimmer	2	Wood-turner	2
Coach-painter	2	Agriculturist	1
Compositor	2	Basket-maker	1
Confectioner	2	Bat-maker	1
Cotton-agent	2	Blacking-maker	1
Crofter(or)	2	Blanket-raiser	1
Edge-tool-maker	2	Boat-builder	1
Embroiderer	2	Boatman	1
Farrier	2	Book-keeper	1
File-cutter	2	Bookseller	1
File-maker	2	Boots (?)	1
Flesher	2	Boot-closer	1
Framework knitter	2	Boot-maker	1
French polisher	2	Bottle-maker	1

Table 4. (*continued*)

Brass-turner	1	Glass-cutter	1
Brazier	1	Groom	1
Brewer	1	Guilder	1
Broker	1	Harness-maker	1
Callender	1	Harness-plater	1
Candle-maker	1	Hat-finisher	1
Card-striker	1	Higler	1
Chimney-sweep	1	Housewife	1
Clock-maker	1	Ink-worker	1
Clog-maker	1	Iron-fitter	1
Cloth-cutter	1	Iron-moulder	1
Cloth-worker	1	Iron-turner	1
Coach-and-wheelwright	1	Keelman	1
Coach-builder	1	Lace-hand	1
Coal-heaver	1	Lace-runner	1
Cotton-band-maker	1	Letter-carrier	1
Cotton-spinner	1	Lime-burner	1
Cow-keeper	1	Locksmith	1
Currier	1	Lodging housekeeper	1
Dairyman	1	Loom-hand	1
Dealer	1	Loomer	1
Die-sinker	1	Maker-up	1
Draper	1	Malster	1
Drayman	1	Mantua-maker	1
Dressmaker	1	Meal-dealer	1
Driller	1	Mechanist	1
Engine-driver	1	Milkman	1
Engine-fitter	1	Musical-instrument-maker	1
Engine-tenter	1	Nail-cutter	1
Excavator	1	Nail-maker	1
Factory overlooker	1	Needle-woman	1
Farm labourer	1	Newsagent	1
File-smith	1	Operative	1
Fishmonger	1	Ornithologist	1
Foundryman	1	Pattern-drawer	1
Framer	1	Pianoforte-maker	1
Framesmith	1	Picker-maker	1
Fringe-maker	1	Piece-master	1
Fruiterer	1	Policeman	1
Gentleman	1	Pork-butcher	1
Gimp-maker	1	Postman	1

Table 4. (*continued*)

Print-colourer	1	Stove-grate-fitter	1
Publican	1	Store-keeper	1
Publisher	1	Tea-dealer	1
Railway constable	1	Tenter	1
Railway porter	1	Throstle-overlooker	1
Roll-coverer	1	Tile-maker	1
Rover	1	Tinman	1
Salesman	1	Tobacconist	1
Sail-maker	1	Trace-maker	1
Seaman	1	Trimmer	1
Shopman	1	Upholsterer	1
Silk-boiler	1	Warp-dresser	1
Silk-winder	1	Warper	1
Silver-chaser	1	Watch- and clock-maker	1
Sinker-maker	1	Whale-bone-cutter	1
Slate-rougher	1	Wheelwright	1
Slubber	1	White-limner	1
Smith and farrier	1	Wire worker	1
Spade-maker	1	Wood-cutter	1
Stamper	1	Wool-sorter	1
Stay-maker	1		
Stone-cutter	1	Total	2289

grievances. One Minster Lovell allottee, who shared the popular conviction that God had created the land for all, was surprised to discover the corollary – 'his allotment had not been cultivated since the days of Adam'! O'Connor's anger gave way to a dispirited sadness, even madness. Attempts to raise rents in order to pay the interest on the mortgages failed, and O'Connor was driven to seek legal redress. James Sweet, who had sunk a great deal of time and money into the scheme, and Thomas Wheeler tried to rescue something from the ruins, and loyal branches rallied round. But, apart from a brief revival in 1849, the impetus had gone. The Company was finally dissolved by an Act of Parliament in 1851. The estates were gradually sold off, to an accompaniment of catcalls from angry shareholders. It was a tragic end to a splendid experiment.

CHARTISM
AND
TRADE UNIONISM

The caution and pragmatism of mid-nineteenth-century trade unionists have become proverbial. 'We are practical men,' declared North Wales miners; religion and politics were rarely discussed at ordinary union meetings. The logic of this was self-evident. 'Their Trades Union was illegal enough at present,' said a London shoe-maker in 1842, 'and they were unpopular enough with the masters, without making them more so.' If they had to make the choice many workmen 'considered it a greater honour to be a Trades' Unionist' than a paid-up member of the N.C.A. The experience of the 1830s, and the events of 1839 and 1842 reinforced the conviction that involvement in radical politics could imperil a union's existence. Miners' leaders in South Wales and the North-east were dismissed on the slightest pretence. Their union, being wise after the event, was one of those which publicly disowned any connection with the Chartist movement.

The Chartists replied with a mixture of respect, frustration, and anger, some of which was clearly related to the events of the mid 1830s. 'I feel that trade societies have done a great deal of good,' said Mr Dodds at the annual festival of the Sheffield Bricklayers' Society in 1839, 'but not half so much as might have been done in the same time and with the same means.' Radicals were wary of the power of trade unionism, and its 'narrow', sectional mentality. O'Connor and Ernest Jones directed their attack at representatives of the 'upper trades', bookbinders, mechanics and other 'exclusive aristocrats' who because of their bargaining power were always 'the last to join in the labour quick-step'. When times were bad or when their unions were threatened, such people considered alliances with other workmen and even political action. But it was reluctant and defensive participation. Ernest Jones and Thomas Clark knew this, and in the early 1850s the former angrily denounced all unions as stupid upholders of the present system (15).

Like everyone else, Jones had to come to terms with the

unions. In London, Glasgow and many other areas, trade societies were the key working-class unit, and here the Chartists could work only by and through them. Hence the appeals of O'Brien and McDouall in the late 1830s and early 1840s: 'with union, success is guaranteed.' 'The Trades are equal to the middle class in talent,' said the 'little Doctor', 'far more powerful in means and much more united in action.' McDouall admired the trade-unionist concern for order, information and respectability, and wished to use their militancy for political ends. In 1841 he tried, through his *Journal* and by lecturing tours, to marshal this 'third class' of the empire behind the Chartist movement. In fact, the L.D.A. and the N.C.A. had branches amongst the tailors, masons, carpenters and boot- and shoe-makers. United trades committees in some northern towns organized the political meetings of 1838, and joined Chartist demonstrations. Dr Alexander Wilson tells us that the huge rally at Glasgow Green on 21 May 1838 was organized by the trades of the town who had done similar work in the early 1830s and who were furious over the spinners' trial earlier in the year. In Nottingham, Newcastle, Birmingham, Sheffield and Norwich, trade societies also collected signatures for Chartist petitions and contributions towards the National Rent and victim funds.

The National Convention of 1839, which made a significantly late call to the trades, was the first of several conventions to stress their importance. The N.C.A. incorporated such an appeal in their political programme, whilst newspapers like the *Charter*, the *Operative*, *McDouall's Chartist Journal and Trades' Advocate* and the *Northern Star* published news of strikes and victimization. Certain Chartists were prominent union leaders – Thomas Hepburn and Martin Jude in the north-east, R. J. Richardson and William Grocott in the Manchester area, William Cuffay and John Parker in London, and many others. These men encouraged trade societies to send deputations to radical associations, introduced Chartist speakers at union conferences, and called public meetings to aid strikers. In 1844 they were involved in the joint Chartist-and-trade-union campaign against the Master and Servant's Bill, and a decade later took a prominent part in the agitation against the truck system.

Chartists knew that their best chance of influencing trade

union attitudes came in years of distress or when union officials were forced by circumstances to seek political help. The debates amongst the London West End Shoe-makers in 1842 and the engineers in 1848 indicate the pressure that could be exerted on the 'no-politics' rule. In the latter year inter-trade delegate meetings openly declared their support for the Charter. Of the individual unions, the Chartists claimed a special relationship with the huge Miners' Association, which was staffed with officers like William Dixon and William Grocott (104). But, of course, this 'deep interest' and the joint tours of Chartist and unionist missionaries were not the same as winning over the corporate trade-union mind and organization, and in the mid 1840s, when the idea of a strike for the Charter was again floated, some Chartist leaders acknowledged their disappointment. They had achieved temporary co-operation where they had wanted conversions. David Swallow and Benjamin Embleton, two prominent radical miners' leaders, spent much of 1843 in organizing a massive campaign to improve working conditions in the pits of the north-east coalfield, where some 700 men had lost their lives during the previous twenty years.

In a situation where union officials were preoccupied by the immediate problems of income and employment, some Chartists believed that it was necessary to change the very nature of trade unions or to by-pass them altogether. James Leach had long recommended such a move; like other radicals he criticized the old union policy of trying to control standards and wages in a world where the masters had the advantages of political power and – in some areas – a large reservoir of cheap labour. Even the celebrated security and victories of the Miners' Association were an illusion. 'Strikes always fail' became a Chartist axiom; they were either broken by blacklegs, or employers and the state recouped their losses later. The following extract is part of an address to the trades from the executive committee of the N.C.A. in 1851:

FELLOW COUNTRYMEN, – A long and bitter experience must have taught you that the great labour question of the artisan can only be solved by the possession of political power. You have adopted every other possible means, but in vain have proved your strikes, however bravely and manfully prolonged. Witness one of the very latest – the sailors' strike at Newcastle. Even, where successful for the moment, the advantage won by such expense and suffering has soon been lost in detail, and you have had to fight the battle over again, with increased disadvantage and redoubled difficulty ... We do not mean to slight your efforts – they were great, noble, and good. We do not mean to say a word against your strikes and unions – without them, possibly you might have been worse off than you are. But we *do* assert this – they have not proved sufficient to save you. They may have *delayed* your ruin, but they have not *prevented* it. Every year, (despite Free Trade!) every year your wages have been falling, through almost every branch of industry ... Every year you have been sinking in the Social scale. Increased work accompanied decreasing wages.

We, therefore, Fellow Countrymen, invite you, without slackening your present co-operative and associative efforts – to imbue them with the political element as well, ... Henceforth let social co-operation go hand in hand with political organisation. Much has been talked about division – much has been preached about union: that is the only division to be dreaded – that is the true union of which we stand in need.

After advice such as this one can appreciate the exasperation and fury of Ernest Jones's attack on William Newton over the expensive engineers' strike of 1851–52.

Instead of having useless confrontations with Capital, many Chartists urged unions to spend their money on solving the problem of labour surplus and on gaining political power. 'Chartism is the only path to social rights' was a slogan which consistently appears in addresses to the trades. By the mid 1840s, when the unions registered several defeats, this message had begun to sink home, and several trades invested money in land and co-operative experiments. National associations of shoe-makers and tailors were established with new aims and with Chartists and Owenites in key positions (110). Alongside these was the National Association of United Trades, a rather unhappy alliance of radical and conservative trades which hoped to avoid strikes by arbitration – 'a very pretty theory', commented William Cooper of the powerloom weavers. This body, which obtained considerable support from framework knitters, nailers, silk-workers and other groups of weavers, campaigned for Boards of Trade and shorter hours, and encouraged self-employment and workers' settlements on the land.

The National Association found survival difficult, especially in the early 1850s, when it was eclipsed for a time by a second movement embodying the radical response to labour relations. This Mass Movement of 1853–4, the climax of several years' hopes and endeavours, was based in Lancashire, and conceived in the context of the ferocious lock-outs at Preston and Wigan. Its primary function was to co-ordinate the work of helping the strikers, but George Harrison, James Williams (Stockport), Edward Hooson and other leading Chartists wanted to give the Movement a permanence and a philosophy. They enthusiastically took up the old radical cry of 'national industrial action' and the suggestion of a Labour Parliament, an institution recommended years previously by O'Connor and McDouall. Much to Marx's delight, Ernest Jones and his friends now appeared to be using the unions as the main weapon in their fight for political and social revolution. But the Parliament of 1854 proved disappointing; trade delegates, uncertain of their role, never shared the confidence of the Chartist organizers, and David Swallow stalked out of the conference hall because of Ernest Jones's arrogant rejection of the miners' views.

This symbolic breakdown in communications should not confuse us. The debates in several union meetings and trade councils of the 1850s and 1860s contained that radicalism and suspicion of Political Economy which the Chartists had tried to inculcate. The two 'new' figures of mid Victorian unionism, William Newton and William Allan, came out strongly for manhood suffrage and attended the last Chartist conference of 1858. Ex-Chartist leaders like Martin Jude, Joseph Linney, Allan McFadyen and Duncan Robertson also continued to make their voices heard in trade matters, and lesser-known radicals helped to establish union branches in their districts. In South Wales and the Black Country, Chartist artisans acted as arbiters in the industrial disputes of the 1850s and urged workmen to exhaust all legal and political forms of protest. At times their advice seemed strangely irrelevant to practical miners fending off hunger and blacklegs, but their order of priorities made a lasting impression.

*

The artisan mentality was at the heart of the Chartist response to economic movements. Whilst some occupational groups could afford to remain craft-conscious and others existed only by charity and the threat of violence, the artisan looked to self-employment and political power as a means of regaining status and independence. The experience of the lower trades, which underpinned this approach, provided much of the dynamism behind Chartism. Of course, not all Chartists joined O'Connor in his bruising battle with Political Economy. Those who had never entered the 'hellish world' of James Leach and George White questioned O'Connor's 'Toryism' and the value of joining the great economic debate. But almost all radicals encouraged the working class to wonder. Dickens may have approved of their rhetoric: 'What kind of country do we want?' 'England is not yet, thank God, wholly composed of manufacturing hells with their long chimneys . . .' said the *Labourer* in 1848. In later years it was more difficult to make these points – the popularity of the 1851 exhibition staggered Samuel Kydd – but Jones and his supporters continued to question the nature of the economic system and the benefits of commercial expansion.

Chartism faced stiff competition from other movements with a more obvious economic programme. The Leeds or Huddersfield weaver could take his choice of some seven or eight solutions to his current problems. His reaction varied from township to township, and possibly from age group to age group. A series of local studies might well support contemporary claims that the success of one organization was related to that of another. Rivalry was certainly keen. When Chartists arrived for the first meeting of the Convention of 1839 they found that a free-trade conference was already in session – an omen of things to come. Out-manoeuvred in 1839, J.R.Stephens carried on a vigorous campaign against 'stupid' southern Chartist schemes (58). 'There has already been too much . . . Political Reform' was his highly relevant message. Several Chartist 'traitors' succumbed to such analyses and left the radical movement. Co-operation, self-employment and land societies were appealing alternatives to artisans in the mid nineteenth century. George Harrison claimed in 1854 that some 300 land societies had been established since the failure of O'Connor's scheme. In 1848 all the various responses hit the headlines. The Chartist Convention of that year relayed news of the deliberations of some 400 trade delegates meeting at Glasgow. The view of unionists, Factory reformers and others was that they offered the prospect of immediate success, whilst a campaign for universal suffrage could be mounted at any time. The events of 1846 and 1847 seemed to bear this out. Chartism received greatest support when other methods were found wanting, or when distress induced a serious reappraisal of attitudes. In these periods Chartism became a series of frantic alliances.

The relationship between Chartism and other movements was a complex one. For a time Chartism was able to absorb or deflate potential rivals, but after 1839 radicals were faced by the thorny problems of obstruction and 'deviation'. Difficulties arose with the Anti-Corn-Law League, but Chartists generally accepted O'Connor's advice not to interfere with trade-union and Short-Time meetings. When W. J. Jackson moved a Chartist amendment at a Ten Hours meeting in Manchester in 1844, Christopher Doyle and James Leach stopped the discussion. The role of the Land Plan involved greater heart-searching. James Leach and several delegates at the 1845 Convention wished to separate the Land Society from the political movement, and there were complaints from London Chartists that O'Connor's missionaries hardly mentioned the six points. But O'Connor never disguised his hopes that 'the Land Plan would have carried Chartism'. Certainly, it helped to keep the political movement alive in the difficult years 1845–7, and possibly opened the way for the establishment of radicalism in new areas. In 1847 many Land branches appointed committees to support election candidates and to collect signatures for the national petition. Through its commitment to the Land Plan, Chartism retained the interest and services of men like George White, Martin Jude, William Rider and Samuel Kydd. O'Connor claimed that the land and Chartism were 'Siamese twins'; they summed up the aspirations of half a century of reformers and caught the current preoccupation with status and the right to work.

Interest in economic movements stimulated a Chartist reappraisal of class terminology and attitudes. Brave James Ackland, the Anti-Corn-Law lecturer, baited the Sheffield Chartists in 1840: 'Denounce the middle classes as you may, there is not a man among you worth halfpenny a week that is not anxious to elevate himself among them . . .' In prosperous times this might be true, but the crises of the late 1830s and early 1840s took a heavy toll of workmen's tolerance and hopes. James Leach now 'denied the assertion that the interests of the middle and the working classes were identical . . . Those who but a short time had been lifted out of the puddle hole were the greatest tyrants.' Slavery acquired a new meaning when Free Trade employers offered to join workmen in the cause of freedom. George White, stalking through Bilston in 1842 at the head of a troop of Chartists, embodied the suspicion of the middle-class reformers. 'This is a new era in the science of humbug,' he shouted, as his vitriolic sentences were punctuated by the deafening hisses of a steam boiler. In the later 1840s Ernest Jones and John Skelton repeated his message that 'the middle classes are our greatest enemies', though they were somewhat embarrassed when Chartist rank-and-file members called for the removal of non-working-class leaders. 'Distinguish between tyrannical employers and the rest of the middle classes,' warned O'Connor the educator; and the approaches of shopkeepers and angry ratepayers in the years of distress gave point to his message.

In this era when economic experience strained loyalty and terminology, politics were in a state of flux. 'Men not parties' – an Oastlerite phrase – became the Chartist motto. Their 'natural' friends, radical M.P.s like Henry Ward and J.A. Roebuck, were tested by their voting record on such issues as the Poor Law and the Ten Hours Bill, and found wanting. The Chartists made brief 'alliances' with politicians as different as Sharman Crawford, M.P. for Rochdale, Thomas Wakley and W.B.Ferrand (55). Thomas Duncombe enjoyed a special relationship with the Chartists. As president of the N.A.U.T. and a director of the Land Company, this 'glorious exception' represented all that the Chartists expected in an M.P. (49). For a time Felden enjoyed the same popularity. Baffled by the range of Chartist ties, some opponents wrongly insisted that the popular radicals had deserted the Liberal cause for the Tory.

Faced by a kaleidoscope of political and economic responses, Chartists remained stubbornly convinced of their own rightness. 'What is the remedy? Trade Union? No, they have been tried and found wanting . . .' said the Chartist mechanics of Manchester. 'Repeal the poor law, the rural police, the game law, the money, or the corn law, or any one single law on the Statute Book and leave the root of the evil untouched, and you will be only dabbling with the effects of class legislation!' Even when, as in 1845–6, Chartist associations were perhaps obliged and willing to take a more tolerant view of rival movements, the message for their own supporters remained the same: 'Agitate for nothing less than the Charter.' The failure of the Land Plan and the strikes of the mid 1840s and early 1850s reinforced the original Chartist contention that the major battle had to be fought at a political level. Without the vote, the working class did not have the power to defeat Capital. The frustration and anger of early Chartists towards their rivals turned to a mixture of arrogance and sadness. When Spitalfield weavers, cruel victims of Political Economy, sought political help from non-Chartist quarters, O'Connor moaned. Worse, he was forced to acknowledge in the mid 1840s that 'ignorant shopkeepers', 'aristocratic trades' and 'former friends' had lost their enthusiasm for the radical cause. In this situation the N.C.A. could be little more than 'a rallying-point', constantly keeping an alternative before the people.

4. TWO THEMES:
VIOLENCE AND FOREIGN AFFAIRS,
1839–48

'Would that I had gone to Australia and thus been saved this work, produced by Tory injustice and Whig imbecility' (Sir Charles James Napier, commander of the army in northern England, 1839). With so much distress and tension in early Victorian society, few were surprised when workmen sought answers and inspiration from outside the spheres of parliamentary politics and home economics. 'Rebellious feelings' were always present in Chartist poetry, and Gerald Massey refused to apologize for them. His friend, Julian Harney, courted insurrection on both sides of the English Channel, and Dr Taylor, the Ayrshire naval surgeon, had even fitted out his own revolutionary ship. Taylor, Harney, McDouall, George Black, the Scotsman Robert Peddie and the other Chartist militants were an elusive group of heroes. They drew on the long British underground tradition and the more immediate physical-force mutterings of the early 1830s, but were often guided by French example.

Chartist interest in foreign reform movements has always been a matter of debate. The N.C.A. executive of this period recognized the internationalism of the previous generation of British radicals, but were understandably reluctant to embody this in their programme and discussions. Irish Repealers, whom O'Connor lured into his movement, had a difficult time making their voice felt at the Convention of 1846, and the poor delegate who raised the topical question of Polish independence was ruled out of order. In general, statements on such matters were left to journalists, pressure groups and committed individuals. Vincent, Cooper, Thomas Clark, Philip McGrath, William Beesley and many others showed a concern for world developments which is hardly recorded in Chartist histories.

Much research is needed before one can speak confidently about Chartist attitudes to violence and foreign affairs. Evidence is sometimes difficult to find and interpret. Here, more than anywhere else in the movement, myths have gathered; and it is now almost impossible to see beyond contemporary publicity hand-outs, Chartist reminiscences and historical prejudice. Mrs Dorothy Thompson, Mr A.J.Peacock and Mr Weisser have began an exhausting but rewarding task (6, 62, 114).

CHARTISM AND VIOLENCE: ATTITUDES

For two consecutive Thursday evenings in the early spring of 1839 the Heckmondwike radicals discussed the question 'How are the people to obtain the Charter, there being a majority of the Commons against it?' This was the problem which permanently taxed the minds of Chartist leaders and drove some of them into revolution. The Convention of 1839 tried to provide an answer, but its voice was lost in a maelstrom of hesitation and indecision. Various forms of action were advocated, some of which, like a run on the banks, had been tried before, and some of which, like exclusive dealing, were to become the stock-in-trade of local Chartist committees. The Convention delegates, uncertain democrats, sought public approval before committing themselves to any open clash with the government. But the rejection of the National Petition on 12 July took away an excuse and called forth a response. After another round of consultation and confusion, the thinned Convention agreed to support a 'sacred holiday', beginning on 12 August. By this time the month's strike, which William Benbow had once thought necessary to bring down the government, had been reduced to three days. Even so, the response proved disappointing. In Bradford, Dewsbury, Mansfield and Durham colliery villages the holiday was celebrated by processions, speeches and violence, but generally the cynicism of Disraeli's Egremont had taken root. The Convention stumbled on until 14 September.

The frustration of Chartists in this kind of situation was almost physical. Joshua Barnard, a veteran of seventy years, compared moral force to 'striving to drive a nail with a feather'. Millennial optimism gave way to anger or resignation. 'I spit in their faces,' said one workman. Three years later, in another Chartist high summer, George Harrison sadly repeated the old question 'What do we do if the Charter is refused?' Many radicals would not talk about it; others wanted to revive the methods of 1832 and 1839. In the frenzied world of 1848 a host of alternatives were considered, including a memorial to the Queen and the impeachment of her ministers, but the dilemma remained. W.J.Vernon, chairing a London meeting in the spring of that year, tried to break the chain of tradition and tolerance. Speaking to the wider Chartist world, he said that 'they should give the House of Commons just one hour to consider whether they would grant it [the Petition] or not'.

At one time or another most Chartist leaders must have caught themselves uttering similar statements. Even Lovett, 'the gentlest of agitators', and Henry Candy were arrested for seditious speeches. Although Chartist lecturers soon acquired a facility for disguising militancy, they admitted occasional 'impropriety of language'. W.E.Adams was not surprised; their new urban leaders had set an example in the Reform Crisis, and Chartist debates in 1838 and 1839 had been infected by the biblical rhetoric of Oastler and Stephens. When several provincial W.M.A.s protested about the frequent references to 'physical force', London Democrats reminded them of the respectability of previous English revolutions and the glory of the French example. The motto of the L.D.A. and the Great Northern Union – 'peaceably if we may, forcibly if we must' – summed up the radical version of history and the Chartist instinct.

The right to arm was justified by scriptural and constitutional texts. The Convention ratified this right on 9 April, after R.J.Richardson had ploughed his way through the 'Mysticism' of English history. Alexander Halley ridiculed his fellow delegates; he 'supposed they would next have a commissariat department, and drill sergeants'. But this was not the point; most Chartists regarded arming as a natural form of protection against another Peterloo. Chartists of all description talked much of government plots and the 'violence' of police and civil authorities. The Rural Police Bill, Irish Coercion Acts and the

'Gagging Act' of 1848 indicated the willingness of the Whig ministers to invade people's rights. By encouraging the establishment of armed associations in 1839, and by the parallel arrest of prominent Chartists, the government gave some weight to a conspiracy theory. The addresses of the first Chartist Convention mirrored the genuine fears that swept the northern counties and South Wales in the first half of 1839: 'Woe to those who begin the warfare with the millions, or who forcibly restrain their peaceful agitation for justice – at one signal they will be enlightened to their error, and in one brief contest their power will be destroyed . . .' Some authorities chose to ignore this warning of a swift, bloodless revolution, and harassed the Chartists with troops, police and spies. The Staffordshire magistrates acquired a special reputation for ruthlessness, and numbered John Mason and George White – imprisoned at least ten times – amongst their victims.

The Chartists replied with a mixture of torchlight processions, camp war-dances, paramilitary guards, defence committees and arms clubs. Almost against their will, many Chartist leaders were led to the very edge of violence. At the massive Kersall Moor meeting in the summer of 1839 their sense of responsibility overcame the call for vengeance. At other times this was more difficult. In March and April 1848 Ernest Jones and his friends performed wonders on the verbal highwire, demanding huge physical demonstrations so that physical force would not be needed. Once again the government and middle classes were given the warning that the presentation of a national petition was 'the finale of moral force agitation', but Russell proved to be another Guizot. Chartists complained bitterly of another 'reign of terror': their petition and memorial were blocked, public meetings were prohibited or policed and their leaders arrested in arbitrary fashion. O'Connor's promise that the Chartists would reply to any attack now stuck in his throat, and he was promptly denounced by some of his former friends.

The onset of violence inevitably highlighted divisions within the movement. When radicals cried 'Name the Day' and workmen took to the streets, middle-class and constitutional reformers brought up the question of advisability, or pulled out of the movement altogether. Lovett spoke for many Chartists in 1838 and 1839 when he said that only violence had prevented workmen from obtaining their rights in the previous ten years. 'Do not be "Bristolized" again' was the cry that echoed through the early 1840s. 'Instead of spending a pound on a useless musket,' said Lovett, 'I would like to see it spent in sending out delegates among the people.' A good number of the delegates at the Convention of 1839 agreed. Dr Wade, one of the first to resign over the use of militant language, explained to his 'constituents' that 'the cry of arms, without antecedent moral opinion and union of the middle classes with you, would only cause misery, blood and ruin . . .' Chartists might rejoice at the loss of such 'namby-pamby luke-warm friends', and express surprise at the over-reaction of men like Cleave and Fletcher who had been prepared to defy the law in the past. But the second part of Wade's sentence appealed to the artisan's sense of morality and order.

None suffered from the inevitable taunt of cowardice more than O'Brien. In the Conventions of 1839 and 1848 he brought to the discussions his own brand of political realism. Ducking under the cross-fire of 'moral' and 'physical force' radicals, he queried the weakness of the government and the support of the people. When Richard Marsden in 1839 asked for only the neutrality of southern workmen in the coming battle, O'Brien was still unhappy. In 1848 Philip McGrath and James Leach took a similar line. Their feeling was that Chartists should not anticipate the public reaction to a rejection of the petition. In parts of Scotland and Wales people resented talk of 'bravado in the streets', especially from the new men in the Chartist movement.

Older leaders had learnt the lesson of 1839. A stay in prison had introduced some of them to the naked power of the British government. Joseph Linney, commenting on the deliberations of the Convention of 1848, said 'some gentlemen appeared wishful to have a taste of prison. I have tasted it . . .' W.J. Vernon ignored the warning but emerged from gaol in 1850 with Linney's doubts over physical force. Chartists in the 1840s often made a fetish of declaring their loyalty to the Queen, and of decorously approaching local authorities for the right to hold public meetings and to act as special constables. In 1842 and 1848 certain members of the N.C.A. executive and the local Chartist leadership tried to control the aggressive instincts of their members and the starving unemployed. Of Henry Candy it was said in August 1842: 'He has been mainly instrumental in preserving the peace of the town of Wolverhampton; the colliers will almost do anything for him.' At Sheffield Isaac Ironside spoke strongly against the 1848 call for 'ten thousand bristling bayonets'. Studies of Carlisle, Merthyr and Norwich reveal a similar pattern (60, 73). Here the official Chartist advice was a mixture of fear – soldiers were present in large numbers – Owenite and religious idealism, and genuine common sense.

By the mid 1840s gradualism had become part of national Chartist policy. 'The Chartists have given up physical force,' said Joseph Barker. This was not strictly true; rather they were more aware of the damaging effects of violence, and more prepared to adopt other methods. After the summer of 1842 lecturers often made positive efforts to show people the extent of their rights and influence. Samuel Kydd and O'Connor developed a pride in British politics which was hardly affected by the French Revolution of 1848. 'With unity the working classes can do anything peacefully' was a satisfying let-out and myth.

Chartist comments on contemporary rioting and arson underlined this lesson. On the one hand, radical leaders tried to understand the motivation behind direct action, even defending its adherents in court. In particular, they gave exceptional publicity to the forgotten protests of rural labourers from the time of the Bossenden Wood affair to the 'miseries' of 1851. Yet the Chartists insisted that they were 'misguided people'. Associations praised themselves for their lack of involvement in such demonstrations as the hunger riots at Glasgow in 1848 and at Exeter six years later. The Rebecca movement, the burning of workhouses, the many attacks on blacklegs in the 1840s and the religious riots of the early 1850s evoked a similar response. 'It would be madness, nay it would be worse; it would be traitorism to the hallowed cause of Chartism to mix it up with the present [Rebecca] movement.' The Rebeccaites should become 'educated in politics'.

The Chartist emphasis on discipline and *national* action also conditioned attitudes. Artisans like J. B. Hanson and Morgan Williams sought in the most difficult situations to harness the

tension of desperate working men and to prevent 'partial outbreaks'. 'Let them keep their temper; and the battle is their
own' was a recurring theme. Perhaps O'Connor exaggerated
Chartist detachment from traditional election thuggery, but
their language and behaviour after 1840 did much to enhance
their claim of being the 'new and moral politicians' (6, 126,
141).

CHARTISM AND VIOLENCE: OUTBREAKS

The character and scale of Chartist violence still baffle the
historian. This should not surprise us; a prominent Hyde town
councillor was only one of many people who were later reluctant
to advertise their 'impulsive, hotheaded . . .' past, and the
records of crucial delegate meetings, class meetings and arms
clubs are inevitably thin on the ground. One would like to know
a great deal more about the persistence of militant radicalism
in places like Bradford, Merthyr and Dundee. Did magistrates,
journalists and novelists unfairly blame the Chartists for much
of the unrest in the 1830s and 1840s? Certainly, the extent of
open insurrection was remarkably small, and associations in
towns such as Cheltenham and Brighton knew its limitations.
'Did [the police] think we should be so foolish as to break
the peace?' said William Miles (Merthyr), trying to disguise his
sadness.

This aggressive miner knew that Chartists took up arms only
in exceptional circumstances. One obvious source of political
militancy were communities with a long tradition of violent
action. In Dewsbury, Ashton, Blackwood (Monmouthshire),
Norwich, Winlaton and other mining and weaving towns there
was little inducement to behave in a peaceful manner (54, 61,
73). Only the presence of soldiers could halt the squalid cycle
of unemployment, strikes and intimidation. When Chartism
reached these 'hell-holes', and invaded the out-townships of
large cities, violent language and the shooting of firearms were
an immediate and natural accompaniment. Here – to para-
phrase the words of Sir Charles Napier – sufficient sanctions
and underground organizations existed to make a concerted

rising possible. The great fear was that Chartists would become acknowledged spokesmen for these violent communities.

Acute distress and frustration helped to fuse these elements. The events of 1842 illustrate the point. 'Better die by the sword than die of hunger,' shouted Marsden in the hot, starving, camp-meeting summer of that year, 'and if we are to be butchered, why not commence the bloody work at once?' The weavers of Yorkshire and Lancashire and the miners of the Midlands took him at his word. They stormed food shops and workhouses, set fire to vicarages and police stations, and brought works to a standstill. Lord Melbourne's 'rebellion' quickly extended as far as Scotland and South Wales, and it even ruffled the Queen's skirts. Privately, the authorities often sympathized with the plight of the working class, but in public the Chartists got it in the neck. Hundreds were imprisoned or dismissed from their jobs; in Nottingham alone 400 men were arrested. Leaders of many associations vanished overnight, protesting that they had only 'flung oil upon the troubled waters'. Some had obviously done more than this; William Aitken, William Stephenson (Staleybridge), John Duncan (Dundee) and Thomas Cooper had tried to politicize the strike at an early date – not always successfully – and they welcomed its belated adoption by the Chartist leadership on 17 August. McDouall and George Black went further, and with infinite optimism scouted for signs of a national rising (105, 107, 108).

Chartist militants recognized the potential explosiveness of working-class frustration. The lack of influence on Westminster politics had already produced a series of angry demonstrations. The riots of the Reform crisis, the despairing protests of dying trades and the widespread opposition to the new police and Poor Law are three significant pointers to the topography of Chartist risings. This resolution at a meeting of Yorkshire and Lancashire Chartist delegates in July 1848 captures the mood of men who had every reason to know the obstinacy and strength of successive governments:

This meeting is of opinion that all former agitations for the obtain-ment of the People's Charter have failed in consequence of being based on moral arguments in opposition to an authority based on physical power, and this meeting is of opinion that no other authority short of that by which the people are opposed will ever gain their rights and privileges.

Increases in the police force and the arrival of London officers in the provinces drove the lesson home. A dozen towns in the North offered stout and prolonged resistance to these 'tools of despotism', and there were legendary battles in the summer of 1839 at Bury, Birmingham and in the north-east coalfield. The presence of London 'thieftakers' at Llanidloes sparked off a full-scale rising; for three days in April 1839 'the mob' controlled this weaving town, which was already notorious for its gnawing distress and perpetual election violence. Although the Chartists were inevitably blamed for the affair, many of their leaders were caught by surprise. They struggled desperately, first to control a difficult situation and, secondly, to escape the law's mechanical grasp. Without success; a score of innocent radicals found themselves on ships to America and Australia (162).

In mid Wales much of the popular anger associated with Chartism sprang from the Anti-Poor-Law Campaign. Here, as in other areas, the press and respectable sections of society had led the furore against the new 'cast iron', 'hellish' bureaucrats. Peter Bussey, Matthew Fletcher and Lawrence Pitkeithley found themselves in good company when they argued that the government had broken its bond with the people. The wave of attacks on Guardians and workhouses in 1837 and 1838 indicates the depth of feeling; assistant-commissioner Power drew in his breath when he heard of another 'outrage' at Bradford, Todmorden and Huddersfield (122). Stephens's call to arms in the summer of 1838 added a new dimension to the story, and the government cautiously stalked him down. As we saw in a previous chapter, some of the leaders, and much of the logic and urgency, of the Anti-Poor-Law movement were carried over into Chartism. Both sides often regretted it; when mobs surrounded workhouses in the Midlands and the West Country instinct and interest told magistrates that they were Chartist-inspired.

In the event *sui generis* Chartist violence was confined to the years 1839–42 and 1848. These were the periods of Chartist anguish; of millennial hopes and crushing setbacks. By the spring of 1839 people had been brought to the 'tip-toe of expectation', and reports of arming and drilling swamped the Home Office. This is James Partington's testimony to the Peterloo atmosphere of Lancashire Chartism:

West Houghton, 3 April 1839

HONOURED SIR,

I consider it a duty incumbent upon me to inform you of the Chartist proceedings on Monday last. About four o'clock P.M. five very splendid flags, Caps of Liberty, Death with Cross Bones, mounted upon poles, a band of music, accompanied with a great number of men, women, boys and girls armed with pikes, some with swords, pistols, firelocks with fixed bayonets arrived and halted opposite the Chapel from Hindley and Wigan road, which Motley Group was joined by a number of the 'Westhoughton Fleet'. After brandishing swords, and discharging firearms several times in front of the Red Lion Inn, they returned by the same road . . . (H.O.40/37).

The arrest of J. R. Stephens sparked off a number of ugly incidents and demonstrations in Lancashire and Cheshire. Chartists now used the Old Testament language of retribution. 'Name the day,' cried Manchester operatives, East Anglian handloom weavers and the militants of the National Convention. 'The sixth of May,' replied the L.D.A., and sure enough, there were parades of strength from the Scottish border to the West Country. Three weeks later, on Whitsun weekend, it was a similar story. But the warnings of the government, the presence of several thousand soldiers and Chartist caution helped to prevent open warfare.

The rejection of the National Petition in July and the arrest of leading radicals and known militants added a touch of desperation to the waiting-game. In places like Bolton, Bradford, Newcastle and Pontypool 'there exists a sullen gulf between two armed camps' – the success of exclusive dealing and fiery clashes with the police testified to the polarization. The failure of the 'sacred month' deceived few people; 'the Chartists *now* go about their work quietly' was the message from the provinces. Magistrates plumbed with spies, and the government fastened its attention on a group of leaders who were trying to fill the vacuum left by the discredited convention.

In September, a month of 'unvarying quietude' (Napier), and October, Peter Bussey, William Cardo, Julian Harney and others made plans for a national rising. Although the nature of their discussions will never be known, subsequent recrimination and the sullen behaviour of local leaders like George Black and David John (Merthyr) suggest that something went very wrong with their plans. Certainly, the towns of the West Riding were warned not to rise, and elsewhere there was only token support for the men of South Wales. The story of the Newport insurrection has been told by Professor David Williams; nothing, it seems, could halt the determination of angry colliers to fulfil John Frost's part of the national bargain (48). Chartist ministers and some lodge officials dived for cover. On the night of 4 November the colliers descended on the sleepy seaport town, and almost took the soldiers by surprise. 'The Chartists swear they will not let the ball drop,' wrote Napier in his journal. 'I believe them, but they must show more pluck to make anything of it: they seem to have shown none at Newport, and nine or ten have been killed' (54).

The arrest and trial of Frost, Williams and Jones helped to keep the ball in the air (33). Now the talk was of 'fire and assassination' with John Taylor, the doctor of revolution in the chair. Delegates rushed across the North Country, frightening some of their friends and opening up a lucrative trade for government informers. Dewsbury appears to have been the centre of operations, but when the Chartists of that town released their balloons on the night of 11–12 January only Sheffield responded. As always on such occasions the East End of London reverberated with revolutionary optimism, but significantly the last attempt to provoke a national rising occurred at Bradford. On 26 January Robert Peddie and his friends intended capturing the town, but Harrison the spy led them straight into gaol (6, 62).

In some ways the Chartist violence of 1848 followed the pattern of 1839–40. Some areas experienced a parallel sequence of expectation and disillusionment. Once again the West Riding and London were to the fore; here, at the beginning of the year shopkeepers and magistrates complained bitterly about the aggressive behaviour of the working class. Dr McDouall and Ernest Jones made frenzied tours round the English and Scottish trouble-spots, and Richard Marsden and George White renewed acquaintances at another round of camp meetings. Their language had changed little over a decade. But there was a difference; since the winter of 1846–7 a growing number of Chartist leaders saw themselves as warriors in a desperate European struggle, and in North Cheshire, South Lancashire and parts of the metropolis Chartist workmen were joined in

1848 by Irish nationalists 'who detested . . . the word petition'. The authorities, with calculated alarm, stockpiled vast armies of specials and soldiers.

O'Connor claimed that the Chartists were not responsible for the subsequent outbreaks and, as if to prove his point, the massive demonstration on 10 April passed off peacefully. Yet hardened campaigners like Harney and William Cuffay, and a host of young zealots, encouraged physical resistance and applauded the formation of National Guards. Vernon and Ernest Jones prayed – not too quietly – for 'a spark to light the fire'. Bradford and South London seemed obvious flash-points; here the talk was of secret class meetings, arms-drilling and ferocious battles with the police. At the end of May the situation worsened dramatically, and the police arrested marked men at a dozen centres from Bingley to Manchester:

> The authorities have for some time been aware that the Chartists at Bradford, Halifax, Bingley, and other towns in the Riding, were arming and enrolling themselves in clubs, which they call 'Life and Property Protection Societies, or National Guards;' and that these clubs regularly assemble, both in and out of the towns, for the purpose of being drilled in military evolutions, and especially in the use of the pike, large quantities of which weapon, it is understood, have been made in different parts of the district. Bradford has been the chief seat of these proceedings . . .
>
> At 4 o'clock [on Monday, 29 May] the whole of the [Bradford] police force, headed by Superintendent Brigg, marched from the Courthouse; they were followed by 1,000 special constables, the mayor and magistrates, 200 infantry with fixed bayonets, and two troops of dragoons. This imposing force proceeded to Manchester-road, their object being to capture all the Chartist leaders residing there, and to search for arms. They met with no interruption until they arrived at the corner of Adelaide-street, the scene of the conflict in the morning. There the Chartists had assembled in great force, completely filling the street, and when the police attempted to force their way a fearful onslaught commenced. The police drew their cutlasses, and the special constables their staves, and they were met by the Chartists with bludgeons, stones, &c. Each side fought desperately for a short time, but eventually the police and special constables were driven back, many of them dreadfully injured. The military, being in the rear, could not act at the onset, and the ranks of the civil power were thrown into confusion and disorder before the dragoons could be brought up . . . The dragoons having galloped into the thick of the fight, very soon terminated the conflict, the Chartists beating a pretty general and precipitate defeat. The police and specials then succeeded in capturing 18 of the most active of the

Chartists, one of whom was armed with a dagger, and with which he attempted to stab several special constables and policemen. (*The Times*, 31 May 1848)

In London and parts of Scotland plans were made for an insurrection on 12 June, but once again the Chartists were out-manoeuvred. Ernest Jones and his friends were arrested, and the subsequent 'outrages' in London, South Lancashire and North Cheshire were led by lesser figures. This 'rising' of mid August was the outcome of distress, Irish anger and sheer political frustration. The spies helped, of course; in London, Thomas Powell and George Davis were at the heart of the conspiracy and even sold guns to militants (1, 134). At Ashton, where a policeman was shot in a bid to capture the town, the government were obliged to offer informers a free passage to Australia. From personal reminiscences, published later in the nineteenth century, it appears that revolutionary plotting continued for several more weeks, but wholesale arrests weakened resolve, and the hopes of a generation vanished forever.

THE CHARTISTS
AND
FOREIGN POLICY

By the late 1840s the fear of Chartist violence was often associated in people's minds with plots and risings in other European countries. The extent and significance of Chartist interest in foreign affairs varied enormously. Certain events like the Canadian rebellion of the late 1830s and the Cracow rising a decade later made a considerable impression, even on outlying Chartist groups. In the larger associations at Nottingham, Newcastle, South London, Todmorden and Sheffield a profusion of 'international committees', addresses and *émigré* funds confirmed the sense of awareness and responsibility. Isaac Ironside, who presented a Sheffield address to the French government in the summer of 1848, returned full of revolutionary enthusiasm, and sporting a beard which he vowed never to shave off until social justice had been granted. Elsewhere there was less passion, and certain Chartist leaders and conventions deliberately encouraged a preoccupation with domestic economics and politics. Historians are left to ponder the dichotomy (27, 94, 114).

In the early days of the movement Chartists displayed a considerable knowledge of, and interest in, foreign affairs. This is G. M. Bartlett at a meeting in Bradford, Wiltshire, in 1841:

> We witness nearly in all parts of Europe the attempts of the human mind to assert the rights and liberties of mankind. Spain, priest-ridden Spain, had awakened to the evil of a hired priesthood, and had abolished tithes. It had also abolished all hereditary privileges – in despite of the intrigues of Louis Philippe and his despicable court . . . Let kings intrigue with each other to uphold their fell dominion; the people have learnt a dear lesson from experience, and their desire is to govern themselves. It is so here; it is so in Norway and Sweden, where the people have succeeded in establishing republican institutions. In Mexico the same desire is abroad; there the priests have lost the power to overawe the multitude, and monarchical institutions are no longer respected. This desire is no more than the spirit of Chartism . . .

Chartists looked to certain countries for inspiration and models; America and, to a lesser extent, Switzerland and the Scandinavian states were admired for their constitutions and political freedom. Although frequently criticized, America was 'still the hope of the nation', the home of universal suffrage, a free press and cheap land. Radicals toasted her constitution, hero-worshipped Generals Washington and Jackson, and publicized her working-class movements. And when times were bad, they emigrated there in large numbers. Almost all the Chartist leaders were deeply shocked by the American Civil War, and tried hard to bring the working class behind the North (103, 130).

France, Poland and Hungary had a different appeal. Chartists praised the revolutionary spirit in these countries, and celebrated the anniversaries of the Polish Revolution of 1830 and the second French Revolution of 1791. For many London and northern Chartists there was 'a charm even in the name of Poland'; they organized meetings in support of Polish independence, and proffered a welcoming hand to each wave of *émigrés*. When Poland failed, France and Spain offered a bevy of incidents, heroes and popular movements which the Chartists often grasped with indiscriminate zeal. 'France will not let us down,' said Harney, even after the excitement of 1848 had passed.

This faith was paralleled by deep suspicion of the British government and its foreign policy. In the tradition of the London Corresponding Society and the N.U.W.C., the Chartists attacked ministers whenever they appeared hostile to one of the 'democratic' states. The war-scares of 1840–41, 1844, 1846 and 1848 were denounced as government follies or diversionary tricks. At such times Chartists took up William Lovett's slogan 'No vote, no musket', established a National Anti-Militia Association and campaigned vigorously against all forms of impressment. British support for the 'ancient powers' of Europe evoked a similar response. Chartists disliked their 'corrupt monarchies and priesthoods' and the reactionary nature of their intervention in the affairs of smaller countries. When the British government debated loans for Austria and Russia, Harney and his friends reminded the working class that the National Debt had been partly created by putting down liberty abroad and at home. The visits to England of 'wily tyrant' Tsar Nicholas and the 'butchers' Louis Philippe and General Haynau were the occasion of bitter Chartist and *émigré* protests.

British colonial policy was also criticized, though a number of Chartists had an ambivalent attitude towards the empire. Some attacked the concept of imperialism; others wanted the working class to have a greater share of its benefits. The Chartists, who extended their search for immorality, corruption and maladministration to the colonies, took an increasing delight in native revolts, and detailed the brutality of Britain's armed forces. Harney's revelations of the Canadian troubles, and the Opium War with China, were followed a decade later by Ernest Jones's lucid accounts of the Indian uprisings (45). Here, public apathy was perhaps the greatest enemy. 'We have looked to France, Hungary or Poland,' said an editorial in the *People's Paper*, 'and have forgotten the Hungaries and the Polands, which we allow our rulers to massacre, in Africa, in Asia, in the Pacific, and in America.' O'Connor brought the lesson nearer home, and tried with some success to place Irish problems in the front of Chartist consciousness (44).

Opposition to the 'vicious and coercive' mentality of Westminster politicians was an important unifying strand among popular reformers. But it hardly disguised the divisions within

F

Chartism over such fundamental issues as war and the relation-ship between radicalism at home and abroad. Certain Welsh and Scottish radicals adopted the near-pacifist line of the L.W.M.A. and attacked the misuse of national resources. In the early 1840s, when 'the horrors and atrocities of war' were on everybody's lips, some of these men moved alongside Joseph Sturge and Henry Richard. Other Chartists made a great deal more of McDouall's distinction between 'just' and 'unjust wars', and were highly suspicious of the succession of middle-class peace movements. 'There are nations so tightly fettered,' claimed the Fraternal Democrats Society, 'that we can see no prospect of their chains being broken without the aid of the sword.' At different times during the 1840s and 1850s Harney led the cry for intervention on behalf of Hungary and Poland. Russophobia, which David Urquhart fanned from his intellec-tual cave in the north-east, culminated in the initial popular support for the Crimean War. 'The veteran ex-Chartist leaders now had their last innings in a common cause,' wrote A.R. Schoyen, 'only O'Brien opposing the war on the ground that it was a ruling class device to distract the working class from its grievances' (47). Austrian support for the allies reinforced his point, and soon other Chartists began to shout 'treason' and demand an 'honest war' to liberate the oppressed nations. The Sheffield and Newcastle Foreign Affairs Committees, which included Isaac Ironside, Robert Peddie and Harney amongst their leading members, were formed in 1854 to promote such a policy. They discovered that many working-class radicals baulked at the actual prospect of fighting for freedom in Europe.

Differences amongst Chartists over the question of involve-ment in the affairs of another country were often related to their views on the nature of their own political movement. O'Connor, McDouall and O'Brien were the spokesmen for those Chartists who believed that Britain had perhaps the worst despotism in Europe and that their first priority should be the rights of Englishmen. 'Let Frenchmen work for France, Russians for Russia, and Prussians for Prussia,' wrote O'Connor. 'I WILL WORK ONLY FOR HOME SWEET HOME.' He believed that cosmopolitan London did not appreciate the British workman's lack of interest in foreign matters. Moreover, too much concern with events abroad only diverted people's attention away from the Charter and the Land Plan. In 1840 O'Connor attacked Thomas Doubleday, the *Northern Liberator* and the 'wild goose-chase' of 'Foreign Policy Chartists'. These radicals put the immediate threat of Russian domination before the long-term objective of the six points. For a while, in the autumn and winter of 1840, large northern and Midland audiences listened intently to passionate speeches by William Cardo, Robert Lowery, J.Warden and other Urquhartists. This is Cardo:

> The Georgians and the Poles had been subdued by the Russian despot, and the Chartists of England would find, that if they made any movement for freedom, the tyrants of the world would be called in to crush them. He looked upon the Charter as the rock upon which they might build every thing good, but he thought it should never be used to shield the basest Government that ever ruled the destinies of England ... Why should we be hurried into a war with France? ... The men of France and England were allied in their interests, and he protested against war with France, because it entailed misery upon the working classes. Some said that this was taking their attention from the Charter. Singular logic this! If they were honest men, every word they heard, every fact that proved that the villainous Government inflicted upon them and mankind, wrongs and oppressions, would be an additional stimulus to hurry them on in the good work of Chartism.

O'Connor and some of his supporters disliked the politicians behind this 'Foreign Policy Humbug' as much as its message, and after a stormy public battle the new movement collapsed. Harney and Jones later received similar warnings about an obsessive interest in foreign affairs. Jones refused to apologize for his association with international committees – 'to wait till we have got the Charter before promoting, organizing, and proclaiming the alliance of peoples, would be suicidal' – but he did accept much of O'Connor's logic: 'the greatest aid we can give [Europe] is to free ourselves'.

Many of O'Connor's antagonists saw Chartism as an integral part of a wider European movement for working-class freedom. Hetherington and Lovett helped to pioneer this approach. 'Seeing that our oppressors are united ...' ran one of the L.W.M.A.'s many addresses to the workmen of other nations, 'why should not we unite in holy zeal ...' In 1844 Lovett, his friends and sympathetic exiles, formed the Democratic Friends of All Nations, which soon merged into the Mazzini-inspired information body known as the People's International League (117). There Thomas Cooper displayed an intense internationalism which is not recorded in his autobiography, and there W.J.Linton began his lonely adventure in mystical republicanism (36).

The founders of the League generally held aloof from another group of Chartist internationalists. On his return to London in 1844 Harney helped to organize the aggressive republicanism of John Skelton, Stallwood and old L.D.A. men like Charles Keen. As Chartism disappointed, they looked abroad for salvation and messiahs. The Revolution of February 1848 exceeded their wildest dreams. 'We have been meeting, talking, and writing for the last ten years,' wrote Harney, 'and have not got our Charter; the French, with three days' work, have obtained the Charter and something more.' Many provincial Chartists stepped onto the public stage for the last time and joined in the applause.

Harney's internationalism had a different quality from that of Lovett: 'the cause of the people in all countries is the same – the cause of labour, enslaved and plundered labour.' The subsequent repression in France and the election of Louis Napoleon, the 'Special Constable of 1848', only emphasized the need for a true social revolution; and Harney continued the L.D.A.'s attempt to educate the British people about the realities of past failures and present European situations. He was helped by the enthusiasm of new young Chartists like J.B.Leno and by the cold analysis of Marx and Engels (89–92). Papers like the *Democratic Review* and the *Red Republican* disseminated the new approach.

The differences within Chartist internationalism were reflected in the relationship between British radicals and foreign refugees. The latter, who numbered perhaps a thousand, fled to this country during thirty years of revolution and persecution (1830–1858). The main nationalities involved were French, Germans, Poles, Hungarians, Italians and Spaniards, all of whom were subdivided by different political and social philosophies. Many settled in London, though Chartist committees found jobs for some of them in Manchester, Halifax, Liverpool, Sheffield, Nottingham, Newcastle, Norwich and Todmorden. Inspired by

William Jones (Liverpool), Thomas Brown (London), Thomas Cooper and Harney, Chartists also set up refugee funds and attended public receptions for such heroes as Captain Marguerite, Kossuth and Garibaldi.

Although the great majority of exiles did not involve themselves in the domestic radical movement, a few of them toured with Chartist lecturers and accepted positions of responsibility. Major Beniowski, the Polish secretary of the E.L.D.A., and Robert le Blond of the N.C.A. Executive were perhaps the best known. Others made contacts with their English counterparts in the many London Democratic Societies and Committees formed in the mid 1840s. The most famous of these was the Fraternal Democrats, a loosely organized body comprising leading Chartists like John Arnott and McGrath, and representatives of most of the *émigré* groups. Its 'Declaration of Principles' summed up much of the sentiment and philosophy of mid-nineteenth-century radicals:

In accordance with the above declaration of the brotherhood of the human race, we renounce, repudiate and condemn all political hereditary inequalities and distinctions of 'caste'; consequently we regard kings, aristocracies, and classes monopolising political privileges in virtue of their possession of property, as usurpers and violators of the principle of human brotherhood. Governments elected by and responsible to, the entire people is our political creed.

We declare that the earth with all its natural productions is the common property of all; we therefore denounce all infractions of this evidently just and natural law, as robbery and usurpation. We declare that the present state of society, which permits idlers and schemers to monopolise the fruits of the earth and the productions of industry, and compels the working classes to labour for inadequate rewards, and even condemns them to social slavery, destitution and degradation, is essentially unjust. That labour and reward should be equal is our social creed.

We condemn the 'National' hatreds which have hitherto divided mankind, as both foolish and wicked; foolish, because no one can decide for himself the country he will be born in; and wicked, as proved by the feuds and bloody wars which have desolated the earth, in consequence of these national vanities. Convinced, too, that national prejudices have been, in all ages, taken advantage of by the people's oppressors, to set them tearing the throats of each other, when they should have been working together for their common good, this society repudiates the term 'Foreigner', no matter by whom or to whom applied. Our moral creed is to receive our fellow men, without regard to country, as members of one family, the human race; and citizens of one great commonwealth — the world. Finally, we recognize that great moral law — 'Do unto thy brother, as thou wouldest thy brother should do unto thee', as the greatest safeguard of public and private happiness.

Harney, Ernest Jones and the incisive Karl Schapper turned this Society into an extraordinarily productive propaganda agency, which issues scores of addresses and strengthened ties with provincial and continental republicans (114). Marx and Engels approved of the second course, but criticised the weakness of the F.D.'s social analysis and revolutionary fervour.

Ironically, the revolutions of 1848 damaged this society, for *émigrés* returned home in large numbers and the British government tightened its restrictions on those that remained. During the international 'reign of terror' of the next few years, Chartists talked vaguely about united action on the part of Irish, American and European reformers. At a local level many of them joined middle-class Liberals in spontaneous demonstrations on behalf of Kossuth, Garibaldi and the 'gallant few'. Harney kept surprisingly close to this popular feeling, but Ernest Jones, O'Brien and lesser figures like G.E.Harris, W.Slocombe and J.B.Leno moved towards those social-democratic international committees and leagues which were such a feature of the mid and late 1850s.

*

The enthusiasm which greeted every continental tremor brought up the old question of priorities. Chartists occasionally thought it necessary to invade peace societies and working-class meetings devoted solely to foreign affairs. The Russophobia and militant pacifism of the 1840s created tensions within the radical movement, and associations fractured at Glasgow, Newcastle and Carlisle. In the aftermath of the French Revolution it was a similar story. 'Old Chartists looked askance at our proceedings,' said the republican, W.E.Adams (31). They regarded the six points as the *sine qua non* of every attempt to change government policy, and suspected certain London Democratic Committees of being no more than instruments to 'supersede the [Chartist] movement'. Ernest Jones had similar doubts about the Home and Foreign Affairs Committees which appeared in the North and Midlands at the time of the Crimean War.

Violence posed a different threat to the Chartist movement; in 1839–40, 1842 and 1848 leaders were imprisoned, and loyalty and unity stretched to breaking-point. At such periods radicals as different as Lovett and Dr Taylor had their chance to make inroads into the movement, both denouncing 'the man [O'Connor] who . . . would not step across the first gutter to obtain [freedom], if there was danger of getting his feet wet'. Disillusionment with the failure of violence and the behaviour of the Chartist leadership caused individuals and even communities to withdraw from the N.C.A. A few reformers complained bitterly that by identifying Chartism with industrial action in 1842 their leaders had done irreparable damage to the movement in parts of Lancashire and Cheshire. Cries of 'coward' and 'traitor' flew thick and fast; at one time or another, Harney, McDouall and even George White were accused of being spies. In Wales there was a further problem – leaders who fled to America or were imprisoned could not easily be replaced. And when some of these joined Neesom, Thomas Cooper and Richard Spurr of the L.D.A. in refuting their earlier extravagant claims the mischief was compounded. 'Moral force – 'Tis all HUMBUG. Physical force – It won't do!' said the *Western Vindicator* in December 1839, and many Chartists now committed themselves to Vincent's 'quiet revolution' or joined O'Connor's national party. Matthew Fletcher was given to sneering.

It was easy for everyone to be wise after the event. Towards the end of his life Harney recalled that the 'consensus of opinion' in 1839 had been in favour of open conflict. Although London seemed an impregnable fortress for much of the Chartist period, in the provinces the overthrow of troops and the barricading and firing of towns were real possibilities (134). The well-known equanimity of Napier and Lord John Russell can be as deceiving as the frantic cries of local magistrates. Did the reprieve of John Frost defuse an ugly situation? (6, 115). The Newport rising shocked the government, and accelerated improvements in the machinery of law and order. Disappointed Chartists, who hated these new developments, devoted much of their energy to publicizing and assisting the victims of 'a cruel police state'.

The events of 1848 – 'one huge monument of misfortune' (McGrath) – ended hopes of a Chartist revolution, but provided their opponents with the chance to complete the character assassination begun by Daniel O'Connell, Socialists and

Repealers. For many justices of the peace, newspaper editors and novelists, Chartism had become synonymous with violence and attacks on property. 'Modern Chartism,' said *The Times* in August 1848, 'has but three points – fire-raising, bloodshed and plunder.' The Chartists were denounced as the counterparts of cowardly foreign assassins and communists, whilst the Whig government was presented as the powerful defender of British freedom. This mixture of fear and contempt produced the myth of 10 April 1848.

The exasperation of Chartists in this situation betrays their inward tension. For radicals in 1848 experienced not only another round of self-examination but a more debilitating crisis of confidence. Doubts over the nature and leadership of the movement, which had been fairly common in London and certain other Chartist centres since the winter of 1846–7, now took on a new significance. Although Ernest Jones called upon Chartists to 'Organize, organize', with as much vigour as O'Connor in 1840 and 1843, there was a growing feeling that a great popular movement was passing away. The events of 1848 had reduced old Chartists like James Leach and Philip McGrath to a quiet cynicism, and many of their friends now set off for Kansas City. For the rest 'we must begin again' was sound but insensitive advice. Some, as always on such occasions, appealed to the trades for help; others rolled near the backwash of middle-class reform. And recent recruits, alive with the fire of European revolution, demanded 'the Charter and something more'. It only remained, as one Chartist put it, 'to bury the carcass'.

5. THE LAST DAYS,
1848 – 60

'We have lived to see the most momentous crisis that has ever occurred in the British democratic movement.' So began Philip McGrath's letter to the Chartists in December 1850. The quality and leadership of Chartism had certainly changed over two years; the more intimidating methods of a mass movement had lost their appeal; and in some areas the integrity and value of political reform had been under continuous assault. 'The Chartist movement has failed – yes, failed,' said O'Brien in 1849, ' . . . it is because a thorough discussion of social rights has not been permitted.' The resignations of the lecturer Samuel Kydd and the directors of the Land Company, and the defensive manoeuvrings of O'Connor indicate the changing structure of the movement. When McGrath addressed the Chartists, a new generation of leaders had already stepped forward with their own publications and order of priorities. In general this group appeared more reluctant than their predecessors to join hands under the six-point umbrella.

At the moment it is impossible to assess the geography and significance of this change. Our knowledge of later Chartism at a local level remains pitifully thin. Many contemporary writers were inclined to end their detailed accounts of the movement in 1848, and newspapers often ignored radical activities in the later period. Current research on Wales and the Black Country suggests that we have underestimated the resilience of Chartism; further work on the West Riding and the north-east may well underline this point (108, 162, 166). In North Wales and parts of the West Country there were even signs that the movement entered upon a new life. A. W. Blackler of Torquay, along with Thomas Clewes (Stockport), John Brown (Newcastle), the veteran Joseph Alderson (Bradford) and Walter Pringle (Edinburgh) campaigned with traditional Chartist vigour. Many of these resented the quarrels over the executive and tried to

escape the divisive pattern of Manchester and London Chartism.
The Scotsmen James Adams and the Reverend A. Duncanson
could accept two views of Chartist progress, and Welshmen
always knew when to close their ears. For them survival was
everything.

In this period it is more difficult than ever to isolate and
quantify the various indices of Chartist activity (see Appendix
V). At Halifax a côterie of enthusiasts – Clisset, Snowden,
Binns and Holt – organized an exciting range of committees
and crusades. But this was exceptional. From scattered references it seems that the N.C.A., which was revived in 1849,
never had more than 4000–5000 members during the following
decade, and probably had many fewer. The executive and
district councils were starved of money. Associations merged,
divided and even dropped the name 'Chartist'. 'It is unfashion-
able to be [a Chartist] in certain quarters,' James Finlen
admitted in 1855, 'or at least to say that you are . . .' In the
same year R. G. Gammage, the first historian of Chartism, was
already lecturing on the 'reasons for the failure of the movement'. Complaints of apathy – sometimes linked directly to
improved economic conditions – poured in from Sheffield,
Birmingham, Ashton and several Scottish centres, and even
the great Blackstone Edge meetings sometimes proved disappointing. William Jackson and his Birmingham disciples
tinkered hopefully with the workings of their association, but
it needed extraneous factors such as the Crimean War and
names like O'Connor and Frost to bring out the people in large
numbers.

In time no doubt the full story of this late and complex period
of Chartism will be told. At present one can do little more than
isolate two main themes. The first is the story of 'Charter
Socialism'. For years Samuel Kydd, John Skelton, Isaac
Ironside and others had made no secret of their belief in 'the
Charter and something more', but after 1848 the new Chartist
leaders openly encouraged the enthusiastic demand for a 'clear
social programme'. O'Connor, predictably, saw this as an un-
welcome continuation of the 'Owenite business', a return to
the days of morality politics, élitism and long-term planning.
By the end of 1852 this new kind of Chartism had lost some of
its impetus, and the second theme is Ernest Jones's struggle

to retain a Chartist identity and organization in the face of working-class apathy and middle-class reform. He 'kept the old flag flying till he was almost starved into surrender' (W.E.Adams).

'THE EARTH MOVES': CHARTER SOCIALISM

'The Chartism of '51 is not that of 1839 or 1848,' wrote Harney in the *Friend of the People* (No. 19). 'The outward and visible form of Chartism perished in 1848 . . . Defeated, disappointed of the political victory they had hoped for in 1848, the hard-working thinkers turned their attention to social questions.' Here Harney describes – with missionary exaggeration – the experience of one group of Chartists. For convenience they can be labelled 'Charter Socialists'; they included in their number some provincial stalwarts and a new generation of London radicals. In their eyes the events of 1848 in Britain and France had reinforced the middle-class lesson of 1846 – political victories and revolution were not enough to halt the forces of reaction. The great need was to prepare for the 'True Republic – Democratic, Social and Universal'. The Convention Address of 1848 pointed the way – 'The social condition of the people of England has been long neglected . . .', and over the next four years Harney, Gammage, James Finlen and Ernest Jones responded with a series of publications devoted to political and social analysis (8, 15, 18).

They were not without help, for the contemporary interest in the labour question had rekindled the popularity of O'Brien and Oastler, and had provided an entrée for Marx, Maurice and lesser mortals like Thomas Frost. The great social debate echoed through London clubland. Some of the dissatisfied Chartists of 1848 appeared stunned by the complexity of arguments. 'Respecting the nature of those [social] rights, there may be a difference of opinion,' the provisional executive reassured them in June 1852. 'There are, however,' it continued, 'two of them upon which there can be no difference, viz., the right of the people to produce wealth for their sustenance, and their right to exchange that wealth as may be most just and convenient to themselves. The first can only be achieved by the nationalization of landed property; the second only by basing their national currency on the amount of consumable wealth which the nation produces.' O'Brien, the first schoolmaster of Chartism, must have smiled at this neat summary.

The Charter Socialists shared the religious confidence of so many socialists and republicans of the early 1850s – 'Our hopes ran mountains high' (Gerald Massey). Stallwood, the poet J. B. Leno and James Finlen dismissed other reformers as 'Sham Radicals', seeking to prevent real change, or as stubborn utopians lost in dreams. With a Marxist calendar and a keen sense of ancient history the Charter Socialists chronicled the centralization of wealth and its predictable consequences.

Although this concept of a social revolution was shared by Chartists in Glasgow, Brighton, Bradford and other towns, London provided the vitality and audience for the new movement. In the early spring of 1850 members of the Metropolitan Delegate Council captured the provisional Chartist executive. This victory brought men like D. W. Ruffy and W. J. Linton back into the N.C.A., and encouraged Gerald Massey and other Christian Socialists to take a more active part in Chartist politics. Harney and O'Brien, cautious allies, now talked vaguely of a union of all social reformers, but at a special Social and Democratic conference the Irishman advised the N.C.A. to stick to its last. Still, the intellectual debate had left its mark; at the Chartist Convention in the spring of 1851 the Charter Socialists scored a resounding triumph, as Gammage recalls:

A few of the delegates were still in favour of agitating for the Charter, and nothing but the Charter. Among these were the delegates from Manchester, Derby, the Potteries, and Northampton; but the great majority were in favour of agitating for the social as well as the political emancipation of the people. It was also agreed that, while the Chartists should not oppose the Financial and Parliamentary Reformers, they should form no alliance with that party. Holyoake, and two or three others, spoke against the latter part of the resolution, but it was carried almost unanimously. It was then resolved – only six delegates dissenting – to alter the Charter so as to make it deprive of the vote, criminals, only while undergoing their sentence. The adoption of such a resolution shows how very imperfectly men observe the movements in which they are engaged, for the principle contained in it had been adopted by the Conference at Birmingham nearly nine years previous, at which time that part of the Charter was altered accordingly. Resolutions were agreed to for another National Petition for the Charter, to be adopted at simultaneous meetings, and signed by the chairman of each meeting; for bringing forward Chartist candidates at the forthcoming election; in favour of the Chartists seeking municipal influence, and for issuing addresses on that subject; for carrying the agitation for the Charter amongst the trades, through the agricultural districts, amongst the colliers, miners, and railway labourers, and the appointment of special missionaries to Ireland. Although the Executive had in their first programme left unnoticed the fundamental principles of social rights, they introduced into the Convention, day by day, propositions regarding those principles. A clause was introduced and adopted in favour of the nationalization of the land by the establishment of a Board of Agriculture; the restoration of poor, common, church, and crown lands to the people; and the empowering of the State to gradually purchase up other land, until all of it should become national property. Another clause went for the separation of Church and State; the existing church property to become national, with a due regard for vested interests. A third clause laid down the principle of national, secular, gratuitous, compulsory education. A fourth asserted the right of Co-operative Societies to registration and enrolment, and expressed an opinion that the co-operative bodies should all be joined in a national union, the profits to be paid into a general fund; the State to open a Credit Fund for advancing money to bodies of working men desirous of associating together for industrial purposes. A fifth clause asserted the right of the poor to substantial relief when out of employment, and to be employed where possible on the land; the aged and infirm to be entitled to relief, either at their own homes, or in special buildings erected by the Government, as they themselves might choose. The sixth clause asserted that all taxes ought to be levied on land and accumulated property. The seventh provided for the extinction of the National Debt by means of the interest being applied as repayment of the capital. The eighth set forth that standing armies were contrary to the principles of Democracy, and dangerous to the liberty of the people; but that it was necessary that a standing force should be maintained for a time, and that a reform in the army was necessary, as also in the navy. The ninth clause asserted the right of every individual to bear arms, and to be afforded the opportunity of military training. The Convention also passed a clause in opposition to capital punishment. The whole of these propositions underwent considerable discussion, and were spoken to by some of the delegates most ably. The discussions too, were generally free from acrimony, nearly every man expressing his opinion in a calm and dignified spirit. The programme adopted by the Convention was vastly superior to any adopted by previous Conventions.

In the enthusiasm for the programme of 1851 it was easy to forget that Chartists still faced the old problems of propaganda and organization. 'Start again,' was the O'Brienite advice of the new leaders, 'with tracts and schools as your main weapons.' Localities were urged to hold regular meetings and open their libraries to the public, and individual reformers were given the responsibility of converting their friends. Young London activists like Leno and E. Miles welcomed this Baboeuvian approach, but Chartists in Wales and the Potteries seemed more concerned with the practical side of communication. The incessant battles for control of the executive had left them stranded. Ernest Jones, an organization-man in the O'Connor mould, took up their complaints, and for several years he and Gammage toured the provinces, restoring the contacts and strength of an ailing N.C.A. and trying – somewhat desperately – to recover the mass appeal of early Chartism.

Charter Socialists were anxious to appeal to social groups and regions which had previously held back from the radical movement. Jones visited Wales, the West Country and the eastern counties. His enthusiastic reports, the spasmodic rural violence of the period and the French experiences all combined to remind the Chartist executive of the importance of the agricultural population to a successful national movement. Of course, other non-artisan groups – miners, railway navvies, etc. – needed to be evangelized, but here the new leaders were faced by an old difficulty, the unions. Gammage, Stallwood, A. A. Walton, Thomas Young (Leicester) and Jones wooed the trades, hoping to break down their exclusiveness and 'produce a COMMUNITY OF ACTION' (15).

A similar attitude was adopted towards the invigorated co-operative movement of this period. James Leach, William Bell and John Gray were just three of many Chartists who enthused over the growing unity of northern co-operative stores and the formation of new Redemption Societies and London Working Men's Associations. Much of this activity was initiated or encouraged by Christian Socialists. John Malcolm Ludlow, Patrick Lloyd Jones and Walter Cooper toured the country on behalf of Maurice's Association movement and turned the *Christian Socialist* into a national co-operative paper. Ernest Jones, a suspicious romantic, disliked their competition and queried their logic (15, 119).

Jones and his friends, Gammage and Finlen, stressed the

limited objectives of non-political working-class movements, and their tendency to create a labour aristocracy at the expense of the poorest sections of society. The events of 1848 and the subsequent talk of prosperity heightened Chartist sensitivity towards this 'great curse'. Charter Socialists, who claimed that crime and death rates were a better barometer of society than wage statistics, often made no secret of their distaste for aspiring labour leaders in the William Newton–George Howell mould. Equally, they despaired of the naïveté of ordinary workmen, and their readiness to spend extra shillings on drink, gambling and 'vicious literature'. When Nottingham, one of the great Chartist centres, fell by the wayside, James Sweet doubted the wisdom of further Chartist campaigns.

Other radicals took a very different view. William Rider and Philip McGrath blamed the barrier 'between popular feeling and Chartism' on self-elected London adventurers, who had insisted on the 'touchstone of social rights' and thus complicated a 'once ABC political creed'. This feeling reached its climax in the winter and spring of 1851, when the Charter Socialists and the 'Manchester School' of Chartists had separate executives, conferences and programmes. The former group emerged triumphant, but in the hour of their victory they fell out amongst themselves (47). Harney, one of the principal contestants, was now prepared to bury the movement, but from hard-working stalwarts like Thomas Wheeler and Samuel Kydd came the usual requests for faith, harmony and leadership. Chartists in Wales, Stockport, Newcastle and the West Riding echoed these sentiments, and advised their new leaders not to lose their Chartist identity and potential friends by 'confusing ends with means', and to remember that Chartism was a *national* movement.

THE STRUGGLE FOR SURVIVAL

The final problem facing the Chartists was perhaps the most cruel of all – how to survive in an age of reform. With politicians committed to some extension of the franchise, it was even more important to prevent them from grasping 'a people's party fit for the ripe seasons of 1852–60'. 'We are disorganized,' admitted Richard Barker, a Chartist from Bacup, 'and our enemies step before us, and cause us to do the work twice over.' Ernest Jones, the dominant Chartist figure of the 1850s, believed that his main task was to rectify this situation. The conference of May 1852 marked the beginning of his attempt. 'He is getting young again, and hearty,' said Jones at the first sign of a revival, and he brought out the *People's Paper* to chart the progress of the new child.

Many radicals were unable to accept his nervous optimism. Their uncertainty, already discernible in the National Convention of 1848, became more obvious in the following years. Towards the end of the next decade a London Chartist claimed that all their agitation had brought them nothing; Thomas Clark, an earlier rebel, had grown tired of the continual round of martyrdom and victims' funds. For many people the seeds of doubt were sown in gaol, and in the aftermath of '1848' another group of 'deserters' were added to that of the early 1840s:

> He is gone: better so. We should know who stand under
> Our banner: let none but the trusty remain! (Gerald Massey)

But this time the defections were more serious, for the local Chartist leadership was already being decimated by death and emigration. In North Shields it was found almost impossible to replace Myers and Robertson. By the mid 1850s veterans like Benjamin Rushton, James Wheeler and John Skevington had passed away, and provincial associations, in some despair, begged 'our young friends' to take their places.

Another problem confronting the leaders of the N.C.A. was that some members – W.H. Chadwick and Samuel Kydd are good examples – dropped out of formal Chartist politics altogether, or gave most of their energy to other movements. In the North and Midlands there were the rival attractions of Urquhartism, the Ten Hours Movement and Ferrand's Labour League. George White, on his Chartist tour in the autumn of 1855, was fairly critical of the old radical leadership which had, in some areas, detached itself from the problems, hopes and mass politics of those whom it claimed to represent:

> SHEFFIELD – Through the various nostrums brought forward from time to time in this important town, and from want of any tangible movement in favour of democratic progress, some of our best Chartists held aloof, whilst others occupied themselves with elections for town

councillors, and a few co-operated with Urquhart. After arriving there I had to spend a few days to bring together a few of the 'old brigade', when it was agreed that a requisition should be presented to the Mayor, requesting him to convene a meeting for the purpose of forwarding Chartist principles. Ultimately a committee was formed and arrangements made to carry out that object . . .

LEICESTER – This town is an enigma – I found those whose names have been paraded as big men in our prosperous days, yawning and gasping their doleful doubts as to the probability of arousing the people. I found some more who had been the *ostensible* 'whole hog', some quietly settling down to the business of small shopkeepers, and bemoaning their 'awful sacrifices' for 'the cause'. Eventually I inserted an advertisement in a cheap local paper announcing a lecture in the 'Pasture' for Sunday at ten o'clock, and, by the request of the meeting, I delivered another address in the evening, at six, on the same ground, and organized a committee for the enrolment of names . . .

All of George White's reports have to be read with care, but the problems which he outlined were common enough. Radical leaders, disillusioned with 'The Apathy of Mankind', found immediate personal consolation, independence and scope for their organizing skills and democratic sensibilities in the expanding co-operative and self-improvement institutions. In some areas the number of Chartist families that founded or ran co-operative, friendly and trade societies in the third quarter of the nineteenth century is quite astonishing. At the same time, militant nonconformity and temperance enthusiasm so affected workmen in certain Chartist strongholds in Wales, the border counties and the Midlands that Henry Vincent was now able to command huge audiences. In this situation Ernest Jones and Gammage could do little more than tack to the wind, and hope to enrol a few dozen supporters.

For some of their old comrades, men like W. E. Adams and Isaac Ironside, local politics provided a worthwhile substitute for Chartist glory, and they injected Chartist methods and energy into the council chamber and parliamentary elections. Some of them responded favourably to Toulmin Smith's notions of the sovereignty of local government. Isaac Ironside's 'anarchist' party turned Sheffield municipal politics upside down for a short time, whilst in South Wales, Northampton and the Black Country Chartist councillors made individual contributions towards the campaigns for cheap rates and better sanitary conditions. Inevitably, even in Bradford, and Oldham, where the character of working-class politics had changed considerably since the early 1840s, these radicals sometimes found themselves working alongside middle-class reformers. In the early 1850s several important municipal alliances were formed and election bargains struck. At Newcastle, where many Chartists retained a preference for local action, Harney and the young Joseph Cowen joined forces.

But a national Liberal alliance over franchise reform was a different matter, for this resurrected the old issues of trust, terms and organization. In 1848–9 middle-class politicians launched a new wave of reform proposals and public meetings, and looked to popular radicals for support. The weakness of the Chartist movement increased the prospect of collaboration, and Vincent, Duncombe and W.J.Fox proved willing intermediaries (49, 52). Hume and Roebuck made the running in Parliament, and the National Parliamentary and Financial Reform Association was established to push the former's 'Little Charter'. When O'Connor and other Chartist leaders joined this body or advocated a policy of non-intervention, George White and James Williams (Stockport) raised their eyebrows. But the atmosphere now was very different from that of 1842 (149). Many people, including James Leach and Peterloo veterans, felt that help was needed from some quarter; if it were impossible to trust the middle class reformers, perhaps, after all, in the post-1846 period their view of history and political progress might not be incompatible with working-class interest. In some areas the recent interest in press censorship, public expenditure, political exiles and foreign affairs had brought both groups closer together. Much to the delight of Thomas Clark, Chartists in Bath, Walsall, Paisley, Glasgow and Newcastle were apparently struck by 'the middle-class disease'; committees were fused, and Reform Leagues established.

Ernest Jones, who visited many of these towns, tried valiantly to oppose the influence of the Parliamentary and Financial Reform Association and of subsequent middle-class organizations like the Administrative Reform Association and Roebuck's rate-paying franchise movement. They are 'our deadliest enemies and our powerless allies' was the gist of his argument. When the Crimean War strengthened the arm of these movements and gave the *Reynolds News* the opportunity to reveal that all evils were related to aristocratic power, Abraham Robinson and George White joined Ernest Jones in a frantic call for independent action. But their hopes were sometimes thwarted by the optimistic assurances of a Washington Wilks – 'he had induced the middle classes, even the oldest Chartists of Carlisle, to sign the Roebuck programme, because he thought it brought them nearer to the attainment of that glorious old document, the Charter' – and the willingness of some radical artisans to join other reformers in a campaign for manhood suffrage alone. There were other temptations, too, for members of the N.C.A.: Lovett's People's League, William Newton's Manhood Suffrage and Ballot party, and more obscure phenomena such as the Central League of National Chartists Brotherhood. James Capewell, the last of the Old Guard in Walsall, bemoaned this process of secession. 'Are we few men,' he asked, 'to divide and redivide our efforts until we become but ropes of sand?'

In his fight to retain a separate Chartist identity Jones faced considerable opposition not only from those ready to 'go for less', but also from Charter Socialists and northern democrats who never accepted his personal view of Chartist politics. The ferocious battles in the Metropolitan Delegate Council in 1852–3 were the first stage of a conflict which continued throughout the decade. Some districts refused to recognize executive decisions. Fellow members of the executive travelled uncomfortably in Jones's wake; Gammage and James Finlen were given to bitterness, John Shaw added a touch of humour. 'Since my election as one of the executive I have never been corresponded with by any of the Chartist body, and I think that it is somewhat strange.' After 1856 Jones posed as the dictator and inspiration of the small Chartist movement. His *People's Paper* kept alive communications between the remaining associations (45).

From the pages of this newspaper it appears that the main centres of organized Chartism in its last days were South Lancashire, the West Riding, the Black Country, London and certain towns in the North-east, Wales, north Cheshire and the West Country. In these areas Edward Hooson, a Manchester wire-drawer, Benjamin Lucraft, a London bookseller, and other prominent new leaders worked hand-in-hand with veterans like

William Hill, George Harrison and Richard Jones (Llanidloes). The revival of the mid 1850s, a product of war and hunger, gave them new confidence. The London Organization Committee redoubled its energies, several international committees were established, and associations were re-formed at Halifax, Stockport, Doncaster, Bradford, Newtown and a score of other towns. George White remained as optimistic as ever about the good sense of ordinary workmen:

> I have heard a great deal lately concerning Chartist apathy, and have been told that now was the time to rouse the people to a sense of duty. I do not feel that there is any reason for despondency, because we have not kept up a continual uproar. The masses in the large towns are pretty well acquainted with our principles and, should an opportunity occur, I have no doubt that they will be prepared to assert them. (May 1855)

But White, Abraham Robinson, George Stobart, James Bligh and other Chartist lecturers still went about their work in the manner of pioneers, and radical tracts were distributed in vast numbers. White and William Mitchell, a leading figure in West Riding Chartism, even brought out their own periodicals, a rare attempt to break the growing middle-class monopoly of provincial publications devoted to political reform. In these middle years of the decade public meetings could be surprisingly large, though over the period as a whole Chartist operations were small and sometimes had an air of despondency about them.

Jones tried hard to give the faithful a sense of direction. His Mass Movement was a positive response to the class warfare of the early 1850s. Equally important were his analyses of the various reform proposals of leading politicians. Jones, an old friend of Disraeli, suggested that the Tories might well offer a more radical measure than their rivals. With a new Reform Bill promised for 1858 Jones renewed his demand for the six points of the Charter, but circumstances and his supporters induced him to take his stand on manhood suffrage alone. As Democratic Political Reform Associations sprang up at Tower Hamlets, Newcastle and several Scottish towns, provincial Chartist leaders like Hooson, Samuel Cook and William Gould openly supported the Sturgeite campaign to influence the government's proposals. A conference was called to cement this alliance. The invitation list included old radicals – Clutton Salt, Vincent and Lovett, rivals – O'Brien, Owen and Kingsley, and possible allies – William Newton, John Bright and Joseph Cowen. The conference, held in the early part of 1858, saw the birth of the Political Reform League and the practical end of the Chartist movement. This is a report of Ernest Jones's crucial speech to the conference:

> Times altered, and as times altered, results altered also, and he now begged to read the second proposition of the programme. He considered that they should meet the middle classes halfway and take what was offered, if what was offered was a reasonable proposition from the middle classes. If they only had a £5 franchise it would be throwing the preponderance into the hands of the middle classes, and widening the distance between them and other working classes. But if the working classes could get the Universal Manhood Suffrage, then they would for a time waive the other points of the charter. If they would obtain the ballot it would be sufficient for a time, and if they could get these two points, it would throw the balance of power into the hands of the working classes, and the other points would soon follow. (*Cheers*) . . .
> If they joined, they would go forward together; and if not they the Chartists would go forth alone, and no time was to be lost. Now the time had come and now the opportunity had arrived. The middle classes had agreed that this movement was best. Let them hold out a friendly hand to them, and insist upon having the fair and honourable rights of the Chartist body. They were not going to abandon the Charter; but they were going to obtain what they could towards it, at the same time agitating for the whole six points . . .

Chartists in central and south London predictably denounced this 'sell-out' and established their own National Political Union for the Obtainment of the People's Charter, and several provincial Chartist groups carried out an old threat to go it alone. The N.C.A. staggered on for another two years, its leader prematurely old and its spirit broken by constant wrangling.

EPILOGUE

Chartism in its ending and beginning was more than its organization. The 'Old Guard' continued to influence local politics in the 1860s, through their work on election committees, reform associations and town councils. Joseph Goody (Ipswich), Henry Thomas (Merthyr) and others did their best to organize and channel the protests of working men (163, 166). In the years 1866–8 many of these Chartists appeared on the platform for the last time, determined to celebrate another

victory over 'Old Corruption'. Liberal politicians like Henry
Richard never underestimated their value nor their attachment
to the old movement. Some Chartists refused to give up the
name, and those who emigrated to America often lived out
their lives together, talking and writing in the old style (103).
Benjamin Wilson recalls how on 7 July 1885 twenty-two
Halifax Chartists sat down to a reunion dinner (39). There
was much to remember, and much to applaud.

'What have we gained?' asked Julian Harney in 1848. 'Is
the reward proportionate to the toil expended?' Most would
have said 'Yes'. It was Ernest Jones's proud boast that the
Chartists had redefined the nature of democracy, and had
challenged everything – from voluntaryism to Christian
Socialism – which might oil the wheels of aristocratic monopoly
and commercial expansion. They did not always succeed, of
course, nor did they carry out their intentions to rewrite
history and capture the co-operative working-class mind. In
particular, it was a matter of common regret that they had not
paid more attention to the women and children who held the
key to working-class progress. 'The Charter will never become
the law of the land,' the ardent feminist Caroline Maria Williams
had once said, 'until we women are fully resolved that it shall
be so.' And certainly, few of the hundred or so women's and
young men's Chartist associations continued into the mid 1850s.
Perhaps, as Engels suggested, the old cry 'Ye *are* slaves' and
the 'obvious and easy' economic alternatives of 1847 came less
frequently in later years from the mouths of comfortable shopkeepers and artisans intent on Improvement. Was there something symbolic in the number of Chartists who found jobs in
insurance? Novelists, newspaper editors and George Meredith
could afford to smile and be charitable.

The Chartist movement has always been dogged by critics
and prophets. In later years rivals and disillusioned participants
pushed home their advantage. Some freethinkers took up
Richard Carlile's old criticism of Chartists as being men with
'no mental manhood'. Bronterre O'Brien, schooled in cynicism
– 'The people always appear doomed to be humbugged' –
claimed that by their obsession with politics and organization
the Chartists had opened the way for the triumph of Liberalism.
Miles Brearley of Dewsbury, an old Stephenite, insisted that the

Chartists had helped to perpetuate the real abuses in society; and perhaps it is significant that in some areas of London and the North this radical movement slipped quickly from popular history. There were other detractors, too: Owenites and trade unionists, who complained of wasted money and effort; Marx and Engels, who talked of a wrong turning; and perhaps most damaging of all, veteran radicals like Lovett, Vincent and Thomas Cooper.

Resentment is at the heart of early Chartist history. Broken hopes and injured pride turned memoirs into thinly disguised denunciations of the Chartist leadership (26, 32, 37). Men who had always been wary of excessive hero-worship attacked 'O'Connorites' for their exaggerated claims of popular support, their obstructionism and inconsistencies, and their willingness to divide the Chartist body and plunge the country into revolution. 'Antagonisms, within and without, have been our greatest curse' (Thomas Cooper). All these points could be, and were, made of the Ten Hours, Anti-Poor-Law and Anti-Corn-Law movements, but – as O'Connor anticipated – historians have generally woven the story of Chartism around them in a unique way.

The Irishman was given to special pleading, but the problems which he faced deserve greater attention. When analysing their peculiar difficulties, O'Connor and Ernest Jones often began with the disunity of the working classes and the individualism of their leaders. The divisions were clear enough: the gulf between the aristocratic trades and the rest, the deference and fear of certain rural and industrial areas, the proud independence of London and the provinces, the tension between town and country, the religious and national feelings of Irish and Scottish radicals, and the diffusion of working-class effort in a myriad of self-help and political activities. Nothing angered Chartists more than the prosperous indifference of the working-class aristo-crats – 'deserters from our ranks' – and the sight of old friends in the pay of rival political groups. Except perhaps apathy; the 'indifference and utter inattention of the multitude' in the 1850s drove poets and Chartist lecturers to the point of despair:

Smitten stones will talk with fiery tongues
And the worm when trodden will turn . . .

So much depended on the leaders of working-class communities and the political feelings produced by local and work situations. Respected and articulate men like Samuel Cook, Matthew Fletcher and Richard Bowen of Cefn Mawr, North Wales, inevitably coloured the response of their districts. O'Connor and Ernest Jones, disappointed with the showing of Birmingham Chartism, put much of the blame on prominent artisans. Such people in such a town often had a wide range of interests and loyalties, as lecturers frequently discovered in the 1850s, and could move in and out of organized Chartist politics with considerable rapidity. We have seen the attraction which self-help societies and other movements held for them; one would like to know more about the effects of sustained periods of mid Victorian prosperity on them, and about the rewards, scope and alliances of independent local politics in the 1840s and 1850s.

The task of bringing together men with varying levels of political and social consciousness was an enormous one. For twenty years Chartists argued over the best means to create a great popular movement, much of the debate turning on the relationship between thought and action. Some believed that propaganda was the first requirement. 'We need to capture the minds of the people,' said Arthur O'Neill; and for this reason some radicals wanted to give the 'dry, abstract' Charter the strength of 'Improvement' or the promise of 'Something More.' In the Chartist press there were long discussions over whether radicals should bring forward a detailed plan of the economic and social reforms which would be initiated by a People's Parliament, or whether potential supporters should be given an immediate demonstration of these benefits. At various times in the 1850s delegate meetings in Lancashire and Yorkshire proposed to dispel the political gloom by establishing Chartist co-operative stores. 'A nation's freedom cannot be gained by talking,' said the Convention of 1846, which considered O'Connor's practical answer to the disappointments and rivalry of the mid 1840s. Some Chartists placed an enormous emphasis on the value of organization. History, experience and other movements had shown the importance of having a national focus, and of keeping a limited programme constantly before the public eye. The problems of organization in this pre-

Liberal era were enormous: finance, communications, the suspicion of professionalism, the pull between local and national action, the strength of commitment and recruitment of the young. Trade unions and other bodies sometimes overcame these difficulties better than the N.C.A., but the Chartists, even of the 1850s, claimed a special achievement – the power to bring out the masses on matters of great moment.

The controversy over Chartist organization and leadership unfortunately draws attention away from parallel developments within popular radicalism. O'Neill, Vincent and O'Brien, stubborn victims of O'Connor's caustic tongue, still enjoyed remarkable local followings in the 1850s. O'Brien's disciples played an influential role in London club life (112). Thomas Cooper, who rejoined the N.C.A. in 1853, Lovett, who refused to do so in 1843 and 1846, and McDouall, all acted out their own particular interpretation of Chartism, with their own prescriptions for success and failure, and their own plans for organization. On the very day of the Kennington Common demonstration of April 1848, Hetherington, Watson, Cooper and others met to elect the officers of a little-known body called the People's Charter Union. These radicals occasionally joined O'Connor's men in the cause of *émigrés* and victims, and at certain public celebrations, protests and election meetings. At the opening of the South London Chartist Hall in December 1843 O'Connor shared the platform with O'Brien and J. H. Parry, both of whom he had recently denounced. On such neutral ground these Chartists could also be seen in the company of Mr R. S. Neale's 'uneasy' and lonely professionals – Dr Wade, Dr Black, Sturge, Solly, Cowen, W. E. Forster and others – who constantly threw out lines and images to the middle and working classes (97). For two brief periods, in the reflective disappointment of 1849–50, and in the excitement of 1858, it seemed that all these people might come together as they had done in the late 1830s.

The radical ideology made such a union possible. At one time or another most reformers saw themselves as part of the battle for the regeneration of society in the face of a debilitating aristocracy. Even in the last days of Chartism, Irish and Scottish landlordism, colonial rape, Negro slavery and the 'Aristocratic

Treason' of the Crimean War kept this feeling very much alive. Factory-owners who aspired to gentility and moved out to splendid suburban villas fitted comfortably into this traditional picture of aristocratic corruption. Although Chartists like McDouall, O'Brien, William Dixon, J.B. Hanson and Samuel Kydd insisted that the real struggle in society was between Capital and Labour, and found proof in the 1840s that the sins of the aristocracy 'are like snow, when compared with the black and damning atrocities of the steam lords', they still accepted the political strategy of a Lovett or Vincent.

Opinions differed over the starting-points for the regeneration of the working class. In the 1850s and 1860s Benjamin Lucraft and his friends campaigned vigorously for changes in education and drinking habits, and the old arguments of Henry Vincent reappear in certain columns of the *People's Paper*. Others believed that nothing could be achieved without an improvement in physical conditions. For O'Connor, Ernest Jones and other Irish and English Chartists who were only one step removed from rural society, land reform was the answer – 'the practical – the only mode of regeneration'. The importance of land figured prominently in Chartist literature of the 1840s and 1850s, and in the letters from fortunate emigrants. This is Joseph Barker, writing from America in 1853: 'I could not bear to be without a farm and to be treated as of an inferior order now. My hatred of the English aristocracy is unbounded. There are no greater criminals on earth.'

What united all these Chartists was the feeling that universal suffrage was the most urgent and effective method of change. Although there were times in the last days of the movement when old stalwarts like James Sweet came near to doubting its value, the importance of political power was deeply embedded in their historical consciousness. James Leach, who was involved in the Ten Hours and co-operative movements, advised hungry workmen 'to pay strict attention to politics, for it was mixed up with every action of their lives . . .' and O'Brien, with youthful optimism, had once promised that 'the moment the people obtain a Parliament of their own, the whole of society will undergo rigid scrutiny'. The message was carried forward into certain Trade Councils and Reform Associations of the mid-Victorian era (53, 124).

For many people an interest in foreign affairs was merely an extension of this radicalism. The lecturers Vincent, Gammage and George Stobart (Newcastle) spoke on the Charter one night, and on European developments the next. '[The aristocracy] cannot divide us, as in the past,' ran a common refrain, 'we are all brethren.' 'If this interest in foreign affairs can be kept sufficiently alive it will one day produce great results,' said Samuel Kydd in 1849. After the mid 1840s there was a growing feeling, stimulated by reports from emigrants in America and Australia, that the greatest problems in society were international in character. O'Connor and his Irish friends, who saw the world from an Atlantic perspective, passionately recorded shifts in American opinion; whilst Kydd and Harney looked to events in Europe to revive the spirit of democracy at home. Although co-operation between Chartism and reforming movements elsewhere was small, apart from the exchange of leaders, programmes and newspapers, Chartists accepted, almost without question, the notion of a western revolution.

In retrospect it is perhaps too easy to remove the emotional and intellectual scaffolding of the Chartist movement. Patrick Lloyd Jones was one of those contemporaries who were later able to appreciate Chartism's 'innocuous' nature, and some historians have been impressed by its 'high middle-class content' and 'respectability', but people at the time rarely thought in this way. They had to contend with the ideological integrity of an O'Brien, the conviction of a George White – 'Nobody needs to prove that they are right' – and the anger of a George Harrison – 'The present history of the working classes is a theme, solemn as death, serious as the grave . . .' It is worth recalling here that some of our key historical witnesses, men like Lovett, Vincent and Lowery, were kept on the fringe of the Chartist movement for long periods, and that some of the temperance and religious Chartists were as anxious as Ernest Jones for a complete change in the social order. Lloyd Jones, when lecturing in the Manchester of 1839, knew precisely what fear, poverty and disappointment could do to rank-and-file Chartists. Here, as elsewhere, opponents of the movement were sometimes subjected to an unpleasant mixture of contempt and intimidation, and their behaviour in moments of crisis was rarely forgotten. What worried 'respectable' people in some areas was the willingness of McDouall, William Miles and other Chartists to work closely with trade unionists in the battle for a just society; one would like to know more about the subsequent careers of such radicals. Recent research has highlighted the extent of militancy in this period, though in the final analysis it is perhaps the caution of Chartist leaders which sticks in the mind.

Chartists, of course, prided themselves on being 'practical men'; this was the message which they took to trade union and socialist meetings. Yet dreams stalk through the poetry which so many of them wrote. Each quiver abroad, each small victory at home, fired the imagination. The millennialism of the early days is difficult to re-create or explain; so is the prodigious optimism of Chartist organizers, and the loyalty and sacrifices which they called forth. As the years passed, and the threat of violent change receded, people readjusted their hopes and strategy, but the faith remained. 'The result IS certain – the Numbers ARE coming – flow the tide DOES – and the future of the Charter is secure' (Ernest Jones, poet and Chartist, 11 December 1852).

This conviction justified Chartist independence. The willingness of Chartists to rely on their own strength is the outstanding characteristic of the movement. At the local level Chartism was often an integral part of the struggle for identity, dignity and improvement. Men like William Hill, William Aitken and William Dixon articulated common feelings about the disruption of family life, the exploitation of women, the waste of talent and the degradation of human beings. 'Am I a Man?' is a question which recurs in one form or another in Chartist speeches and poetry. Workmen, who were committed to education and self-help, had their own set of fears, values and objectives (144). In their support for Chartist schools, halls, churches, newspapers and estates; in their campaigns against capital punishment, army flogging and impressment; and in their belief that science and machinery should ultimately be harnessed for the benefit of all, we catch a glimpse of an alternative society – egalitarian, humane and harmonious. Much of the interest of Chartism in its last days is in the protests by Ernest Jones, James Williams (Stockport) and William Mitchell over the inadequacy of those agencies consciously propagating a working-class view of society and progress in the face of an enveloping middle-class culture.

Contemporaries were impressed by the initiative and independence shown by working men in the movements of this period. One suspects that some historians have underestimated the power, discretion and class feelings of ordinary Chartist members. It was a central text of the Chartist faith that – 'with individual exceptions' – the political salvation of the country lay with the working class. The scepticism and independence which faced Dr Black, the American reformer, on his first excursions into artisan London still confronted him in the 1850s. Ernest Jones, who treaded warily between free-traders, protectionists, Christian paternalists and Urquhartists, did his best to foster these feelings. It was a measure of Chartist independence that they could work so closely to the various reform movements of those years, and yet retain 'the hot talk of the vote' and the demand for labour representation. At the parliamentary elections of the 1850s a small number of Chartist candidates once again tried to win support in favourable constituencies. Their failure, even to recapture Nottingham, should not blind us to their other achievements in local politics. Henry Hyndman had every reason to be impressed.

Many Chartists had an annoying habit of subjecting non-working-class friends and M.P.s to searching cross-examinations. In the *Northern Star* O'Connor dissected these people with a skill that a political scientist might envy; even the most Advanced Whig would be reminded of an old vote for the Poor Law Amendment Act of 1834 or an odd phrase in favour of Irish coercion. O'Connor and Ernest Jones encouraged their followers to query rival organizations at every opportunity. 'What would you have the middle classes to do?' asked the *Bradford Observer* in some desperation. George White, of course, revelled in the confusion of middle-class reformers. 'Let them gnash their teeth and yell out "Chartist Obstructions", "Tory Chartists", "Demagogues", &c. &c., in their disappointed rage,' he wrote in 1855. 'We have them! Glorious thought! Heavenly consolation!' Even when Chartists and Radical Whigs spoke the same language, and when necessity and interest brought them together, the former were aware of differences in emphasis, meaning and power. Chartists had an exaggerated respect for truly independent politicians like Thomas Duncombe and Sharman Crawford, but ultimately their preference was to 'rely on ourselves alone'.

If some radicals took a rather narrower definition of this principle than O'Connor would have liked, this was perhaps inevitable. The history of Chartism after his fall from power revealed, even more obviously than before, that each person had his own order of priorities, his own definition of freedom, and his own views of the relationship between power and knowledge and between the individual and the state. For this reason Chartists reacted differently to the economic and political progress of the mid-Victorian era. Some settled down to an Advanced Liberalism; some moved into independent Labour politics, and others retired in confusion and bitterness (30, 31, 39, 112, 146). But almost all of them retained that tough and independent spirit which had made them 'Irreconcilables' in Robert Owen's lunatic world.

APPENDICES:

CHARTIST ORGANIZATION

I. THE ADDRESS AND OBJECTS OF THE LONDON WORKING MEN'S ASSOCIATION, JUNE 1836*

ADDRESS

Fellow Labourers in the pursuit of knowledge and liberty

We are anxious to express our grateful acknowledgements thus publicly, to those associations who have addressed us in the spirit of fraternity, and especially to those individuals who have so kindly assisted our missionaries in their exertions to form other associations.

It is a pleasing evidence of the progressive knowledge of those great principles of democracy which we are contending for, to find kindred minds prepared to appreciate, and noble hearts seeking their practical development in the remotest parts of the kingdom.

But we would respectfully caution our brethren in other societies strictly to adhere to a judicious selection of their members – on this more than on any other of their exertions harmony and success will depend. Let us, friends, seek to make the principles of democracy as respectable in practice as they are just in theory, by excluding the drunken and immoral from our ranks, and in uniting in close compact with the honest, sober, moral, and thinking portion of our brethren.

Doubtless, by such selections our numbers in many instances will be few compared with the vicious many, but these few will be more efficient for the political and social emancipation of mankind than an indiscriminate union of thousands, where the veteran drunkard contaminates by his example, and the profligate railer at abuses saps by his private conduct the cause he has espoused.

In forming Working Men's Associations, we seek not a mere exhibition of numbers unless, indeed, they possess the attributes and character of *men!* and little worthy of the name are those who

* Copy in the Lovett Collection in the Birmingham Public Library.

have no aspirations beyond mere sensual enjoyments, who, forgetful of their duties as fathers, husbands, and brothers, muddle their understandings and drown their inte'' t amid the drunken revelry of the pot-house – whose profligacy makes them the ready tools and victims of corruption or slaves of unprincipled governors, who connive at their folly and smile while they forge for themselves the fetters of liberty by their love of drink.

We doubt not that the excessive toil and misery to which the sons of labour are subject, in the absence of that knowledge and mental recreation which all just governments should seek to diffuse, are mainly instrumental in generating that intemperance, the debasing influence of which we perceive and deplore. But, friends, though we possess not the political power to begin our reformation at the source of the evil, we cannot doubt the efficacy of our exertions to check by precept and example this politically-debasing, soul-subduing vice.

Fellow-countrymen, *when we contend for an equality of political rights,* it is not in order to lop off an unjust tax or useless pension, or to get a transfer of wealth, power, or influence, for a party; *but to be able to probe our social evils to their source, and to apply effective remedies to prevent, instead of unjust laws to punish.* We shall meet with obstacles, disappointments, and it may be with persecutions, in our pursuit; but with our united exertions and perseverance, we must and will succeed.

And if the teachers of temperance and preachers of morality would unite like us, and direct their attention to *the source* of the evil, instead of nibbling at the effects, and seldom speaking of the cause; then, indeed, instead of splendid palaces of intemperance daily erected, as if in mockery of their exertions – built on the ruins of happy home, despairing minds, and sickened hearts – we should soon have a sober, honest, and reflecting people.

In the pursuit, therefore, of our religious object, it will be necessary to be prudent in our choice of members; we should also avoid by every possible means, holding our meetings at public-houses; habits and associations are too often formed at those places which mar the domestic happiness, and destroy the political usefulness of the millions. Let us, then, in the absence of means to hire a better place of meeting – meet at each others' houses. Let us be punctual in our attendance, as best contributing to our union and improvement; and, as an essential requisite, seek to obtain a select library of books, choosing those at first which will best inform of our political and social rights. Let us blend, as far as our means will enable us, study with recreation, and share in any rational amusement (unassociated with the means of intoxication) calculated to soothe our anxieties and alleviate our toils.

And, as our object is universal, so (consistent with justice) ought to be our means to compass it; and we know not of any means more efficient, than to enlist the sympathies and quicken the intellects of our wives and children to a knowledge of their rights and duties; for, as in the absence of knowledge, they are the most formidable obstacles to a man's patriotic exertions, so when imbued with it will they prove his greatest auxiliaries. Read, therefore, talk, and politically and morally instruct your wives and children; let them, as far as possible, share in your pleasures, as they must in your cares; and they will soon learn to appreciate your exertions, and be inspired with your own feelings against the enemies of their country. Thus instructed your wives will spurn instead of promoting you to accept, the base election bribe – your sons will scorn to wear the livery of tyrants – and your daughters be doubly fortified against the thousand ills to which the children of poverty are exposed.

Who can foretell the great political and social advantages that must accrue from the wide extension of societies of this description acting up to their principles? Imagine the honest, sober and reflecting portion of every town and village in the kingdom linked together as a band of brothers, honestly resolved to investigate all subjects connected with their interests, and to prepare their minds to combat with the errors and enemies of society – setting an example of propriety to their neighbours, and enjoying even in poverty a happy home. And in proportion as home is made pleasant, by a cheerful and intelligent partner, by dutiful children, and by means of comfort, which their knowledge has enabled them to snatch from the ale-house, so are the bitters of life sweetened with happiness.

Think you a corrupt Government could perpetuate its exclusive and demoralizing influence amid a people thus united and instructed? Could a vicious aristocracy find its servile slaves to render homage to idleness and idolatry to the wealth too often fraudulently exacted from industry? Could the present gambling influences of money perpetuate the slavery of the millions, for the gains or dissipation of the few? Could corruption sit in the judgment seat – empty-headed importance in the senate-house – money getting hypocrisy in the pulpit – and debauchery, fanaticism, poverty, and crime stalk triumphantly through the land – if the millions were educated in a knowledge of their rights? No, no, friends; and hence the efforts of the exclusive few to keep the people ignorant and divided. Be ours the task, then, to unite and instruct them; for be assured the good that is to be must be begun by ourselves.

G

OBJECTS OF THE ASSOCIATION

1. To draw into one bond of *unity* the *intelligent* and *influential* portion of the working classes in town and country.

2. To seek by every legal means to place all classes of society in possession of their equal political and social rights.

3. To devise every possible means, and to use every exertion, to remove those cruel laws that prevent the free circulation of thought through the medium of a *cheap and honest press*.

4. To promote, by all available means, the education of the rising generation, and the extirpation of those systems which tend to future slavery.

5. To collect every kind of information appertaining to the interests of the working classes in particular and society in general, especially statistics regarding the wages of labour, the habits and condition of the labourer, and all those causes that mainly contribute to the present state of things.

6. To meet and communicate with each other for the purpose of digesting the information required, and to mature such plans as they believe will conduce in practice to the well-being of the working classes.

7. To publish their views and sentiments in such form and manner as shall best serve to create a moral, reflecting, yet energetic public opinion; so as eventually to lead to a gradual improvement in the condition of the working classes, without violence or commotion.

8. To form a library of reference and useful information; to maintain a place where they can associate for mental improvement, and where their brethren from the country can meet with kindred minds actuated by one great motive – that of benefiting politically, socially, and morally, the useful classes. Though the persons forming this Association will be at all times disposed to co-operate with all those who seek to promote the happiness of the multitude, yet being convinced from experience that the division of interests in the various classes, in the present state of things, is too often destructive of that union of sentiment which is essential to the prosecution of any great object, they have resolved to confine their members as far as practicable to the working classes. But as there are great differences of opinion as to where the line should be drawn which separates the working classes from the other portions of society, they leave to the Members themselves to determine whether the candidate proposed is eligible to become a Member.

II. AIMS AND RULES
OF THE
NATIONAL CHARTER ASSOCIATION*

A PLAN FOR ORGANISING THE CHARTISTS OF GREAT BRITAIN

Agreed upon at a meeting of delegates appointed by the people, and held at the Griffin Inn, Great Ancoats-Street, Manchester, on Monday, July 20, 1840.

DESIGNATION OF THE ASSOCIATION

1. That the Chartists of Great Britain be incorporated into one Society to be called 'The National Charter Association of Great Britain'.

OBJECTS

2. The object of this Association is to obtain a 'Radical Reform' of the House of Commons, in other words, a full and faithful Representation of the entire people of the United Kingdom.

PRINCIPLES

3. The principles requisite to secure such a Representation of the people are:— The right of voting for Members of Parliament by every male of twenty-one years of age and of sound mind; Annual Elections; Vote by Ballot; no property qualifications for Members of Parliament; Payment of members; and a division of the kingdom into Electoral Districts; giving to each district a proportionate number of Representatives according to the number of electors.

MEANS

4. To accomplish the foregoing object none but peaceable and constitutional means shall be employed, such as public meetings

* *Northern Star*, 1 August 1840. Compare this with the shorter revised plan of February 1841; ibid., 27 February 1841.

to discuss grievances arising from the present system; to show the utility of the proposed change, and to petition Parliament to adopt the same.

Conditions of Membership

5. All persons will become members of the Association on condition of signing a declaration, signifying their agreement with its objects, principles and constitution, when they will be presented with cards of membership which shall be renewed quarterly, and for which they shall each pay the sum of twopence.

Registration of Members

6. A book shall be kept by the Executive Council (hereinafter described) in which shall be entered the names, employment and residence of the members of this Association throughout the kingdom.

Classes

7. Wherever possible, the members shall be formed into classes of ten persons; which classes shall meet weekly or at any other stated periods, as most convenient; and one out of, and by, each class shall be nominated as leader (and appointed by the Executive as hereinafter ordered) who shall collect from each member the sum of one penny per week, to the funds of the Association.

Ward Divisions

8. Each town, wherever practicable, shall be divided into wards and divisions according to the plan of the Municipal Reform Act. Once in every month a meeting of the members of the said ward shall be held, when addresses shall be delivered, and Society's business transacted. The leaders within the said wards shall attend the said monthly meetings, and give such a report of the state of their classes as they may deem best, provided always that such report be given in temperate and lawful language.

Election of Ward Collector

9. At the first meeting of each ward or division, a collector shall be nominated (afterwards to be appointed by the Executive as hereinafter ordered) to whom shall be paid the monies collected from the classes by the leaders; and the said collector shall pay the said money to the Treasurer (assistant) of the town or borough, at the weekly meeting of the council.

Local Officers

10. Each principal town, with its suburban villages, shall have a council of nine persons, including an assistant treasurer and secretary.

Duties of Local Treasurer

11. The aforesaid local treasurer shall receive the money from the ward collectors, and all the monies subscribed for the Association in the said township and suburbs; he shall keep an exact account and transmit the proportion (one moiety) due once a month to the General Treasurer.

Duties of Local Secretary

12. The aforesaid secretary shall keep a minute book of all the transactions of the Town Council, and a record of all meetings connected with the Society in his jurisdiction, and shall, with the sanction and under the direction of the said Council, transmit for publication such portions of the said minutes or records as may be deemed necessary.

Duties of Local Council

13. The Town Council shall meet for the transaction of business once every week, and shall have the power of appropriating to the purposes of the society in their own locality a sum not exceeding one half of the subscriptions and other monies received in the said locality. They shall also see that the recommendations and instructions of the Executive Council are carried into effect, and they shall have full power to adopt such means as may seem to them meet, provided such means are in conformity with the fundamental rules of the Association and do not contravene the decisions of the Executive Council.

County and Riding Government

14. In each County or Riding there shall be a council, the number to be according to the circumstances and population of the said County or Riding, with a sub-treasurer or secretary.

General Government

15. The general government of this Association shall be entrusted to a General Executive Council, composed of seven persons including a Treasurer and Secretary.

G*

Duties of General Treasurer

16. The General Treasurer of this Association shall be responsible for all monies entrusted to him, in such penal sum as may be determined upon by the Executive Council; he shall keep an exact account of all monies received and expended by the Association, and shall once every month, publish a statement of the same in the 'Northern Star', 'Scottish Patriot', and in such other of the Chartist newspapers as may be selected by the Executive Council, and once every three months a full balance sheet, which shall be first examined by auditors appointed for the purpose by the Executive Council.

Nomination and Election of the Executive Council

17. The nomination of candidates for the Executive Committee shall take place in the Counties and Ridings, each County or Riding being allowed to nominate one candidate on the first day of December each year – the names of the persons so nominated shall be returned immediately by the secretary, called sub-secretary of the County or Riding to the General Secretary – (this year to the Secretary of the Provisional Committee who have full powers to carry this plan into effect in the best possible manner) – and a list of the whole to be transmitted by him, per post, to all the local (assistant) Secretaries, who shall take the elections of their localities on the first day of January following, and immediately forward the result of such election to the General Secretary, who shall lay the same before the Executive for examination, and by their order publish within one week of receiving the whole of such returns in the 'Northern Star', 'Scottish Patriot', and in any other Democratic Journal, a list of the majorities, and declare who are the persons duly elected. The Executive Council shall be elected for twelve months, when a new Council shall be chosen in the manner and at the period aforesaid, outgoing members being eligible for re-election.

Power and Duties of the Executive

19. The Executive Council shall be empowered to adopt any measure for the advancement of the objects of this Association as may be consistent with its fundamental laws, for which purpose they shall have the disposal of one half, at least, of the monies collected throughout the Society and lodged with the general Treasurer. They shall appoint all the members of the County or

Riding and Local Councils, and all officers throughout the Association, in the appointment of whom, however, they shall be confined to those who may be nominated by the members resident in each place.

TIME OF NOMINATION AND APPOINTMENT
OF SUBORDINATE COUNCIL AND OFFICERS

20. To prevent any interruption of the election of the Executive Council, the nomination of County or Riding Councils shall annually take place on the 1st day of February of each year, and the appointment on the 1st day of March following.*

REMUNERATION OF OFFICERS

21. The General Secretary shall be paid for his services the sum of £2 per week, and each member of the Executive Council the sum of £1. 10s per week during the period of their sittings.

COMPENSATION

22. The members of the Executive shall be entitled to compensation for the loss consequent upon their acceptance of office, either by being employed as missionaries during any recess that may happen while they continue in their official capacity, or in such other way as may be most convenient for the Association; the question of compensation to be determined by the County or Riding councils. When members of the Executive shall be employed as missionaries, their salaries shall be the same as when employed in the Council. Coach-hire, and one half of any other incidental expenses shall be paid to them in addition, by the parties who may request their services, or in the event of being employed by the Executive to open new districts, the same proportion of expenses shall be allowed out of the general fund.

SOME MEANS FOR THE ATTAINMENT OF THE GREAT END

1. The People shall, wherever convenient and practicable, put in operation Mr O'Brien's plan of bringing forward Chartist candidates at every election that may hereafter take place, and especially select, where possible, those as Candidates who are legally qualified to sit in Parliament.

* This clause, it will be seen at once, must be carried into effect for the present year as *soon* as can be by the Provisional Committee.

2. The Members of this Association shall also attend all public Political Meetings, and there, either by moving amendments, or by other means, enforce a discussion of our rights and claims, so that none may remain in ignorance of what we want, nor have an opportunity of propagating or perpetuating political ignorance or delusion.

3. It is urgently recommended that strict sobriety be observed by all members and officers of this Association.

4. The diffusion of Political Knowledge.

III. RULES AND REGULATIONS OF THE CHARTIST LAND CO-OPERATIVE COMPANY*

To consist of an unlimited number of shareholders. Shares, £2 10s. each.

To be paid in weekly settlements of 3d., 6d., 1s., and upwards.

OBJECTS OF THE SOCIETY

To purchase land on which to locate such of its members as may be selected for that purpose, in order to demonstrate to the working classes of the kingdom – firstly, the value of land, as a means of making them independent of the grinding capitalists; and, secondly to shew them the necessity of securing the speedy enactment of the 'People's Charter', which should do for them nationally, what this society proposes to do sectionally: the accomplishment of the political and social emancipation of the enslaved and degraded working classes being the peculiar object of the Society.

MEANS

Good arable land may be rented in some of the most fertile parts of the country at the rate of 15s. per acre, which might be bought at twenty-five years' purchase – that is, at £18 15s. per acre; and supposing £5,000 raised in shares of £2 10s. each, this sum would purchase 120 acres, and locate sixty persons with two acres each, besides leaving a balance of £2,750, which would give to each of the occupants £45 16s. 8d., £30 of which would be sufficient to build a commodious and comfortable cottage on each allotment; one half of the remaining £15 16s. 8d. would be sufficient to purchase

* *Northern Star*, 3 May 1845.

implements, stock, &c., leaving the residue as a means of subsistence for the occupant until his allotment produced the necessaries of life. These allotments, with dwellings, might be *leased for ever* to the members of the society at an annual rental of £5 each, which would be below their real value. The gross annual rental would thus amount to £300. This property, if sold at twenty years' purchase (which would be far below the market value), would yield to the funds of the society £6,000, which sum, if expended in a similar manner to the first, would locate other seventy-two persons on two acres of land, provided with *homes*. These seventy-two allotments, sold at the rate of the first, would bring £7,200; and this sum, laid out in the purchase of other land, building of cottages, &c., at the original rate, would locate 86 and two-fifths persons. These 86 two-fifths allotments, if sold, would realise £8,634 8s.; and with this amount of capital the society could locate other 103 one-sixth persons. These 103 one-sixth allotments, would produce £10,317 3s. 4d.; and the last named sum, expended as before, would locate 123 one-third persons. Thus the original capital of £5,000, would more than double itself at the fourth sale: and so on in the same rates. The benefits arising from the expenditure of the funds in the manner above stated may be seen at a glance in the following summary: –

	£	Purchase	Locate
Original capital	5,000	120 acres	60 persons
First sale produce	6,000	144 ,,	72 ,,
Second ,, ,,	7,200	172 ,,	86 ,,
Third ,, ,,	8,634 8s.	206 ,,	103 ,,
Fourth ,, ,,	10,317 3s. 4d.	246 ,,	123 ,,

Continuing to increase in the same proportion until the tenth sale, which would realise £37,324, and locate 372½ persons. Thus the total number which could be located in ten sales – which, if the project is taken up with spirit, might easily be effected in four years – would be 1,923 persons; in addition to leaving in possession of the society an estate worth at least, in the wholesale market, £37,324, which estate could be resold, increasing at each sale in value and capability of sustaining the members, until, in the space of a few years, a vast number of the 'surplus labour population' could be placed in happiness and prosperity upon the soil of their native land, and thus become valuable consumers as well as producers of wealth.

1. – *Membership.*

All persons are eligible to become members of this society, by taking out a card of membership, and a copy of these rules, for which the sum of fifteen-pence shall be paid; one shilling to be an instalment of the share.

2. – *Government of the Society.*
The government of the society to be vested in a board of directors consisting of a president, treasurer, secretary, and four others.

3. – *Qualification for the Board of Directors.*
No person shall be eligible to become a member of the board of directors who is not at the time of election, and has been for three months previously, a paying member to the funds of this society.

4. – *Mode of electing the Board of Directors.*
The board of directors to be balloted for annually by the members of the society.

5. – *Duties of the Board of Directors.*
It shall be the duty of the Board of Directors to transact all the monetary and other business of the society; and when the sum of £5,000 is subscribed, to purchase a suitable plot of land, containing about 120 acres, which shall be divided into 60 equal allotments, erect the necessary habitations, and furnish each allotment with the required implements, stock, &c. They shall then apprise the members of the society, and instruct them to select, by lot, occupiers, to whom the several allotments, with the buildings, &c., shall be let at a rent of £5 per annum, on lease for ever. They shall then effect a sale of the land, buildings, &c., at the rate of twenty years' purchase on the rent paid, and carry the proceeds, after defraying unavoidable expenses, to the credit of the society, to be again employed in the purchase of more land, the building of more dwellings, the purchasing of stock, &c., to be again divided in allotments to the members, and so on in continuity.

6. – *Appointment of Trustees and their Duties.*
The members at the first general meeting shall appoint five persons as trustees, whose duties shall be to keep a cheque against the general treasurer of all monies placed by him in the bank to their names and credit; and when the Board of Directors shall, in accordance with the rules of this society, be cognisant that there is £5,000 in the said bank, they shall notify the same to the general treasurer, whose duty it shall be to make application on their behalf to the trustees of the society, requesting their sanction to the withdrawal of the same.

7. – *Appointment of General Auditors and their Duties.*

Two auditors shall be appointed by the members of the various district committees, whose duties shall be to audit the accounts of the society.

8. – *Election of District Committees.*

District Committees, consisting of from five to nine persons, shall be chosen by the members in the several localities where they may be resident. Notice of such election, with their names and address, shall be forwarded to the secretary of the Board of Directors. Localities not having a sufficiency of members to elect a District Committee, may appoint a secretary and treasurer to transact their business.

9. – *Duties of the District Committees.*

To collect subscriptions from the members; to assist the Board of Directors when required with their advice; and otherwise exert themselves in forwarding the objects of the society.

10. – *Appointment of the District Secretary and his Duties.*

A secretary shall be appointed by the members of the District Board, and his duty shall be to register the names of the members of the district, to keep account of the income and expenditure, and conduct the correspondence of the district. He shall also transmit to the general secretary, along with the £2 remittance of the treasurer, a clear specification of the names and the amount of the money paid by each shareholder.

11. – *District Treasurer and his Duties.*

A treasurer shall be appointed by the members of the district committee. He shall keep a correct account of the receipts and disbursements of the shares in his district; and remit to the general treasurer the receipts when they amount to the sum of two pounds. Notice thereof to be forwarded to the general secretary.

12. – *District Auditors and their Duties.*

Two auditors shall be appointed by the members of each district, whose duties shall be to audit the accounts of the district once per quarter.

13. – *Selection of Occupants.*

The selection of occupants for the allotments to be by lot from amongst those who may have paid up their shares, in the following manner. The central committee to issue as many tickets to the localities as there may be shares paid up. The prizes to be regulated in proportion to the number of shareholders in the locality. The local boards shall then call a meeting of all shareholders, who have paid up their shares, and decide by lot who shall be holders of the prize allotments. If the capital of £5,000 shall have been raised prior to a sufficient number of shares having been paid up, the lot shall take place amongst those who have paid the highest sums.

14. – *Certificate of Payment of Shares.*

When a member has paid up his share, he shall be furnished by the general secretary with a certificate in the following form: –

Certificate of Chartist Co-operative Land Fund Contribution.
No. —   Value £2 10s.
We, the undersigned officers of the above association hereby certify that John Jones, member of the Nottingham branch of the above association, has paid to the above fund the sum of two pounds ten shillings, for a share in the above association.

Witness our hands this third day of November, 1845.

—, General Secretary.

15. – *Time allowed for paying up Shares.*

Subscribers at 1s. per week	1 year
Subscribers at 6d. per week	2 years
Subscribers at 3d. per week	4 years

Members not having paid up their shares within the time specified, to pay a fine of threepence per week until the rule be complied with. All arrears, with fines included, to be paid up within three months after the expiration of the above-named time, or the money they have paid in shall be forfeited to and for the use of the members of the society.

16. – *Disposal of Shares.*

Members wishing to dispose of their shares may do so by giving notice to the district secretary. He shall immediately notify the same to the general secretary, with the name and address of the party to whom the share may be transferred. In the event of the death of any member, the share will be transferred in accordance with the directions in his will; or, in the event of his dying intestate, be transferred to the next of kin. Members leaving and neglecting to transfer or dispose of their shares, such shares shall become the common property of the society.

17. – *Defrayal of Expenses.*

The expenses consequent upon the formation and conducting the business of the society, to be defrayed by a contribution of 2s. upon each share, which contribution will (in most cases) be paid by the weekly instalments in the following manner: – A subscriber of one shilling per week will, in one year, have paid £2 12s., or the share and 2s. expenses. The sixpenny and threepenny subscribers in like manner, no deduction being made on the £2 10s. for any incidental expenses.

18. – *Appointment of Arbitrators.*

At the first general meeting of the members of the society, five persons shall be elected as arbitrators for the settlement of any disputes which may occur between the society and any of its members, none of which arbitrators shall be directly or indirectly beneficially interested in the funds of the society.

19. – *Selection of Arbitrators.*

In case of any dispute, not less than three of the said arbitrators shall be chosen by ballot, for which purpose the names of the arbitrators shall be written on a piece of paper, and placed in a box, or glass, and the three whose names are first drawn out by the complaining party, or some one appointed by each party, shall be arbitrators to decide the matter in dispute, and their award shall be final, and all expenses attending the arbitration shall be paid as may be fixed by their decision.

IV. THE NATIONAL REGISTRATION
AND CENTRAL ELECTION COMMITTEE*

At a meeting of its members held at the Assembly Rooms, 83, Dean Street, Soho, on Tuesday evening, July 20 [1847], Mr. John Simpson in the chair, Messrs Stallwood and Grassby reported that Mr. Hume had agreed to present the Derby petition to the House of Commons. It was announced that Mr. McGrath had resolved to contest Derby at the coming general election. A letter was also read, setting forth that the people of Sheffield were making arrangements to take Mr. Thomas Clark to the poll for that borough. On the motion of Mr. Stallwood, it was resolved that Mr. Julian Harney be requested to comply with the wish of the men of Tiverton, and offer himself a candidate for the representation of that borough in Parliament. A letter was read from the Chairman of the Halifax Election Committee, setting forth the moral certainty of Mr. Ernest Jones' return in conjunction with Mr. Miall, and requesting the support of the committee. A sum of money was immediately voted for that purpose. A letter was likewise read from the secretary of the Nottingham Election Committee, stating the increased and increasing prospect of Mr. O'Connor. The secretary was instructed to write, congratulating the men of Nottingham, and assuring them of the Central Committee's best support. It was then resolved that as it was already determined to contest Nottingham, Halifax and Derby, to the poll, in the persons of Feargus O'Connor, Ernest Jones and Philip McGrath, that an earnest appeal be made to the country for pecuniary support, in order that those gentlemen may be returned to the Commons House of Parliament free of expense. A letter was also read from Mr. John Williams, stating that he had accepted an invitation to contest a manufacturing town, on the principles of the People's Charter, with the brightest prospect of success. It was also resolved that the following gentlemen having pledged themselves to the principles of the People's Charter, our friends in the

* *Northern Star*, 24 July 1847.

several cities and boroughs for which they are candidates, are requested to give them an earnest and cordial support:–

FINSBURY – T. S. Duncombe, T. Wakley
OLDHAM – J. Fielden, Halliday
ROCHDALE – W. S. Crawford
COVENTRY – W. Williams
NOTTINGHAM – F. O'Connor
BLACKBURN – W. P. Roberts
MARYLEBONE – D. W. Harvey
TOWER HAMLETS – George Thompson
HALIFAX – E. Jones, E. Miall
DERBY – Philip McGrath
BRADFORD – Colonel Thompson
LEEDS – Joseph Sturge
SHEFFIELD – Thomas Clark
TIVERTON – G. Julian Harney
IPSWICH – Henry Vincent
WORCESTER – J. Hardy
NORWICH – W. Simpson
BOLTON – Dr. Bowring
BIRMINGHAM – G. F. Muntz, W. Scholefield and John Williams

V. CHARTIST ORGANIZATION
IN 1853*

HALIFAX, 22 March,

BROTHER DEMOCRATS,

I have before me the names of fifty-eight provincial localities that have joined since our reorganisation; I respectfully call upon the Chartists in every one of these to rally to the rescue; is there one of them that cannot raise one pound, either amongst members, or members and their friends combined? These, with the London localities number nearly seventy. I give the names of all so as not to make invidious distinction: – Cheltenham, Bristol, Tiverton, Bridgewater, Collumpton, Exeter, Torquay, Totness, Merthyr Tydvil, Llanidloes, Newtown, Yarmouth, Coventry, Foleshill, Birmingham, Hanley, Macclesfield, Stockport, Leicester, Nottingham, New Mills, Glossop, Staleybridge, Ashton, Oldham, Rochdale, Manchester, Bacup, Todmorden, Halifax, Bradford, Midgley, Thornton, Clayton, Cinderhills, Pudsey, Keighley, Bingley, Darlington, Durham, Crook, South Shields, North Shields, Sunderland, Newcastle, Greenwich, Buckingham, Padiham, Bolton, Haworth, Cumnock, Glasgow, Paisley, Edinburgh, Gorgie Mills, Alexandria, Dumbarton, Dundee, Arbroath, Blairgowrie, Aberdeen, Huddersfield. There may be others. I quote from memory, and these are all I recollect.

But in addition to these, there are a number of other places in which organised localities do not exist, but where the paper [*People's Paper*] has numerous friends. Among these are: – Ripponden, Illand, Farnhill and district, Derby, Sutton in Ashfield, Northampton, Norwich, Ipswich, Colchester, Brighton, Portsmouth, Southampton, Loughborough, Leeds, Wakefield, Doncaster, Sheffield, Mossely, Hyde, Lees, Plymouth, Devonport, St Austle, Truro, Redruth, Penzance, Barnstaple, and Swansea. I trust that next week there will be a worthy response from the whole of these . . .

R. G. GAMMAGE

---

* *People's Paper*, 26 March 1853. Gammage was probably exaggerating the strength of the N.C.A., but this kind of information is rare and valuable.

BIBLIOGRAPHY

A comprehensive bibliography of the Chartist movement, drawn up by Professor J.F.C.Harrison and Mrs Dorothy Thompson, should be published shortly. Chartist publications are amongst those being catalogued by the University of Warwick Project on the Labour Press. See the *Bulletin of the Society for the Study of Labour History*, No. 25, 1972. A detailed account of recent work on Chartism can be obtained from the annual biographies in the same journal, and from F.C.Mather's Historical Association pamphlet, 'Chartism', 1973 edition. The bibliography below covers only the more obvious and accessible sources.

ORIGINAL SOURCES

There is a vast amount of documentary material on Chartism. Most record offices and the larger municipal libraries contain relevant newspapers and manuscripts. Two of the largest collections of Chartist documents are to be found in London as follows:

1. Public Record Office. See, in particular, the Home Office Letters and Papers, and the Treasury Solicitor's Papers. The main series are H.O. 40, 41 and 45, and T.S. 11. These are particularly useful for Chartist trials, riots and sedition, but they provide little information on the last days of the movement.
2. British Museum. The main sources here are the Francis Place Newspaper Collection, and various Additional MSS, notably 27, 819-21, 34,245 and 37,773.

Other libraries which contain large deposits of Chartist material, and which have been used by the author, include the Birmingham Public Library, the Cardiff Public Library and the Central Library, Derby.

Some of this documentary material has been published in the following books:

3. G.D.H.Cole and A.W.Filson, eds., *British Working Class Movements, Select Documents, 1789–1875*, Macmillan, 1951
4. M.Morris, ed., *From Cobbett to the Chartists, 1815–48*, Lawrence and Wishart, edition of 1951.
5. D.J.Rowe, ed., *London Radicalism 1830–43*, London Record Society, 1970
6. D.Thompson, ed., *The Early Chartists*, Macmillan, 1971

CHARTIST PUBLICATIONS

The following journals are available on microfilm from the British Museum or have been reprinted recently by the Merlin Press, London, the Greenwood Reprint Corporation, Westport, Connecticut and Augustus M.Kelley, Publishers, Clifton, N.C.

7. *Chartist Circular*, 1839–42
8. *Democratic Review*, 1849
9. *English Chartist Circular*, 1841–2
10. *Labourer*, 1847–8
11. *London Mercury*, 1836–7
12. *McDouall's Chartist Journal and Trades' Advocate*, 1841
13. *Northern Liberator*, 1837–40
14. *Northern Star*, 1837–52
15. *Notes to the People*, 1851–2
16. *Operative*, 1837–9
17. *People's Paper*, 1852–8
18. *Red Republican and Friend of the People*, 1850–51
19. *Reynold's Political Instructor*, 1849–50
20. For a commentary on the most famous Chartist journal, see D. Glasgow, 'The Establishment of the Northern Star Newspaper', *History*, new series, xxxix, 1954.

The following Chartist publications have also been recently reprinted:

21. J.B.O'Brien, *The Rise, Progress and Phases of Human Slavery* (1885), Kelley, Clifton, New Jersey, 1969
22. J.Collins and W.Lovett, *Chartism, a New Organisation of the People* (1840), Leicester University Press, 1969
23. F.O'Connor, ed., *The Trial of Feargus O'Connor Esq., and Fifty-Eight Other Chartists on a Charge of Seditious Conspiracy* (1843), Kelley, Clifton, New Jersey, 1969

HISTORIES OF CHARTISM

The best general accounts in English are:

24. A.Briggs, ed., *Chartist Studies*, Macmillan, 1958
25. H.U.Faulkner, *Chartism and the Churches*, F. Cass, 1916
26. R.G.Gammage, *History of the Chartist Movement*, F. Cass, 1854
27. R.Groves, *But we shall rise again; a Narrative History of Chartism*, Secker and Warburg, 1938
28. M.Howell, *The Chartist Movement*, Manchester University Press, 1918
29. F.F.Rosenblatt, *The Chartist Movement in its Social and Economic Aspects*, F.Cass, 1916
30. J.West, *A History of the Chartist Movement*, Kelley, Clifton, N.J., 1920

CHARTIST MEMOIRS

The most interesting and substantial memoirs are:

31. W.E.Adams, *Memoirs of a Social Atom* (1903), Kelley, Clifton, N.J., 1968
32. T.Cooper, *The Life of Thomas Cooper* (1872), Leicester University Press, 1971
33. T.A.Devyr, *The Odd Book of the Nineteenth Century*, Privately printed, New York, 1882
34. T.Frost, *Forty Years Recollections*, Sampson Low, 1880
35. J.B.Leno, *The Aftermath*, Reeves and Turner, 1892
36. W.J.Linton, *Memories* (1895), Kelley, Clifton, N.J., 1970
37. W.Lovett, *Life and Struggles of William Lovett*, 1876
38. H.Solly, *These Eighty Years*, 2 vols, Simpkin and Marshall, 1893
39. B.Wilson, *The Struggles of an Old Chartist*, John Nicholson, Halifax, 1887

BIOGRAPHIES OF CHARTIST LEADERS

There are a great number of Chartist biographies. The most accessible are:

40. A.G.Barker, *Henry Hetherington*, G.W. Foote & Co., 1938
41. G.D.H.Cole, *Chartist Portraits*, Macmillan, 1940
42. W.J.Linton, *A Memoir of James Watson* (1879), Kelley, Clifton, N.J.
43. A.Plummer, *Bronterre; a Political Biography of Bronterre O'Brien 1804–1864*, Allen & Unwin, 1971
44. D.Read and E.Glasgow, *Feargus O'Connor, Irishman and Chartist*, Arnold, 1961
45. J.Saville, *Ernest Jones, Chartist*, Lawrence and Wishart, 1952
46. J.Saville and J.M.Bellamy, eds., *Dictionary of Labour Biography*, vol. I, Macmillan, 1970. This contains an excellent account of Henry Vincent's life and work.
47. A.R.Schoyen, *The Chartist Challenge*, Heinemann, 1958
48. D.Williams, *John Frost: A Study in Chartism*, University of Wales Press, Cardiff, 1939

OTHER USEFUL BIOGRAPHIES

49. T.H.Duncombe, *The Life and Letters of T.S. Duncombe*, Hurst and Blackett, 1868
50. S.Hobhouse, *Joseph Sturge, his Life and Work*, Dent, 1919
51. G.J.Holyoake, *Byegones Worth Remembering*, T. Fisher Unwin, 2 vols, 1905, and other works
52. R.E.Leader, *Life and Letters of J.A. Roebuck*. E. Arnold, 1897
53. F.M.Leventhal, *Respectable Radical: George Howell and Victorian Working Class Politics*, Weidenfeld & Nicolson, 1971
54. W.F.P.Napier, *The Life and Opinions of General Sir Charles Napier*, 4 vols., Privately printed, 1857

55. S.S.Sprigge, *The Life and Times of Thomas Wakley*, Longmans Green & Co., 1897

56. C.M.Wakefield, *Life of Thomas Attwood*, Privately printed, 1885

57. G.Wallas, *Life of Francis Place* (1898), Allen & Unwin, 1925

58. J.T.Ward, 'Revolutionary Tory, the life of J.R.Stephens of Ashton-under-Lyne', *Transactions of the Lancashire and Cheshire Antiquarian Society*, LXVIII, 1958

REGIONAL STUDIES

These are increasing at a tremendous rate. Some of the most valuable publications which have appeared since 1958 are:

59. J.Cannon, *The Chartists of Bristol*, Historical Association, Bristol, 1967

60. J.K.Edwards, 'Chartism in Norwich', *Yorkshire Bulletin of Economic and Social Research*, 1967

61. W.H.Maehl, 'Chartist Disturbances in North-eastern England in 1839', *International Review of Social History*, VIII, 1963

62. A.J.Peacock, *Bradford Chartism 1838–40*, Borthwick Papers, 1969

63. I.J.Prothero, 'Chartism in London', *Past and Present*, 44, 1969

64. D.J.Rowe, 'The Failure of London Chartism', *Historical Journal*, XI, 1968

65. D.J.Rowe, 'Some Aspects of Chartism in Tyneside', *International Review of Social History*, XVI, 1971

66. J.Rule, 'Methodism and Chartism among the Cornish Miners', *Bulletin of the Society for the Study of Labour History*, XX, 1971

67. J.Salt, *Chartism in South Yorkshire*, University of Sheffield Institute of Education, 1967

68. P.Searby, *Coventry Politics in the Age of the Chartists*, Historical Association, Coventry, 1965

69. R.N.Soffner, 'Attitudes and Allegiances in the Unskilled North 1830–50', *International Review of Social History*, X, 1965

70. T.Tholfsen, 'The Chartist Crisis in Birmingham', *International Review of Social History*, III, 1958

71. P.Wyncoll, *Nottingham Chartism*, Nottingham Trades Council, 1966

For the Scottish, Irish and Welsh aspects of Chartism, see:

72. R.O'Higgins, 'The Irish Influence in the Chartist Movement', *Past and Present*, 20, 1961

73. D.J.V.Jones, 'Chartism in Welsh Communities', *The Welsh History Review*, vol. VI, no. 3, 1973

74. J.H.Treble, 'O'Connor, O'Connell and the Attitudes of Irish Immigrants towards Chartism in the North of England, 1838–48', in J.Butt and I.F.Clarke, eds., *The Victorians and Social Protest: A Symposium*, David & Charles, Newton Abbot, 1973

75. A.Wilson, *The Chartist Movement in Scotland*, Manchester University Press, 1970

NOVELISTS AND WORKING-CLASS RADICALS

76. J.Burnley, *Looking for the Dawn*, Simpkin, Marshall and Co., 1874
77. T.Carlyle, *Chartism* (1839), Chapman and Hall, 1905
78. J.M.Cobban, *The King of Andaman*, Methuen and Co., 1895
79. C.Dickens, *Hard Times* (1854), Penguin Books, Harmondsworth, 1970
80. B.Disraeli, *Sybil* (1845), Peter Davies, 1927
81. G.Eliot, *Felix Holt, the Radical* (1866), Penguin Books, Harmondsworth, 1972
82. E.C.Gaskell, *Mary Barton* (1848), Penguin Books, Harmondsworth, 1970
83. C.Kingsley, *Alton Locke* (1850), Dent, 1970
84–5. For an interpretation of the above, see especially R.Williams, *Culture and Society*, 1961, and his article 'Dickens and Social Ideas', in M.Slater, ed., *Dickens 1970*, Chapman and Hall, 1970

CHARTIST POETRY

86. P.Collins, *Thomas Cooper, the Chartist: Byron and the 'Poets of the Poor'*, Leicester University Press, 1969
87. I.V.Kovalev, *Anthology of Chartist Literature*, Printed in Moscow, 1956
88. L.James, *Fiction for the Working Man, 1830–50*, Oxford University Press, 1963

See also the various poetical works of Ernest Jones, Gerald Massey and J.B.Leno. Most of the Chartist journals contained poetry.

ENGELS, MARX AND CHARTISM

89. F.G.Black and R.M.Black, eds., *The Harney Papers*, International Institute for Social Studies, Amsterdam, 1969
90. P.Cadogan, 'Harney and Engels', *International Review of Social History*, x, 1965
91. H.Collins and C.Abramsky, *Karl Marx and the British Labour Movement*, Macmillan, 1965
92. D.Torr, ed., *Marx and Engels, Select Correspondence, 1846–95*, Lawrence and Wishart, 1934
Two important Marxist interpretations are:
93. A.L.Morton and G.Tate, *The British Labour Movement, 1770–1920*, Lawrence and Wishart, 1956
94. T.Rothstein, *From Chartism to Labourism*, Dorrit Press, 1929

RECENT INTERPRETATIONS

95. B.Harrison and P.Hollis, 'Chartism, Liberalism and Robert Lowery', *English Historical Review*, LXXXII, 1967

96. S.D.McCalman, 'Chartism in Aberdeen', *Journal of Scottish Labour History*, 2, 1970

97. R.S.Neale, *Class and Ideology in the Nineteenth Century*, Routledge & Kegan Paul, 1972

98. I.J.Prothero, 'The London Working Men's Association and the "People's Charter"', *Past and Present*, 38, 1967

99. D.J.Rowe, 'The London Working Men's Association and the "People's Charter"', *Past and Present*, 36 and 38, 1967

100. D.J.Rowe, 'Chartism and the Spitalfield Silk-weavers', *Economic History Review*, 2nd series, xx, 1967

101. A.Tyrell, 'Class Consciousness in Early Victorian Britain: Samuel Smiles, Leeds Politics, and the Self-Help Creed', *The Journal of British Studies*, ix, 1970

102. A.Wilson, 'Chartism', in J.T.Ward, ed., *Popular Movements, c. 1830–50*, 1970

NEW WORK ON CHARTISM

103. R.Boston, *British Chartists in America*, Manchester University Press, 1971

104. R.Challinor and B.Ripley, *The Miners' Association; a Trades Union in the Age of the Chartists*, Lawrence & Wishart, 1968

105. J.M.Golby, 'Public Order and Private Unrest: a Study of the 1842 Riots in Shropshire', *University of Birmingham Historical Journal*, xi, 1968

106. A.M.Hadfield, *The Chartist Land Company*, David & Charles, Newton Abbot, 1970

107. F.C.Mather, 'The General Strike of 1842', in J.H.Porter, ed., *Exeter Papers in Economic History*, 6, 1972

108. L.M.Munby, ed., *The Luddites and Other Essays*, Katanka, Stanmore, 1971

109. S.Pollard, 'Feargus O'Connor – as seen by a Contemporary', *Bulletin of the Society for the Study of Labour History*, 24, 1972

110. I.J.Prothero, 'London Chartism and the Trades', *Economic History Review*, vol. xxiv, no. 2, 1971

111. D.J.Rowe, 'The Chartist Convention and the Regions', *Economic History Review*, xxii, 1969

112. S.Shipley, *Club Life and Socialism in Mid-Victorian London*, Ruskin College History Workshop, 1971

113. D.Thompson, 'Notes on Aspects of Chartist Leadership', *Bulletin of the Society for the Study of Labour History*, 15, 1967

114. H.Weisser, 'Chartist Internationalism, 1845–48', *The Historical Journal*, xiv, 1971

115. Various articles by Dorothy Thompson, David Goodway and others on Chartism, published in the *Bulletin of the Society for the Study of Labour History*, 20, 1970

COMPARATIVE STUDIES

The following list contains some of the more useful studies:

116. W.H.G.Armytage, *Heavens Below*, Routledge & Kegan Paul, 1961
117. P.Brock, 'Polish Democrats and English Radicals, 1832–62', *Journal of Modern History*, xxv, 1953
118. D.Bythell, *The Handloom Weavers*, Cambridge University Press, 1969
119. T.Christensen, *Origins and History of Christian Socialism, 1845–54*, Universitetsforlaget, 1962
120. G.D.H.Cole, *A History of Socialist Thought*, vol. i, Macmillan, 1953
121. C.Driver, *Tory Radical: The Life of Richard Oastler*, Oxford University Press, 1946
122. N.C.Edsall, *The Anti-Poor Law Movement, 1834–44*, Manchester University Press, 1971
123. G.B.A.M.Finlayson, *England in the 1830s*, Arnold, 1969
124. F.E.Gillespie, *Labour and Politics in England, 1850–67*, F.Cass, 1922
125. J.L.Godechot, ed., *La Presse Ouvrière 1819–50*, Société d'histoire de la Révolution, 1966
126. T.R.Gurr and H.D.Graham, eds., *The History of Violence in America*, The New American Library, 1969
127. B.Harrison, *Drink and the Victorians*, Faber & Faber, 1971
128. J.F.C.Harrison, *Robert Owen and the Owenites in Britain and America*, Routledge & Kegan Paul, 1969
129. J.F.C.Harrison, *Learning and Living*, Routledge & Kegan Paul, 1961
130. R.Harrison, *Before the Socialists*, Routledge and Kegan Paul, 1965
131. E.J.Hobsbawm, *Labouring Men*, Weidenfeld & Nicolson, 1964
132. P.Hollis, *The Pauper Press: A Study in Working-class Radicalism of the 1830s*, Oxford University Press, 1970
133. J.Marlow, *The Tolpuddle Martyrs*, André Deutsch, 1971
134. F.C.Mather, *Public Order in the Age of the Chartists*, Manchester University Press, 1959
135. R.C.O.Matthews, *A Study in Trade Cycle History: Economic Fluctuations in Great Britain, 1833–42*, Cambridge University Press, 1954
136. N.McCord, *The Anti-Corn Law League, 1838–46*, Allen & Unwin, 1958
137. A.E.Musson, *British Trade Unions, 1800–75*, Macmillan, 1972
138. S.Pollard and J.Salt, eds., *Robert Owen: Prophet of the Poor*, Macmillan, 1971
139. D.Read, *The English Provinces, c. 1760–1960*, Arnold, 1964
140. W.W.Rostow, *British Economy of the Nineteenth Century*, Oxford University Press, 1948

141. G. Rudé, *The Crowd in History: Study of Popular Disturbances in France and England, 1730–1848*, Wiley, 1964

142. B. Simon, *Studies in the History of Education, 1780–1870*, Lawrence & Wishart, 1960

143. N. J. Smelser, *Social Change in the Industrial Revolution*, Routledge & Kegan Paul, 1959

144. W. C. Taylor, *Notes on a Tour of the Manufacturing District of Lancashire*, (1841) F. Cass, 1968

145. T. Tholfsen, 'The Intellectual Origins of mid-Victorian Stability', *Political Science Quarterly*, LXXXVI, 1971

146. E. P. Thompson, 'Homage to Tom Maguire', in A. Briggs and J. Saville, eds., *Essays in Labour History*, Macmillan, 1960

147. E. P. Thompson, *The Making of the English Working Class*, Gollancz, 1963

148. E. P. Thompson and E. Yeo, eds., *The Unknown Mayhew*, Merlin Press, 1971

149. J. R. Vincent, *The Formation of the British Liberal Party*, Constable, 1966

150. J. T. Ward, *The Factory Movement, 1830–55*, Macmillan, 1962

151. W. R. Ward, *Religion and Society in England, 1790–1850*, Batsford, 1972

152. R. F. Wearmouth, *Some Working-Class Movements of the Nineteenth Century*, Epworth Press, 1948

153. J. H. Wiener, *The War of the Unstamped, 1830–36*, Cornell University Press, 1969

Certain newspapers and periodicals are also valuable for comparison. See, for example:

154. *Annual Register*, 1839, 1842 and 1848

155. *Anti-Bread Tax (Corn Law) Circular*, 1839–42

156. *Fleet Papers*, 1841–4

157. *Leeds Intelligencer*, 1838–52

158. *Manchester and Salford Advertizer*, 1835–48

159. *New Moral World*, 1834–45

160. *Poor Man's Guardian*, 1831–5

161. *Times*, 1839–48

THESES (1960–72)

162. O. R. Ashton, 'Chartism in Mid-Wales', M.A., University of Wales, 1971

163. G. J. Barnsby, 'The Working-Class Movement in the Black Country, 1815–67', M.A., University of Birmingham, 1965

164 J. Bennett, 'A Study in London Radicalism: the Democratic Association 1837–41', M.A., University of Sussex, 1968

165. R. O'Higgins, 'Ireland and Chartism', M.A., University of Dublin, Trinity College, 1959

H

166. A.V.John, 'The Chartists of Industrial South Wales, 1840–68', M.A., University of Wales, 1970

167. T.M.Kemnitz, 'Chartism in Brighton', D.Phil., University of Sussex, 1969

168. R.S.Neale, 'Economic Conditions and Working-Class Movements in the City of Bath, 1800–50', M.A., University of Bristol, 1962

169. I.J.Prothero, 'London Working-Class Movements, 1825–48', Ph.D., University of Cambridge, 1967

170. D.J.Rowe, 'London Radicalism, 1829–41', M.A., University of Southampton, 1965

171. J.Salt, 'Isaac Ironside and Education in the Sheffield Region in the first half of the Nineteenth Century', M.A., University of Sheffield, 1960.

INDEX